SEEING THROUGH

CYNICISM

A Reconsideration of the Power of Suspicion

DICK KEYES

IVP Books

An imprint of InterVarsity Press
Downers Grove, Illinois

InterVarsity Press
P.O. Box 1400, Downers Grove, IL 60515-1426
World Wide Web: www.ivpress.com
E-mail: mail@ivpress.com

InterVarsity Press® is the book-publishing division of InterVarsity Christian Fellowship/USA®, a student movement active on campus at hundreds of universities, colleges and schools of nursing in the United States of America, and a member movement of the International Fellowship of Evangelical Students. For information about local and regional activities, write Public Relations Dept., InterVarsity Christian Fellowship/USA, 6400 Schroeder Rd., P.O. Box 7895, Madison, WI 53707-7895, or visit the IVCF website at <www.intervarsity.org>.

Scripture quotations, unless otherwise noted, are from the New Revised Standard Version of the Bible, copyright 1989 by the Division of Christian Education of the National Council of Churches of Christ in the USA. Used by permission. All rights reserved.

The Doonesbury comic strip on p. 12 is ©1996 G. B. Trudeau. Reprinted with permission of UNIVERSAL PRESS SYNDICATE. All rights reserved.

The Gilbert Meilander quote on pp. 198-99 is used by permission.

Design: Cindy Kiple
Images: Blake Little/Getty Images

ISBN-10: 0-8308-3388-9
ISBN-13: 978-0-8308-3388-7

Printed in the United States of America ∞

Library of Congress Cataloging-in-Publication Data

Keyes, Dick.
  Seeing through cynicism: a reconsideration of the power of
suspicion/Dick Keyes.
    p. cm.
  Includes bibliographical references.
  ISBN-13: 978-0-8308-3388-7 (pbk.: alk. paper)
  ISBN-10: 0-8308-3388-9 (pbk.: alk. paper)
  1. Providence and government of God. 2. Cynicism. 3. Skepticism.
  4. Suspicion 5. Belief and doubt. I. Title.
  BT135.K49 2006
  231'.5—dc22
                                                              2006013024

| P | 19 | 18 | 17 | 16 | 15 | 14 | 13 | 12 | 11 | 10 | 9 | 8 | 7 | 6 | 5 | 4 | 3 | 2 | 1 |
| Y | 22 | 21 | 20 | 19 | 18 | 17 | 16 | 15 | 14 | 13 | 12 | 11 | 10 | 09 | 08 | 07 | 06 |

CONTENTS

118508

Part One

THE ANATOMY OF CYNICISM

INTRODUCING CYNICISM

No matter how cynical you get, it's never enough to keep up.

LILY TOMLIN

There is a shrewdness *which, almost with pride, presumes to have special elemental knowledge of the shabby side of existence, that everything finally ends in wretchedness.*

SØREN KIERKEGAARD

THIS BOOK BEGAN SEVERAL YEARS AGO in our kitchen when one of my students asked, "Can you read the newspapers, watch television and generally try to keep informed about what is going on in the world—without becoming cynical?" My response to her convinced neither of us. I had always felt a strong attraction to cynicism but had leaned against it, being suspicious of its cleverness and wary of its consequences. I began to think that cynicism needed to be taken more seriously.

Cynicism is all around us. The pressure of fearless, open-eyed honesty seems to drive us toward it. Yet at the same time we might sense an intuitive counterpressure warning us that cynicism might give away too much, too easily to the dark side of life. What is cynicism? How is it justified? What does it deliver? Let's start with an everyday event.

The "Sick Day"

Take the problem posed by cynicism in its simplest form: a "sick day." Someone tells you that he or she is sick today and asks you to free them from their normal responsibilities. Perhaps it is a coworker or an employee who cannot possibly make it to work. Perhaps it is your child who feels much too miserable to go to school. How do you understand the request for the sick day?

You might take it at face value. People of all ages and occupations do, after all, get sick. People who are sick often cannot continue with life as usual. They need time to rest in order to recover. Sicknesses do not arrange themselves according to convenient moments for the patient or for those who have to take up the slack for the patient. "I'm sorry to hear that you're feeling badly. Yes, of course, take the day to rest. I hope you feel better tomorrow."

On the other hand, you might feel inclined not to take it at face value. You can see through the face value of the request and unmask it. It is easy to fake being sick—especially over the telephone. It may be frustrating, but you cannot argue with or contradict someone who claims to feel nauseated, utterly exhausted or have a splitting headache. Perhaps there is some dreaded event that your patient wants to avoid today at work or school. Or could it just be laziness? Bogus sick days have happened before. Once upon a time you may have used strategies like this yourself to avoid feared events. "Well, let's see, what *exactly* are your symptoms? Have you seen a doctor? What does the *doctor* say?" "How much do you think it would it hurt you to go to work (or school)?" "It would be really hard not to have you at work. Can't you come anyway?"

How do you understand the simple request for the sick day? Straightforwardly, as an ordinary, sincere request to be granted with sympathy and without questions? Or with suspicion, further inquiry and innuendoes that you have seen through to ulterior motives?

If you feel a tension between these two ways to interpret the sick day, you have felt the problem posed by cynicism. Of course the way we respond to a sick day has a great deal to do with the patient and what we know of his or her trustworthiness. But it also has a lot to do with you as an interpreter of sick days, people in general and reality itself. If you understand the sick day at face value, you are being sympathetic, trusting and kind. It is the way you hope to be treated yourself when you feel awful. On the other hand—maybe you are being conned, taken for a ride and will even be mocked for your naiveté after the "patient" hangs up the telephone and heads for the beach with friends.

The experienced voice of cynicism says, "Watch out, don't be taken in." Suspicion is shrewd and necessary to life. Cynicism promises a more sophisticated way of seeing. It promises to protect you from getting conned or disgraced or from letting your hopes be smashed in disillusionment. There is something deeply appealing about cynicism—especially in a world where we have to cut through so much sham, phoniness and spin. If we did not have a fairly high level of suspicion, commercial advertising would bankrupt us all in no time. Isn't cynicism an honest, reliable and necessary guide for living in this world?

This makes some sense, yet cynicism has its own risks. Maybe the patient whom you subjected to a cynical interrogation turned out to be completely sincere and extremely sick. Perhaps the child you packed off to school with a stiff-upper-lip motivational speech had to be taken to the hospital emergency room by somebody else later that day. It turns out that cynicism is not foolproof or embarrassment-proof.

Of course the claims of cynicism reach far beyond sick days. The chances are that you can hear the voice of cynicism in your own head as you think about your relationships with other people, as you listen to politicians' moral pronouncements, corporate executives' glowing promises or church leaders' far-reaching assertions. Cynicism can call into question all that you value as most important in life, and so shape your world.

What Is Cynicism?

Cynicism, as we use the word today, has to do with seeing through and unmasking positive appearances to reveal the more basic underlying motivations of greed, power, lust and selfishness. It says that every respectable public agenda has a hidden private agenda behind it that is less noble, flattering and moral. Is this idea dangerous, destructive, misguided? Or is it shrewd, courageous and truthful, the last stopping place of the honest mind?

One dictionary defines *cynic* as "a person who believes that only selfishness motivates human actions and who disbelieves in or minimizes selfless acts or disinterested points of view," and *cynical* as "distrusting or disparaging the motives of others."[1] The philosopher Peter Sloterdijk writes that cynicism "is the universally widespread way in which enlightened people see to it that they are not taken for suckers."[2]

Take a classic cynical statement, as in the words of the Preacher in the book of Ecclesiastes: "Then I saw that all toil and all skill in work come from one person's envy of another" (Eccles 4:4). The Preacher sees through the façades of hard work and expertise, and sees behind them the mainspring of their motivation—the competitive struggle for status. He is not going to be taken in by anybody. People may work with diligence and develop superhuman skills and abilities, even in public service or charity, but it is all because they desire to catch up to, keep up with or get ahead of their neighbors.

It is not exactly startling to be told that *some* people are driven by envy in *some* of their skill and hard work—*some* of the time. But all people, all of the time? What makes the statement a cynical statement is the little word *all*—"all toil" and "all skill" of (implicitly) all people. It is a cynical judgment of human nature itself. It is a totalizing way of thinking, applicable to all people.

Look at this *Doonesbury* cartoon from the mid-1990s, of the Clinton White House.[3]

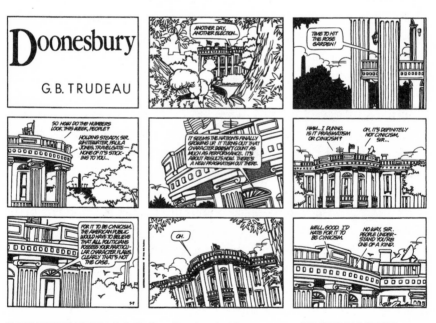

Cynicism in this case would rest on a nationwide survey done with psychological x-ray vision, revealing to you a negative picture of the character of all politicians. Such cynicism would be able to see through the sham and pretense of apparent public service and virtue. Cynicism is not the broad pessimism of the person who is always sure that it is going to rain on the weekend. It is a narrower pessimism focused on the motivations and purposes of others, which are normally hidden from the observation of the uninitiated and naive.

There is another popular use of the word *cynical* that I will not be using in this book. Some call a politician "cynical" if he or she shamelessly grabs money or power in open, unapologetic violation of law and moral principle. I would call this politician "shameless," but not necessarily cynical. I will use the word *cynical* to mean a specific attitude of "seeing through others" rather than to any specific behavior—although shameless behavior will certainly invite cynical attitudes in anyone who is watching.

Cynical Privilege: Immunity from Prosecution?

One of my reasons for writing this book is that cynicism does not get the scrutiny it deserves. I have wondered whether it has some privileged position that makes it immune to serious challenge. Four possible reasons for this come to mind.

Fish don't notice the water. One reason that cynicism receives little criticism is that many people do not even realize that it exists in their own thinking and conversation. Cynical insights, perspectives and critiques are so much a part of modern vocabulary that we get used to them; they are nothing special, unusual or needing particular recognition, let alone justification.

One way that critics dismiss films as beneath contempt is to call them "feel-good movies." Are all films that can be said to have positive moral messages feel-good movies? Or are only certain moral values deserving of contempt when discovered in film? Are worthy films meant to be feel-*bad* experiences? These questions do not get asked because cynicism about many moral principles is not noticed in the air we breathe.

In some groups, particularly those associated with media and higher education, cynicism seems to have the status of common sense or self-evident truth. It becomes the default setting of many conversations. We don't think to question it when it is all around us. We don't see our eyeglasses, we only see everything else through them.

Cynicism as a moving target. Second, there is the elusive character of cynicism. It is not a school of philosophy or of systematic thought in any sense. It is promiscuous, and so it can cohabit with many different worldviews. It can live in some areas of your life and thinking and leave others alone. It can come and go, or it can be a permanent fixture in your life. You can be dominated by its insights one moment and disown them the next. At the most trivial end, it can come with low blood sugar and leave with a cup of good coffee.

Cynicism is also elusive because it is essentially a negative judgment. It stakes out no positive turf that it would then have to defend. It can make withering exposures of pomp, selfishness or hypocrisy, then count on an intuitive disgust for those vices in its hearers. It can also count on a response of satisfaction and catharsis when it exposes pompous, selfish hypocrites. It only needs to unmask somebody's phoniness to make its case. Cynicism may then be able to ride for months or years on that established authority.

The humor connection. So, how can you criticize someone who makes no positive assertions to criticize? Or even more difficult, how do you do it when his or her negative judgments are funny? Much of the power of cynicism comes through wit and humor. To question the truth claims of cynical judgments often requires an awkward and unnatural shift of your whole state of mind or of the momentum of any given conversation. Imagine questioning the truth of some of the claims of the political satire on *Saturday Night Live*. You may object that this is just light entertainment, and so of course you cannot "argue" with caricatures as if it was serious political discussion. But that is just the point. It is entertainment, but nonetheless it is powerful in communicating ideas and impressions about important subjects and people. Presidential candidates have altered their campaign strategies as a result of watching the way they were being satirized on *Saturday Night Live*.

In the early twentieth century, cynicism became known as "debunking." In 1923 William Woodward wrote a novel called *Bunk*. He is credited with coining the word *debunk*. His hero spoke of "taking the bunk out of things," of "intellectual deflation" as the "science of reality."[4] You can always query whether a specific cynical judgment is valid, whether what is debunked really had been bunk in the first place. But it is an uphill point to make if the debunking came with humor.

This is a phenomenon not lost on cynics. The hero of the novel *Bunk* says:

> You put new ideas over by making people laugh. All new ideas are looked upon as dangerous, and people fight them as they fight tigers. But all clowns are considered harmless. So you get a man laughing and before he knows it you've passed your idea on to him.[5]

Humor disarms criticism. Can you imagine the futility of wagging your finger at John Cleese and telling him that he should not be so cynical?

Fear of the return strike of cynicism. Finally, there is a serious disincentive to criticizing cynicism in the first place. This is one of cynicism's most powerful shelters of immunity. It is the fear of the return strike. There are warnings of this danger going all the way back to the wisdom literature of the Bible: "Whoever corrects a scoffer wins abuse" (Prov 9:7). If you question or argue against cynicism, you invite abuse; you risk provoking the cynical counterattack. The cynic, if provoked, is often very good at using humor to make an opponent look naive, earnest, stupid or uncool. It is much, much safer to leave the cynic undisturbed and unchallenged.

It is like the old revolutionary flag picturing a coiled rattlesnake with "Don't Tread on Me" written underneath it. Cynicism says, "If you step on me, I can make you look really out of it."

My Own Agenda

I should say a word about my own history with cynicism. It goes back as far as I can remember. On a scale with cynicism at one end and sentimental optimism at the other, I have always been much closer to the cynicism pole. My instincts and internal voices have always gravitated toward suspicion when there is any doubt.

I became a Christian in my early twenties both because of my cynicism and in spite of it. Unlike other worldviews that I had considered, I never felt the God of the Bible was asking me to put on rose-colored glasses to upgrade what was wrong with the world. Even the heroes of the Bible were described unsparingly in appalling moral failures—lies, sexual aberrations and murders. I did not have to give up the honesty and realism that I had valued. Cynicism claimed that the world—both inside and outside of our heads—was profoundly broken and bent. I realized that the Christian faith had been saying this for two thousand years, and Judaism for longer than that.

On the other hand, faith in Christ challenged my cynicism. There was something too facile about cynicism. It seemed too complete in its tidy and convenient dismissal of virtue. I realized that many of the key cynical judgments I had made were overreaching what I could actually know. Faith ran with cynicism for some distance and then made a turn in a different direction.

Most of my working life has been in Christian residential study centers operated by L'Abri Fellowship in Switzerland, England, and in northeastern United States.[6] This has meant teaching and writing, but more importantly, many hours spent one-on-one with those who have come to study at L'Abri. Among the enormous variety of people of all ages and origins who have stayed with us, more and more seem to be wrestling with the claims and consequences of cynicism. You might find some of their ideas familiar. Some embrace cynicism with pride and defiance. Others suffer from a cynicism that they do not want but feel forced to adopt by honesty. Still others fight against it with whatever they find handy, and far more drift into it by accident with little awareness of what has happened.

Cynicism has been the only way some have found to protect themselves from other people or from what they felt was reality itself. Legitimate expectations were smashed; they have been burned by religious groups, corporations, educational institutions or government agencies. Many were driven into cynicism by seeing their high ideals for public service or service to God battered into disillusionment. There may have been hypocrisy with brutal consequences, cruelty, legalism, honest and urgent questions dismissed by condescension or rejection. Trust became a dangerous, unrealistic and unwanted possibility.

Given the far-reaching consequences of cynical ideas and commitments, evaluations of cynicism have been surprisingly neglected. The idea of this book is to put a brighter spotlight on cynicism. It is to offer help in responding to the question, Can you be informed about the modern world, be honest—and not be cynical? I will begin in the first part with a look at the breadth of cynical attitudes in our society, then shift to examine cynicism more critically and finally to explore the possibility of an alternative.

CYNICISM

Cynicism dominates the assumptions of our political and cultural life. We not only do not recognize the cynicism; we confuse it with democratic deliberation and political wisdom.

JEFFREY GOLDFARB

If you want a friend in Washington, get a dog.

HARRY TRUMAN

WHERE DID CYNICISM COME FROM? How has it become so widespread in the modern world? Before we look at modern forms of cynicism, consider some of its patriarchs in classical Greece and those who have carried it into our own time.

"Used" Cynicism

The word *cynicism* traces back to classical Greece in the fourth century before Christ. It had a colorful beginning. The first Cynic to bear the name was Diogenes of Sinope. What we know about him is an uncertain mixture of myth and historical information. He lived much of his adult life in Athens but died in Corinth on the same day as the death of Alexander the Great in 324 B.C.

He had been exiled from Sinope, possibly because of some scandal associated with his father or possibly for having defaced the coins of the city. "Defacing the currency" became something of a metaphor for his philosophical vocation. He dedicated himself to driving out the counterfeit currencies of vain philosophy to make room for what was real.[1] Diogenes may be best known for roaming the streets of Athens in broad daylight with a lighted lantern held high. When asked what in the world he was doing, he replied,"I am looking for an honest man."[2] There are many stories about his eccentric, humorous, coarse and confrontational ways, but they were shaped by certain basic ideas that he tried to live out and propagate. The most basic truth for him was the reality of nature as expressed by the behavior of animals. As people tried to lift their lives above the simplicity of animal behavior, they left the path of virtue and became corrupt and arrogant.

Since the ideal was to live according to nature defined in this way, Diogenes saw through the civilized and sophisticated life of most Athenians as artificial, hypocritical and so requiring exposure and mockery. It needed to be defaced or, as we might say today, deconstructed. He opposed wealth, not out of compassion for the poor or for their economic benefit but for the spiritual benefit for the rich who would be better off without the stuff. He renounced all property himself, lived in a barrel near the temple of Cybele, and did not wear much clothing. At one point, when he noticed a peasant boy drinking from his cupped hands, he destroyed his own single possession, a wooden bowl, having realized that he didn't really need it.

Diogenes was known less for his philosophical doctrines than for his style of living—outrageous humor, shamelessness, repartee and street theater. Although he had disciples, he founded no philosophical school. His impact was on different philosophical schools, most importantly on the development of Stoicism after his death. It was said that Alexander the Great, in his early years, met Diogenes and wanted to show the philosopher his respect. He asked what he could do for Diogenes. Diogenes, who was sunbathing at the time replied,"Get out of my light."

Diogenes was called a"dog,"probably because of his shameless repudiation of social conventions and his habit of performing bodily functions whenever and wherever he felt like it. He embraced the idea of the"dog." It became his badge or symbol. It is from the Greek word for"dog"that our word *cynic* came. They became known as"disciples of the dog."Like good guard dogs, Cynics would chase away those unfit to do philosophy. His shamelessness gave him superiority in his own eyes over other Athenians with their artificial respectability, convention and wealth. Diogenes said that he was a dog whom all admired, but with whom few dared go hunting.[3] "Other dogs bite their enemies. I bite my friends, for their salvation."[4]

His mission was to see through and expose by his mockery all attempts to rise above nature. Wisdom was found in unmasking or defacing the thoughts and ways of the majority of humankind, from philosophers to aristocrats to slaves. Criticism from others was received with a laugh. Poverty and disrepute were aids to achieving self-knowledge and self-control.

Crates of Thebes was Diogenes' most influential disciple. He taught that "we should study philosophy until we see in generals nothing but donkey drivers."[5] His reputation was for being less harsh and more winsome than his master. He began to develop a Cynic literature of tragedy, dialogue, parody and satire. He did more jesting and laughing than "biting" and confrontation, and seemed to specialize in mediation between neighbors and family members.[6]

There was a revival of Cynicism later through its influence on Stoicism, but there is no direct line of descent of ideas from that era to our own. In every age and place there have been people who have looked with deep suspicion at human nature, motivation and achievement, whether or not they have ever heard the name Diogenes or the word *cynic*. Farrand Sayre, in his book *The Greek Cynics*, suggested, "It is probable that the first man who shaped a stone hammer was jeered at by cynics who claimed that unshaped stones were better."[7] But the words *cynic* and *cynicism* became attached to this tendency to deface the currency, to see through positive appearances to their underlying selfish, sinister, silly or sordid purposes.

New Cynicism

What is cynicism today? Modern cynicism bears little resemblance to the lifestyle of the early Cynics. The austerity and asceticism of Diogenes, his renunciation of property and the pleasures of this world are—to say the least—not the "draw" for cynicism in the twenty-first century. Having met many cynical people, I have never met one who decided to live in a barrel.

Diogenes' cynical critique and exposure of others was not because he was a malicious person. He was not just biting his friends, he was biting them for their salvation. To the extent that they were civilized, he believed that they were falling short of the simplicity and virtue of nature as seen in animal life. So, nature was the platform ideal from which he launched his cynical assault. All cynics, new and old, have needed platform ideals to stand on, from which to throw rocks at whatever they were trying to criticize. It is impossible to throw rocks with either accuracy or power if you are in a free fall.

The mainspring of cynicism today is not nature as the ideal as it was for Diogenes. Many different ideals now work as baselines or platform ideals for cynicism. Even those who claim with Diogenes that nature is all that exists do not limit their ideals to the behavior of animals. The most powerful cynical voices today seem to come from ideals of freedom, honesty, authenticity, love or justice. They are the platform ideals from which the rocks of modern cynicism are thrown at oppression, dishonesty, hypocrisy, cruelty and injustice.

Although the standards or ideals are different now, the way of thinking is much the same in its strategy. Cynicism still sees through respectable false appearances to the lower motivations beneath them, but it uses different tools to pry open the secrets of human motivation. Hidden motivations are exposed of which we are likely to be ashamed.

Another important difference from the time of Diogenes is that today the cynic is no longer the outsider, functioning as a gadfly "missionary" to the society at large. The air that we breathe has become cynicism friendly, so that when *Time* magazine recently did a feature story on happiness, they included a page of one-liners to keep things in perspective. Here are some of them:

- "Happiness in intelligent people is the rarest thing I know." (Ernest Hemingway)
- "Happiness serves hardly any other purpose than to make unhappiness possible." (Marcel Proust)
- "Happiness is good health and a bad memory." (Ingrid Bergman)
- "The secret of happiness is to face the fact that the world is horrible, horrible, horrible." (Bertrand Russell)[8]

Cynicism is well-established in centers of cultural power. Some of its most important tools of critique were formed and now thrive in higher education. Unlike the experience of Diogenes, it is easier in many circles today to shock people with a noncynical perspective than with a cynical one.

Today's cynicism is slippery and elusive. It is not, after all, a fixed set of doctrines, a philosophical system or a set of ethical rules. Cynicism has no card-carrying membership, parliament, priesthood or system of tenure. It cannot be compared fairly to various schools of philosophy, psychology or social theory. It is not a school of thought at all but a voice of doubt in your ear, a predisposition for seeing through people and things, a negative idea about human nature, a mood or attitude of suspicion, or friends with a particular sense of humor.

Cynicism can influence any one of us by filtering the way we interpret the motivation for sick days and hard work as well as all other human virtues, thoughts and activities. It is a free-floating pattern of totalizing, confident suspicion that can come and go without particular warning or obvious reason. It is also contagious.

How Does Cynicism Come to Us?

Cynicism has been carried to Americans through the delightful humor of Mark Twain's stories, the caustic wit of H. L. Mencken's essays and the compressed bleakness and power of Hemingway's narratives. It has come to television viewers through sitcoms like *Seinfeld* and the satire of *Saturday Night Live*. It is alive and well on the Web, with Internet versions of newspapers such as *The Onion*. We will not find it restricted in narrow, tidy categories and locations. Cynicism has become virtually stock-in-trade for much journalism, particularly in its political commentary. Think of the influence of Watergate and all subsequent "gates" on cynicism about our highest leadership. Cynics often have heroic status as triumphant deflaters of morally overinflated balloons. Cynicism can feed voraciously on attacks made against it and on remedies suggested for it. It is pretty easy, especially with humor, to make most attacks on cynicism look naive and ridiculous.

We see adolescent cynicism in J. D. Salinger's *Catcher in the Rye*, as Holden Caulfield can see only "phonies" among the people around him. We find cynicism also in the life of the disillusioned idealist whose shattered dreams form the bitter ground floor of a suspicion of the whole human project. Cynicism can come from the exhaustion of or disillusionment with religious belief or of whatever story gave meaning to life. To some, the truth of cynicism seems self-evident. Oscar Wilde said, "I am not at all cynical, I'm only experienced—that's pretty much the same thing," and Anton Chekov, "No cynicism can outdo life."[9]

Attempts to escape our own internal cynical voices are not easy. Often our honesty and sensitivity to truth and beauty keep pulling us back to cynicism, making resistance to it feeble. Douglas Coupland captured this in *Life After God*. While drinking weak coffee on a concrete front step, his friend tells him:

> You know—I'm trying to escape from ironic hell: cynicism into faith; randomness into clarity; worry into devotion. But it's hard because I try to be sincere about life and then I turn on a TV and I see a game show host and I have to throw up my hands and give up.[10]

Coupland was not dealing here with the power of cynical ideas as much as with the experience of living in a world saturated in artificiality, spin and banality. We do not have the strength or energy to understand this artificiality or resist it, let alone change it. Nor do we understand the inevitable sense of disappointment and disillusionment that comes with it.

Could it be that cynicism also grows out of expectations that were naive and doomed to disillusionment from the start? Daniel Boorstin, a social historian, wrote about the "extravagant expectations" that are a part of modern life. His reflection is unsettling in that it seems so much more true today than when he first published it in 1962.

> When we pick up our newspaper at breakfast, we expect—we even demand—that it bring us momentous events since the night before. We turn on the car radio as we drive to work and expect "news" to have occurred since the morning newspaper went to press. . . . We expect our two-week vacation to be romantic, exotic, cheap, and effortless. We expect a faraway atmosphere if we go to a nearby place; and we expect everything to be relaxing, sanitary and Americanized if we go to a faraway place. . . .
>
> We expect anything and everything. We expect the contradictory and the impossible. We expect compact cars which are spacious; luxurious cars which are economical. We expect to be rich and charitable, powerful and merciful, active and reflective, kind and competitive. We expect to be inspired by mediocre appeals for "ex-

cellence,"to be made literate by illiterate appeals for literacy. We expect to eat and stay thin, to be constantly on the move and ever more neighborly, to go to the"church of our choice"and yet feel its guiding power over us, to revere God and to be God.

Never have people been more the masters of their environment. Yet never has a people felt more deceived and disappointed. For never has a people expected so much more than the world could offer.[11]

Extravagant expectations are not a full explanation for modern cynicism. But they guarantee a disappointment that makes fertile ground for it to grow.

Before evaluating cynicism, we should have a closer look at the questions that began the first chapter. What is cynicism? How is it justified? What does it deliver? If we consent to cynicism, it should at least be an "informed consent." To understand cynicism, it is easier to break it down into parts. Cynicism does not have only one sphere of operation but works in three theaters: cynicism about individual people, about institutions of society and about God.

SEEING THROUGH PEOPLE

We are caught within a web of cynicism that makes us question whether there could be any higher purpose besides material self-interest and looking out for number one.

MICHAEL LERNER

I said in my consternation, "Everyone is a liar."

ANONYMOUS PSALMIST

A cynicism deeper than Freudian cynicism may have once seemed hard to imagine, but there it is.

ROBERT WRIGHT

THE CYNICISM THAT FIRST SPRINGS TO MOST peoples' minds is cynicism about the motivations of other people. It is the first theater of cynical operation. Is anyone immune from being a target for cynical criticism today? Certainly no public figures are spared. Even Mother Teresa before she died was given the full treatment.[1] That voice of cynicism can come to us from many different and sometimes opposite angles.

Cynicism and Experience of Life

When other people fail to meet our important expectations of them, it can be unbearably painful—so much so that it can turn us to cynicism about all other people. I have hoped in someone, invested in a relationship,

counted on my family, given years to my employer, served my church—
only to get kicked in the teeth. If we have been disappointed, betrayed or
disillusioned enough times or even once in a big enough way by a significant enough person, cynicism may come naturally to us.

When a young boy is regularly dragged out of bed at night and beaten
by a drunken father, it should not surprise us that he finds it difficult to
even want to trust anyone's good intentions when he grows up. When
people are abandoned by their spouse just when they contract a chronic
illness, it should not surprise us that they see other people through a cynical lens. When we see CEOs retire with megamillion-dollar bonuses
while leaving lower management and the rest of the employees without
the pensions they had been promised, cynicism comes easily. Cynicism
will not only appear believable, but it will feel self-evidently true—like
common sense or an attitude that is necessary for survival. The dread of
further disappointment outweighs the pain of loneliness as we withdraw
from the risk of hope in new relationships.

The perspectives of people who live in the ex-Marxist countries of Eastern Europe are extreme examples of this pattern. They have been lied to
and oppressed for so long, in so many ways and with such painful consequences that cynicism about anyone outside the immediate family may be
second nature to them. The same experience is shared by some members
of minority groups in our own country.

Cynicism about other people is fed also by the transient character of
modern life. How many relationships do we expect to last a long time?
We move our home. We change jobs. We no longer see the people that
we used to see five years ago. We adjust our sense of what is normal to
adopt lower expectations for most relationships. Even marriage relationships do not carry the expectation of permanence that they did fifty
years ago.

Cynicism and money. Cynicism has many strategies for "defacing the
currency" of apparent virtue. One of the most common lenses used to see
through people is to believe that they are, at bottom, out for money. Beneath all respectable veneers, money is the motivation that drives them
all. It can seem that the conscience which speaks with high moral rhetoric
is powerless to restrain greed. Can you think of anything that somebody
has *not* tried to sell?

I was once trying to buy some land for L'Abri Fellowship from a neighbor and a real estate agent soberly advised me, "Just wave a blank check in front of his face. Everybody has their price." Happily I had the sense to not follow this advice, but I have often heard this mantra, "Everybody has their price." Everybody is for sale if the price is right. Is this true?

Think of how often the reason given to get an education has become "to get a good job." What is a "good job"? It is usually a job that will allow you to shop freely and retire early in comfort and with freedom to travel. Is this really the main goal of education?

Cynicism and sex. "The first time a boy comes calling on my daughter, I'll be out on the front porch just casually cleaning my shotgun. Because I was his age once and I want him to know that I know what he knows—and I know what he's after."[2] (A vow made by a father anticipating a new stage in the life of his family.) In his plan, the father assumes that he sees accurately through the potential (as yet unknown) boyfriend of his daughter. He knows a thing or two, so he is not easily fooled. He knows that the driving force beneath all other motivations is sexual desire. It will be hard to convince him otherwise.

The media also provides reliable encouragement to the idea that all motivation is at bottom sexual. Check the magazine racks in your local bookstore or airport. In the most popular prime time television shows, think of how the narratives are driven by sexual attraction, sexual anticipation, sexual obsession, sexual conquest and sexual disillusionment. These themes now make up an enormous amount of the American diet of public stories. It is predictable that sex would be used by advertisers to sell skimpy clothes and exotic vacations. But you get a better picture of the power of sexual motivation in our society when you realize that sex is also used to sell milk and snow tires. All of this gives support to the father on his front porch with his shotgun. Does he have it right?

Ideas That See Through People

Although cynicism itself is not a formal school of philosophy, certain schools of thought, scientific ideas and social theories include cynical conceptions of human nature and behavior. If we believe them, they give us the tools to see through and unmask the face value of the thoughts, words and actions of our neighbors and ourselves.

Cynicism and moral excellence. The fate of moral excellence is a good weathervane to show the depth and direction of cynicism about people. It may be relatively easy to see through some of our friends, neighbors and politicians. But what about those people who are singled out for exceptional moral character or achievement? Are there no heroes whose lives resist cynical deflation?

The human sciences offer us various tools to accomplish this translation from apparent heroic altruism to motivation by instinct or self-interest. Cynicism must somehow explain the exceptional quality of the hero's behavior—whatever made him or her stand out from and above the crowd. A heroic rescue might have been motivated by the need to compensate for some deficit, such as lack of love from parents at an early age or perhaps by an excessive need for attention. When the cynic is finished the person who has done something heroic is no longer to be admired or emulated but rather to be pitied as a neurotic. Psychological dysfunction was at the root of moral excellence.[3]

Cynicism and evolutionary psychology. Continuing in this same direction, a still deeper form of cynicism is taught by a form of evolutionary theory. It is a modification of traditional Darwinism that has attracted a great deal of excitement and allegiance in recent years. The idea was first popularized as "sociobiology" in the work of Harvard entomologist E. O. Wilson. It is now better known as "evolutionary psychology" and has been spread with missionary zeal by E. O. Wilson, Robert Wright and Richard Dawkins among others.[4]

One of the distinctive contributions of evolutionary psychology is that it uses the theory of evolution to account not just for our physical structure but also for much of our psychological and social behavior as well. It claims to account for a vast range of human behavior and emotion— among these, our fear of snakes, prohibition of incest, both sexual promiscuity and chastity, double sexual standards for men and women, altruism, styles of gossip (especially about sex and conflict) and belief in God.

The claim is that natural selection has randomly selected genes which make us *feel* that certain behavior choices are good not bad, right not wrong and attractive not abhorrent because those genes have turned out to be best at reproducing themselves over thousands of generations. So, both moral values and the idea of human dignity itself are in fact, face value

fictions. They are really biologically caused feelings and reasoning that encourage us to perform in such a way that our specific genes are most likely
to replicate themselves, a trick played on us by our own biology.[5]

Although there are significant differences in the camp, evolutionary
psychologists offer a very thorough form of cynicism at a biological level.
Robert Wright, in his popular work *The Moral Animal*, celebrated this cynicism and drew specific parallels with postmodernism:

> What is in our genes' interests is what seems "right"—morally right,
> objectively right, whatever sort of rightness is in order.
>
> In short: if Freud stressed people's difficulty in seeing the truth
> about themselves, the new Darwinians stress the difficulty of seeing
> truth, period. . . . A cynicism deeper than Freudian cynicism may
> have once seemed hard to imagine, but there it is.
>
> This Darwinian brand of cynicism doesn't exactly fill a gaping cul-
> tural void. . . . Already many people believe what the new Darwinism
> underscores: that in human affairs, all (or at least much) is artifice, a
> self-serving manipulation of image. And already this belief helps
> nourish a central strand of the postmodern condition: a powerful in-
> ability to take things seriously. . . .
>
> What is to be avoided at all costs in the postmodern age is ear-
> nestness, which betrays an embarrassing naiveté. . . .
>
> Thus the difficult question of whether the human animal can be a
> moral animal—the question that modern cynicism tends to greet
> with despair—may seem increasingly quaint. The question may be
> whether, after the new Darwinism takes root, the word *moral* can be
> anything but a joke.[6]

I have called evolutionary psychology a deeper level of cynicism than
other schools of thought. In most other forms of cynicism, the cynic exposes the "real" agenda of selfish motivation that I have been consciously
or unconsciously concealing—let us say, my desire for sex, power, money
or approval. But when the evolutionary psychologist has seen through
me, the conscious *I*, with all its layers of motivations, is irrelevant. The only
real game in town is played by my genes, guiding my responses in order
to guarantee their own reproduction. My own conscious *I* is only a spec-
tator to the process of my life, which is directed by biological forces

embedded in my genes, of which I am unaware.

Evolutionary psychology is a relatively new discipline. We have yet to see what its long-term reception will be in the scientific community or what the impact of such profound cynicism will be on the general culture. My guess is that if it continues to gain authority, it will, along with neuroscience, have a far greater contribution to the cynicism of future generations than to our own.

What if I have a moral choice in which doing the "right thing" seems to be against my self-interest? For example, let's say that I must decide whether to blow the whistle on corporate or political corruption—but at risk to my future employment possibilities if not to my safety. If I believe the doctrines of evolutionary psychology, I must understand my own moral convictions about moral "rightness" as coming only from emotions hard-wired into my genes by the accidents of the late hunter-gatherer society. That is, my convictions originate in biological contingency, not in any actual moral order of reality to which I might be responsible. It is hard to imagine that this self-understanding would not decrease my incentive to blow the whistle. After all, one of the most aggressive adherents of this theory suggests that it might make morality itself into a joke.

Cynicism, Self-Marketing and Postmodernism

It is interesting that in the passage quoted (see p. 29), Robert Wright saw a parallel between evolutionary psychology and the idea that all of human affairs are dominated by a self-serving manipulation of image, an analysis that he associated with postmodernism.

In 1959 Erving Goffman wrote an influential book on this theme called *The Presentation of Self in Everyday Life*. In it he looked at human life as a theatrical performance. Goffman described our attempts to control our image in the minds of others as "impression management."[7]

To illustrate his point, Goffman quoted at length from a novel by William Sansom, *A Contest of Ladies*. It tells of an Englishman, called Preedy, on vacation, making his appearance on a Spanish beach:

> He took care to avoid catching anyone's eye. First of all, he had to make it clear to those potential companions of his holiday that they were of no concern to him whatsoever. He stared through them,

round them, over them—eyes lost in space. The beach might have been empty. If by a chance a ball was thrown his way, he looked surprised; then let a smile of amusement lighten his face (kindly Preedy), looked round dazed to see that there *were* people on the beach, tossed it back with a smile to himself and not a smile *at* the people, and then resumed carelessly his nonchalant survey of space.

But it was time to institute a little parade, the parade of the Ideal Preedy. By devious handlings he gave any who wanted to look a chance to see the title of his book—a Spanish translation of Homer, classic thus, but not daring, cosmopolitan too—and then gathered together his beachwrap and bag into a neat sand-resistant pile (Methodical and Sensible Preedy), and tossed aside his sandals (Carefree Preedy, after all).[8]

The author, with x-ray observation into the working of Preedy's mind, saw through all the impression management of our tourist and gave us a running commentary on his contrivance, projection and attempts to manipulate his audience. The author takes off the masks and reveals the "kindly," the "ideal," the "methodical," the "sensible" and the "carefree" Preedy to be actually an insecure, uptight and very self-conscious guy on a Spanish beach.

While Goffman wrote of impression management as a universal human tendency, our own time has created an industry of teaching people how to do it on purpose. You can see this in success literature going back to the 1930s. Dale Carnegie's *How to Win Friends and Influence People* sold eight million copies between 1936 and 1971.[9] Intriguingly, Dale Carnegie, despite his irrepressible buoyancy, began with a pretty condescending view of "other people." He wrote, "When dealing with people, let us remember we are not dealing with creatures of logic. We are dealing with creatures of emotion, creatures bristling with prejudices and motivated by pride and vanity."[10]

From those assumptions he offered advice that if followed would bring success. It was in the form of rules: Be interested in other people. Smile. Remember that a person's name is the sweetest and most important sound in the English language to that person. Be a good listener. Encourage others to talk about themselves.[11]

Sincerity poses a problem. What if you are sincerely not interested and do not really want to smile, repeat someone's name many times or listen to them at length? Success requires sincerity. Well, not quite. Success only requires the *impression* or *appearance* of sincerity. In *The Culture of Cynicism* Richard Stivers points out that this style of success literature advocates the disintegration of the self into multiple selves, teaching us to consciously play roles to get the results that we want in personal interactions. It "extends the self-manipulation of the mind-power ethic to the other: I manipulate myself so that I can manipulate everyone else."[12]

Postmodern thinking has expanded Erving Goffman's insights about human life as a performance into one of its most basic doctrines. There is no mind and no self, just a body with desires and the capacity to play roles or performances in different social settings. What becomes of the value of being a sincere or authentic person? It becomes obsolete. In this view there is no inner, essential self to be honest or sincere. If I think that I *am* a sincere person—thinking, feeling and acting from some essence of who I am and what I believe to be true—I have only conned myself. I have believed my "sincere person" act and have succeeded in fooling *myself* with my own performance.

We are only bundles of desires and the masks worn to satisfy those desires. There is no unique essence of who I am that is durable over time. I am the product of countless accidental factors in my culture and individual experience. I am fluid. I do not struggle to find or discover myself. I choose to invent myself. This is no cause for despair but for relief and exhilaration. It is exciting. I am free to project what images I want into the world to make the world work the way I want.

In *The Saturated Self* Kenneth Gergen described the experience of a friend, who said:

> On Saturday I went shopping with my teenage daughter. I needed a dress for a party the next week. I saw a very attractive dress, black, a daring cut, and with silver sequins. I was very excited until I tried it on. Dejectedly I had to tell my daughter that I just couldn't take it. It just wasn't me. My daughter responded with gentle mockery, "But Mom, that isn't the point. With that dress you would really *be* somebody."

Gergen pointed to the two different worlds illustrated. The mother is a

modernist. She has a sense of her essential self and chooses clothes to express that idea of herself. The daughter is more postmodern, without any
internal sense of herself to which she must be loyal. Her sense of self is all
possibility and flexibility to be shaped by image, style and fashion.[13]

In 1988 Tom Wolfe published a bestselling, satirical novel called *Bonfire
of the Vanities*, in which his all-seeing eye reduced everyone to one dimension—self-marketing.[14] It is the story of a high-flying bond trader on Wall
Street in the 1980s whose life comes unraveled. Each character is transparent before the gaze of the author. He assumes x-ray vision, sees through
them all, and when the masks are off there is nothing but selfishness, artifice and vanity. It is a seven hundred page narrative illustration of Erving
Goffman's thesis—the main human activity is impression management.

Each character is unmasked in an almost formulaic manner. There is
the assistant district attorney who interrogates a beautiful woman but is
more concerned that he positions himself to show off his neck muscles
(he lifts weights) than with the legal substance of the interview. The main
character walks his daughter to the school bus but is less interested in his
daughter than with the impression he gives to bystanders as the ideal
specimen of humanity, the fulfillment of their fantasies. As the story develops vanity consistently overpowers all moral concern, love and social
responsibility. There are no heroes. No one is spared the unmasking of
their pursuit for approval, money, sex, fame and power. Leaders of the
corporate world, politicians, ministers, lawyers, journalists, teachers, civil
rights leaders, high society and low, black and white, the cynics and the
naive—all are exposed.

The strategies of self-marketing offer the power to influence people in-
tentionally in ways that can seem to help us. But the other side of the
equation is that it leads us toward a universal cynicism that imprisons us
between the self-conscious artifice of constructing our own image and the
suspicion of deconstructing the images of others. Can I ever get past cynicism to know a person as he or she really is, or will I always be dealing
with a person's expertise in self-branding, projecting an image that is cal-
culated to impress me? And what is he trying to sell me? These doubts are
not exhilarating or exciting but corrosive to the kinds of relationships that
we consider meaningful.

Have you ever had someone who looked only vaguely familiar approach you and act like a long-lost, intimate friend? Then, before the conversation was over, you discovered that there had been an agenda all along. Was it to sell you financial services, real estate, life insurance (you can never have enough) or Tupperware? We hear of the "commodification of everything."[15] Surely, friendship is one of the easiest things to turn into a commodity, but when exposed it produces a painful sense of betrayal. Again, an invitation to cynicism.

SEEING THROUGH INSTITUTIONS
Government, Family and Church

Political parties, journalists, and institutions have all earned our cynicism. By now, we might well start to understand that this is something like a permanent condition.

WILLIAM CHALOUPKA

Their only plan is to bring down a person of prominence.

KING DAVID

The overwhelming majority of people who shape our national media hold the belief that human beings are rarely motivated by anything beyond material self-interest. Media moguls and national columnists tend toward this view with the same ferocity and irrationality that they attribute to religious fundamentalists.

MICHAEL LERNER

If you work for the government, it's dog eat dog. If you work in the corporate world it's just the other way around.

ANONYMOUS RADIO ANNOUNCER

SOMETIMES OUR MOST SEVERE DISAPPOINTMENTS are with people who represent important institutions. We have the highest expectations of them. They also possess a power and authority that make their failures or rejection all the more painful, disillusioning and destructive.

One of the identifying characteristics of our time is a widespread loss of a respect for the authority of our public institutions and of confidence in what they do. It is called the "delegitimization" of institutions. If enough of our major cultural institutions are widely under suspicion for being destructive in their impact or corrupt in their motivation—"in it for power" or "in it only for money"—then there is a general loss of cultural authority. This is no small development. We live in and through institutions. Like them or not, we cannot escape them. If our major institutions cannot be trusted to serve the public good, we will move toward an individualism that will trust only ourselves and perhaps our close friends but invest nothing in public life.[1]

Think of the cynical critiques of sports, education, politics, medicine, the arts, religion, entertainment, media and law as well as of the corporate world—all "in it for the money" or "only in it for power." We will look specifically at cynicism about three institutions: government, the family and the church.

Seeing Through Government

Political scientist William Chaloupka wrote, "Whatever else Americans are cynical about, we are hugely cynical about politics."[2] We live in a fairly constant drizzle of clichés that bear this out. Think of what "It's all politics" means. Washington is "Hollywood for ugly people,"[3] "Politics is about lying." Think of the distinct genre of lawyer jokes. For many, their cynicism is the conviction that politics has nothing to do with public service but only money and power.

Wagging the dog. The 1997 film *Wag the Dog* is a good place to start on political cynicism. It showed the president of the United States who was (justly) accused of having had a sexual relationship with an unwilling teenage girl who had been visiting the White House. It was eleven days before the presidential election. Damage control people were brought in. They decided to stage a virtual war with Albania to distract the public from the sexual scandal and make the president look presidential. The "war" would take place in a TV studio and be sent out on national news.

It pictured the wheels of government guided by amoral techniques for retaining power, in complete and shameless disregard for truth, honesty, justice and human life. Yet the message sent out to distract the public was dripping with high moral principles and sentimentality. The most substantial involvement of the president himself was a long discussion about the color of the kitten (white) that a young girl would carry in the studio-simulated war scene for a TV news release. The cynical bite of the film was first aimed at the unprincipled practitioners of electoral politics, but secondarily at the American people for their mindless gullibility and sentimentality.

Political cynics had a windfall of confirmation in 1998. President Clinton ordered rocket attacks on the Afghanistan camps of Osama bin Laden just as he was having to admit that he lied to the public about his relationship with Monica Lewinsky. He then bombed Iraq just as impeachment proceedings were beginning against him. They were, as far as I know, real rockets and real bombs. The cry went up that real life "out does" art.

Cynicism about citizenship. I heard a National Public Radio piece in the week before a presidential election offering ten reasons to vote. The first five will give you the idea: Why vote? (1) It is free. (2) It is painless. (3) It won't be very crowded. (4) It will be a good place to meet your neighbors. (5) The voting booth is a pleasant place of peace and quiet, no one is allowed to hassle you there. Of course it was intended to be humorous, but what does it communicate about the responsibility of citizenship? The person naive enough to think that their vote matters is mocked by its irony.

There is a standing invitation to political cynicism in that the power of politics is constantly overlobbied, oversold and overpromised, while government necessarily underperforms by comparison. This pattern is now part of the scenery. So many of the major domestic problems the nation faces have shown themselves to be intractable problems to both political parties. Promises of a fix inspire suspicion.

Cynicism and news media. The news has become one of the most important forms of entertainment for Americans. It is now called "infotainment." This produces tensions that have driven those within the industry to pretty cynical evaluations of their own craft. This is what Roger Ailes has concluded about campaign coverage:

> Let's face it, there are three things that the media are interested in:
> pictures, mistakes and attacks. It's my orchestra-pit theory of poli-

tics. If you have two guys on a stage and one guy says, "I have a solution to the Middle East problem," and the other guy falls into the
orchestra pit, who do you think is going to be on the evening
news?[4]

Journalism, which is responsible for bringing us so much of our version
of the world, is controlled by having to entertain. That need commits news
to a cynical slant. A journalist is a slacker who does not look behind obvious appearances to find what the subjects of the news had to gain personally from what they said or did. The reporter who only saw a person at
"face value" and did not find an underlying ulterior motive may have been
soft, unsophisticated, duped, lazy or even "paid for."

Sincere people with integrity, just doing their jobs, do not make news,
let alone "good" news. We want something more interesting. We cannot be
so foolish as to protest that journalism has caused culture-wide cynicism.
Journalists give us what we are looking for, and we pay them well to give
it to us. We would feel cheated if journalism did not feed our cynicism.

William Chaloupka wrote:

> The reporter is America's archetypal cynic, dedicated by professional
> standards of conduct to persistent doubt and disbelief. The news
> media have become so important to the political world that the two
> share, and darken, each other's stains. Everyone—politico, reporter,
> and audience—knows that words and images rule. They also know
> that those who generate words and images can and do misuse
> them.[5]

Modern political cynicism is fed by the public demand for the real story
behind the appearances. Glutted on hype, spin and image management,
we are starved for something unscripted, spontaneous, real—"cringe moments" and words spoken when someone didn't know the mike was
turned on.

While the public demands the cynical, backstage view, we are also cynical about the news media ourselves precisely because of its cynicism. We
think of journalists as sharks and complain of the feeding frenzies when
they smell blood in the water of a public figure who is down. We want reality TV but are suspicious that it too is staged.

Seeing Through Marriage and Family

The shortfall between ideals of the family and real family life is vast. The sheer size of the hopes dashed ensures that cynicism about the family will be filled with bitterness and betrayal.

Cynicism about the family. In our pluralistic society it is impossible to define *family* or *marriage* to everybody's satisfaction. Part of the call to redefine these words comes from a strong cynical voice against what has been called the "traditional family." The traditional family is made up of husband and wife living together with their children, if they have children.

Listen to Douglas Coupland in his description of a conversation in a bar.

Claire stopped in midmotion and came back to the bar, where she lifted her sunglasses and confided in me, "You know, I really think that when God puts together families, he sticks his finger into the white pages and selects a group of people at random and then says to them all, "Hey! You're going to spend the next seventy years together even though you have nothing in common and don't even *like* each other. *And,* should you not feel yourself caring about any of this group of strangers, *even for a second,* you will feel just *dreadful.*" That's what I think. What about *you?*[6]

Think of the Academy-Award-winning film *American Beauty,* with its picture of the family with the husband and wife dismembering each other in their dinner-time conversation. They were two people who were perfectly capable of civility—with those outside the family. But in the family they were locked helplessly in a pact of mutual destruction, with their daughter caught between them.

You can hear the cynicism of young people about families that they have not chosen to be born into. They are caught without realizing it in prisons that are destroying them with double-binds, manipulation, revenge and open malice. They later see through the aura of warmth and sentimentality that surrounds the public image of the family and feel mocked by the Norman Rockwell images of happy families. As I have listened for years to the stories of young people, I am often amazed— given their experience—that their cynicism about the family is not deeper than it is.

Cynicism about marriage. A divorced man strategized, "Instead of getting married again, I'm going to find a woman that I don't like and just give her a house."Much of the cynicism about marriage relates to the high rate of divorce. It surrounds one element of marriage—its permanence. But it can come from different directions.

Some look with cynicism at themselves and what they see as our whole population given over to dysfunction and selfishness. They say that the commitment of the futures of both partners" 'til death parts us"is tragically both essential to marriage and also completely unrealistic. Divorce is a catastrophe. I think of the people who have come to be with us in L'Abri who have lived through the divorce of their parents. One man said,"There has been nothing in my life so painful and traumatic as my parents' divorce. But my parents tried hard to make their marriage work. I've got plenty of problems myself. Why should I think my own future marriage would be any more likely to succeed? Why would I ever wish my experience on children of my own?"

Others look with cynicism on the institution of traditional marriage itself and praise the high divorce rate. They speak for adults, with less attention to the children's perspective. The high divorce rate shows that people are at last valuing what really matters in marriage—the quality of the relationship instead of permanent marriage as a public show or a grim duty. They say that the promise" 'Til death parts us"actually encourages manipulation, dishonesty and a stifling of growth—forty years of holy deadlock. Postmodern ideas about the "fluid self"—that you can invent and reinvent yourself many times in the course of your life—contribute to cynicism about any such naive long-term commitment. From this perspective traditional marriage vows are both ignorant and arrogant. How can you pretend that you know who you will be years later in your life? Or to know who your spouse will be? Why make such irresponsible, unfulfillable promises?

Law professor Thomas Morgan pointed out that the laws of the land themselves are cynical about the permanence of marriage:

> It is easier in these United States to walk away from a marriage than
> from a commitment to purchase a used car. Most contracts cannot
> be unilaterally abrogated; marriages in contemporary America can

be terminated by practically anyone at any time and without cause.[7]

Increasingly, traditional marriage is seen as just one lifestyle option among several. Although the rate of divorce is no longer rising, the rate of cohabitation is. Childbearing and marriage are ever more detached from each other, and the pressure for same-sex marriage assumes the authority for people to redefine the institution of marriage itself. Even when marriage is not attacked directly with cynical criticism, its cultural authority is profoundly weakened by the widening acceptability of the alternatives.

Seeing Through the Church

In chapter five we will consider cynicism aimed directly at God. Closely related is cynicism about the church, an institution made up of people who claim to represent God on earth. A well-worn path leads from cynicism about God to cynicism about his church. Of course, if you have decided that the God of biblical faith does not exist, then you already believe that the church of Christ is self-deceived. But there is a cynical path that runs in the other direction also. It looks first at the church, sees through it in disgust and then concludes that it can extend that cynicism all the way up to God.

The walk doesn't match the talk. The church of Jesus Christ makes extraordinary claims, which almost seem to invite cynical response. Christians say that this transcendent Creator has stooped to make personal contact with their fragile, morally twisted lives through what Jesus of Nazareth did two thousand years ago in his life, death and resurrection. They teach that through him their lives can be meaningful at a cosmic level because of his forgiveness, care and love for them—extending even beyond their physical deaths to eternal life spent with him. They say that this same God will bring human history to completion in a final accounting and fulfillment.

The internal life and external mission of the church have always depended on the credibility of these extraordinary claims. The question is, which is more believable, the truth of the church's words or the possibility that these people are not in contact with God at all but only with their own projections, compensations, consolations and self-interest? Which is more plausible, that the church is really the "people of God" or that it is just the social club designed to sustain that illusion?

Cynicism about the church finds a grotesque dissonance between the church's claim and its reality, between its talk and its walk. As a result, the church's claim need not be taken seriously except as something to be rejected. It says, "Hey, for all the righteous talk, you are just as materialistic, corrupt and have just as many problems as the rest of us, but the church is more dangerous because it thinks it has God on its side." Discussions of jihad, religious wars, crusades, inquisition and witch hunts quickly come into the discussion.

The betrayal of grace. There is a story that C. S. Lewis was once asked to participate in a discussion about what, if anything, was unique about the Christian faith. He evidently said just one word: *grace.* Grace is the great theme of Old and New Testaments.

Jesus' best-known parable, the prodigal son (Lk 15:11-32), is about grace. It tells of a young man whose father meets him as he comes home asking for forgiveness after having blown his share of the family fortune and disgraced the family name. The father hugs him, brings him back to the house and has a banquet to celebrate his son's return. The grand miracle of the Bible is that in Jesus of Nazareth, God joined the human race to secure this forgiveness by his death and resurrection, to establish grace as the path of return to God. Jesus, as he was being crucified, prayed for the forgiveness of the very men who crucified him.

Some of the most common and bitter cynicism I encounter against the Christian church happens when people go to a church, hungry for this message. Instead of being met by a celebration of the extraordinary grace of God, they are met, in certain churches, with an experience of shame, guilt and rejection. Along with rules, rules and still more fine-tuned rules, in some churches a person can encounter a profound spirit of judgment and self-righteousness. To cite a trivial but telling example, a man went to a church seeking a place of grace but made the mistake of wearing a lapel button which read "I Quit Smoking." Rather than receiving any encouragement or acceptance, he was sternly criticized for ever having smoked in the first place.

There are churches where you need to be pretty well scrubbed, clean and prosperous. If you have children, they'd better not be in any trouble—and preferably no body piercing, loud music, black leather or questions that sound hostile to the Christian faith. In churches specializing in the moral molehills, attention is inevitably distracted from the moral mountains of pride, greed, injustice and neglect of love. Those who step into churches like this, or those who grow up in them, are high-risk for cynicism about both the church and then also its God.

The cynicism that sees through to unmask institutions can feel affirmed in a world where they all appear to use high ideals as propaganda to cover some form of self-interest. It is difficult to argue against the slant of the news, the innuendoes of the witty and the experience of widespread institutional failure.

SEEING THROUGH GOD

Even when I cry out, "Violence!" I am not answered; I call aloud, but there is no justice.

JOB

Fate (or whatever it is) delights to produce a great capacity and then frustrate it. Beethoven went deaf. By our standards a mean joke; the monkey trick of a spiteful imbecile.

C. S. LEWIS

If Jesus Christ were to come today, people would not even crucify him. They would ask him to dinner, hear what he had to say, and make fun of him.

THOMAS CARLYLE

SO, WHAT DOES IT MEAN TO BE CYNICAL ABOUT GOD? Basically, it is exactly the same as being cynical about any other person. God in reality does not measure up to God as advertised. His "goodness" is a ploy that is transparent to us. There is a vast range of ideas and attitudes that express this project, and their most popular forms change over time.

It is not surprising that the God of the Bible would become the object of cynical targeting. He is presented as both source and judge of moral perfection itself. He is presented as Creator of heaven and earth, as the providential Sustainer of our present world order, and as the Source of justice and love. No one else could ever have so far to fall under cynical criticism. In addition, if cynicism cannot bring him down, he remains as a certain challenge or threat—a potential transcendent meddler in and judge over human affairs. In this chapter we will examine the cynical criticism of his management of the world, and in chapter six we will look at cynicism about human knowledge and experience of God.

Seeing Through God's Character: Grievances with Providence

If you believe that God is both loving and powerful on earth, an immediate tension is created. If this wonderful God is really there, then why is there so much suffering, sin and evil on his watch? This problem comes with a thousand variations, whether you are reading of the suffering of others far away or whether you are in the midst of an agonizing, life-jarring tragedy yourself.

The problem is not new. It has been a timeless tension for any who believed in a loving and powerful God, and who were too honest to minimize or ignore the horror of evil and suffering. The tension can escalate from doubt to unbelief to hatred against the very idea of such a God—or to an exhausted indifference.

The Bible records promises made by God about himself and his commitments. They are not evasive, timid or shy:

> The LORD will not forsake his people;
>   he will not abandon his heritage. (Ps 94:14)

> The LORD is gracious and merciful,
>   slow to anger and abounding in steadfast love.
> The LORD is good to all,
>   and his compassion is over all that he has made. . . .
> The LORD upholds all who are falling,
>   and raises up all who are bowed down. (Ps 145:8-9, 14)

The voices of cynicism are quickly heard. They say: Really? Not when I was falling! Is God *really* our helper and redeemer? Does he *really* love me? If he does, why doesn't he respond to my prayers? Why in the world doesn't he help? He does what I wouldn't do to *my* children, or to any one that I loved! Perhaps he doesn't really care. Maybe he is impotent to do anything even if he does care. Maybe God is actually malicious or has lost contact with us or is indifferent to both our suffering and well-being.

These are not necessarily the thoughts of enemies of God. We find them on the pages of the Bible itself, in the minds and mouths of some of the greatest heroes of faith as they struggle to live by faith as broken peo- ✝ ple in a very broken world.

Job. Job, whose faithfulness God himself had recognized, lost his children to violent death, his wealth and public reputation in the same disasters. He then lost his health, with painful boils all over his body. His wife advised him to get it over with, curse God and die. The friends in his philosophy club told him it was all his fault. He had sinned in some dreadful way, which had caused these disasters. If he would only confess, he would be back on his feet in no time. At the same time, and making matters worse, Job could see openly wicked enemies of God prospering.

> The tents of robbers are at peace,
>   and those who provoke God are secure,
>   who bring their god in their hands. (Job 12:6)

He felt that he had become God's bitter enemy, the archery target in God's back garden. Job did not curse God, but his questions and accusations certainly came from a deep suspicion of God's intentions. Archibald MacLeish wrote his own interpretation of the story of Job in a play called *J.B.* One of the characters says, "The one thing God can't stomach is man, that scratcher at the cracked creation."[1]

Asaph. Asaph was a musician and poet who led worship in the congregation of Israel at the time of King David, around 1000 B.C. He was the author of a number of the psalms of the Old Testament. He too wrote of the clash he felt between God's promises and his own experience in the world.

> I was envious of the arrogant;
>   I saw the prosperity of the wicked.
>
> For they have no pain;
>   their bodies are sound and sleek.
> They are not in trouble as others are;
>   they are not plagued like other people.

Therefore pride is their necklace;
    violence covers them like a garment. . . .
They set their mouths against heaven,
    and their tongues range over the earth.

Therefore the people turn and praise them,
    and find no fault in them.
And they say, "How can God know?
    Is there knowledge in the Most High?"
Such are the wicked;
    always at ease, they increase in riches.
All in vain I have kept my heart clean
    and washed my hands in innocence.
For all day long I have been plagued,
    and am punished every morning. (Ps 73:3-6, 9-14)

As with Job, Asaph grieved that virtue is not rewarded in this world, and looked with a cynical eye at the payoffs for faithfulness to God. A life honoring God is "all in vain"; it leaves you worse off than if you mocked God. Asaph seemed even to anticipate a postmodern exhaustion about trying to figure it all out: "But when I thought how to understand this, / it seemed to me a wearisome task" (Ps 73:16). Both Job and Asaph struggled with the providence of God. How difficult to trust God's own version of things—that he is faithful to his promises, that his plans for us are for good and not evil. How much more plausible, sometimes, is a cynical reading of God's influence on the world!

C. S. Lewis. C. S. Lewis, a professor at Oxford and Cambridge, living three thousand years after Asaph, experienced the same problem at the death of his wife following her long and agonizing battle with bone cancer. Afterward, he wrote a small book called *A Grief Observed*.

Not that I am (I think) in much danger of ceasing to believe in God. The real danger is of coming to believe such dreadful things about him. The conclusion I dread is not "So there's no God after all," but "So this is what God's really like. Deceive yourself no longer."

Fate (or whatever it is) delights to produce a great capacity and then frustrate it. Beethoven went deaf. By our standards a mean joke; the monkey trick of a spiteful imbecile.

Sooner or later I must face the question in plain language. What reason have we, except our own desperate wishes, to believe that God is, by any standard we can conceive, "good"? Doesn't all the *prima facie* evidence suggest exactly the opposite?[2]

These men all wrestled with cynical doubts about God's character to the point of real challenge to their faith. Yet in different ways, each came through that doubt and eventually reached a resolution in faith. They even proceeded to teach others about God's goodness after these words were written.

Seeing Through God's Character to His Nonexistence

But there are others who found no resolution. The tension was too much, and belief in God snapped. The crisis over God's character was so extreme they concluded that there was no such God at all. By different paths they saw through faith in God as a mistake or as so problematic that it had to be indefinitely suspended.

Stephen Crane. Stephen Crane (1871-1900), son of a Methodist minister, is best known for his Civil War novel *The Red Badge of Courage.* He also wrote a short story called "The Open Boat," an account of his own experience of several days rowing in a tiny boat with three other men, trying to get to the Florida coast after a shipwreck in January. It is an agonizing story of alternating hope and despair as they approached the shore in heavy surf. He wrote as a refrain: "If I am going to be drowned—if I am going to be drowned—If I am going to be drowned, why in the name of the seven mad gods who rule the sea, was I allowed to come thus far and contemplate the sand and the trees?"[3]

He struck out against a god who had for him become the same as fate or the forces of nature. This god seemed at first to be malicious but then later indifferent to him.

When it occurs to a man that nature does not regard him as important, and that she feels she would not maim the universe by disposing of him, he at first wishes to throw bricks at the temple, and he hates deeply the fact that there are no bricks and no temples.[4]

Mark Twain. Mark Twain was well known in many roles to a wide range of the American public. He gave us some of the most memorable characters in American literature. He was a river boat captain, a storyteller, a stand-up entertainer and comedian, a social critic, a failed entrepreneur and a cosmic cynic. He was known for his cynicism about human nature, God and God's hypocritical followers. Later in his life, after deep tragedies and losses, he wrote openly of his profound bitterness, and not with his characteristic humor or irony by which so many had known him.

> There is no God, no universe, no human race, no earthly life, no heaven, no hell. It is all a dream—a grotesque and foolish dream. Nothing exists but you, and you are but a thought, a useless thought, a homeless thought, wandering forlorn among the empty eternities.[5]

At his death in 1910 he spoke for many in the twentieth century who would not only see through the God of the Bible but through the whole human project—as a "grotesque and foolish dream."

Battles over believing in the providence of God and in the meaningfulness of human life have been voiced for as long as we have record of voices. Cynical judgments about God either temporarily threatened or permanently derailed faith. The central grievance was the appalling injustice and suffering in a world in which God claimed to be both good and powerful. In MacLeish's words in *J.B.*, "If God is God, He is not good. If God is good, He is not God."[6] God is an ogre or a weakling. Either way, it is a godforsaken world.

But there is another turn in the history of cynicism about God. It is cynicism about human belief in God. It is actually not a discussion directly about God at all but of human knowledge of God. It has probably done more to undermine confidence in God than the questions about his providence.

SEEING THROUGH
HUMAN KNOWLEDGE OF GOD
The Masters of Suspicion

In former times one sought to prove that there is no God—today one indicates how the belief that there is God could arise and how this belief acquired its weight and importance: a counterproof that there is no God thereby becomes superfluous. When in former times one had refuted the "proofs of the existence of God" put forward, there always remained the doubt whether better proofs might not be adduced than those just refuted: in those days atheists did not know how to make a clean sweep.

FRIEDRICH NIETZSCHE

I have tried to show that religious ideas have arisen from the same need as have all the other achievements of civilization: from the necessity of defending oneself against the crushingly superior force of nature.

SIGMUND FREUD

FROM THE MIDDLE OF THE NINETEENTH CENTURY another strand of cynicism has gained enormous power in peoples' minds. It is cynicism not so much about God himself but about human knowledge and experience of God. The idea is that belief in God is actually a twisted and inflated misunderstanding of ourselves and our needs. It is built on the notion of an ideology critique.

The Ideology Critique

I can remember being the object of an ideology critique once when I had just finished graduate school. My wife was seven months pregnant and we were still uncertain about where we would live or how we would support ourselves. I mentioned to an older friend that we were trusting that God would direct us. She paused, and with a look of mild annoyance replied, "Oh, I see you need the security of believing that." I quietly ground my teeth at her condescension, but only later realized what a significant response she had made. I had spoken of God. She had made an instant translation and heard me speaking only of my own insecurity about the future. What lay behind her translation were staggering certainties—that knowledge of God can be reduced to a human psychology of weakness. She had spoken without reflection, without ever having read the thinkers whose ideas had become second nature to her.

What is this ideology critique? Imagine yourself trying to dissuade a group of people from some serious self-deception. Let's say you are unable to persuade them to change their minds by rational argument, and you can't call them liars. They are not lying. They are deceived. But their error is widespread and persistent. It contains prejudices and internal strategies that counter or explain away all objections to it. What can you do?

One way to cure them of their errors is to ignore the whole question of the untruth of their self-deception but suggest an uncomplimentary explanation of *why* they believe what they do. You could try to show them the hidden (preferably embarrassing, shameful or immoral) motivations that are the *cause* of their beliefs. If those hidden motivations can plausibly account for the belief, they will abandon it as a liability. Believers will retreat in shame and disgrace—undeceived. Of course there is a certain intellectual violence and arrogance in this strategy. Some may be convinced but others may take offense and entrench themselves even more deeply in their errors.

It is just this strategy that has been used by several very influential thinkers from the midnineteenth into the twentieth century—to undeceive believers in the God of the Bible, to free them from the power of their persistent superstitions. They stood at the end of the tradition of Enlightenment modernism. They have been called the "masters of suspicion." Theirs was a cynicism that started by assuming that there was no

God that we need to worry about. It then saw through and tried to explain the curious but persistent existence of religion in the absence of God. Its interest was less with God himself than with a suspicious examination of the origin of peoples' ideas and alleged experience of God.

This strategy has been called an "ideology critique." An ideology is a system of ideas that you hold not so much because you know that it is true but because it brings a practical benefit or advantage to you as a result of believing it. It has a pragmatic value or payoff. An ideology critique aims to expose religious beliefs as merely ideologies, and so to discredit the integrity of my beliefs because of my (self-serving) motivations for believing them. So, the assumption of my friend had been that my insecurity about my future was a sufficient explanation for my belief in God.

Peter Sloterdijk explained that an ideology critique declares war on the consciousness of the person or group in question, though it pretends to be unbiased and scientific. The idea is to outflank or go behind "opponents" by revealing their own hidden intentions to them and to whomever else is watching.[1] In even the thumbnail sketches of some of the men called "the masters of suspicion," you will see that they use variations on two challenges to theism. Belief in God is motivated by either the need for consolation in loneliness and disappointment (the need for a crutch in weakness) or a need to justify self-interest (the need for a sanctifying smokescreen for selfishness). It is either a palliative for inner fears or a legitimation for external aggression—and sometimes both. There were four men whose writing was especially far-reaching and powerful in its suspicion.

Ludwig Feuerbach. Ludwig Feuerbach, a German philosopher, began as a student of theology. He became a student of Georg W. F. Hegel and an inspiration to Karl Marx. His most influential work was published in 1841, *The Essence of Christianity.*[2] He taught that we are corrupt and helpless creatures, bound for death. To minimize the painful awareness of these realities, we project the idea of God into the sky. Where we are corrupt, God is perfect. Where we are helpless, God is powerful. Where we will die, God is immortal and is the giver of eternal life. He walked through most of the major Christian teachings showing how they were rooted in felt human psychological needs, not in divine reality.

From this perspective the proper study of theology is really the study of human psychology. God has no objective or independent existence. He exists only as an aspect of a human psychological apparatus—a safety-and-comfort mechanism. People believe in him not because he is really "there"but because the world is unbearably fearful, bleak and comfortless *without imagining* that he is there. Faith in God becomes a crutch for those without the strength, courage or honesty to face themselves and the cold world as it is.

Karl Marx. While Feuerbach held that faith was motivated by the need for consolation and compensation, Karl Marx used the other strategy of cynicism. Religion legitimizes and sanctifies selfishness. Religion is suspect not for its psychological payoffs as much as for its economic and social incentives. He is famous for saying that "religion is the opiate of the masses," meaning that it is a depressant to inhibit the desire for social and economic change for which the masses should be striving. Religion, and by *religion* Marx meant Christianity, encourages the status quo. So God was the sanctifying smokescreen for economic self-interest of those in power.

The doctrine of divine providence had been used to teach the poor that their low station in life was a direct expression of the will of God. Any attempt to change it is rebelling against God's providential order and care. In the words of Peter Sloterdijk, speaking for Marx, "Religion has the sole task of establishing a permanent, mute willingness to sacrifice in the hearts of the subjugated."[3] Belief in a blissful afterlife is an added disincentive to making disruptive social and economic changes in this world. Providence is also used by the rich to give them peace of mind as they maintain domination and oppression of the poor. Christianity is an ideology in which the special interests of the few in power are made to seem as if they were the common good.

Friedrich Nietzsche. Friedrich Nietzsche, whose father and both grandfathers were Lutheran pastors, made his most powerful critique not from science as a foundation but from an intuitively grounded and passionate assault on Christian morality. Christianity was the weak seeking revenge against the powerful. Priests who were jealous and resentful of the intelligent and powerful invented Christian slave morality to oppose the success of the strong. God was dead, but love, humility and justice lived on as the only way the weak were able to control the strong and at the same time hide from themselves their own frustrated will to power. He laughed at those who were "weaklings who thought themselves good because they had no claws."[4] He wrote:

> They are clever, their virtues have clever fingers. But they lack fists, their fingers do not know how to fold into fists. To them, virtue is what makes modest and tame: with it they make the wolf into a dog and man himself into man's best domestic animal.[5]

Nietzsche saw Christians as those who embrace cowardice, weakness and safety in order to not have to take the risks of mastery. The great pay-off of the Christian faith is that it provides self-respect and social acceptability for helplessness and cowardice.

Nietzsche mastered the use of what we have called the ideology critique, going behind the conscious and rational arguments of his opponents to expose the motivations for their belief. He was then able to make a "clean sweep."[6]

Sigmund Freud. Sigmund Freud's version of the ideology critique was that a Father in heaven was an infantile projection that offered a person a certain neurotic consolation. He also saw belief in God as a way to hide from ourselves an awareness of our own sexual and aggressive impulses that would make us ashamed if we recognized them. Our moral principles are more likely to blind us to our own motives than to heighten our awareness of them. God and morality, far from offering redemption, lead us into illusion and neurosis.

Freud reiterated the ideas of Feuerbach that God functioned as a compensation or crutch for our fears and inadequacies. As our childhood fears and feelings of helplessness are eased by the belief in the power and competence of our parents, so adults believe in God in order to sustain such childhood feelings of security in the "grown up" world. He was particularly aware of God as a counterweight to the fear of death and as a consolation for the sacrifices necessary to live in civilization.

In his battle with religious faith he saw that he could be most persuasive not by engaging the truth of the theological issues themselves but by getting someone to feel ashamed of their motivations for believing their theology. As the philosopher Susan Neiman put it, "Of course we long for a world to feel at home in. Freud makes the desire seem not deep but embarrassing."[7]

The Cynical Impact

An ideology critique, if successful, unmasks faith to be only"instrumental faith."Instrumental faith does not address a real God who is really there. It is rather a pragmatic human strategy or ideology that uses belief in God as an instrument to achieve some practical end. That end becomes the highest goal, and God is important only insofar as he serves that goal. God is no longer the Maker of heaven and earth. He is the one who, by believing in him, can provide me with the crutch for peace of mind or the smokescreen of feeling and appearing justified in my selfishness. In instrumental religion the question of truth is in the background; practical benefits of belief are center stage.

The cynicism of the various ideology critiques lies not in its perfectly valid exposures and criticisms of instrumental religion functioning as ideologies. It is in the much more radical claim that *all religion* is instrumental religion. There is no other. Cynical judgment is a totalizing judgment. There is no equivalent to the biblical distinction between true and authentic faith and false, bogus religion. To the cynic it is all false intrinsically and by definition. Remember that these men set out to explain how, given God's absence, there could be persistent faith in him. Since there is no God, then of course any faith that existed could only have been inspired by some *other*, lesser, instrumental motivations. All belief in God must necessarily have been an exercise in some kind of useful illusion.

It is hard to overestimate the impact of these men on modern attitudes and discussion about God. As early as the 1920s Walter Lippmann wrote in *A Preface to Morals* that in churches influenced by these ideas, something profound was lacking—"the conviction that religion comes from God."[8] Faith had become a human fabrication. But it was considered a fairly useful fabrication as long as its moral teaching matched the accepted wisdom of the time. These ideas are now in the air we breathe.

In the tradition of the Enlightenment, the masters of suspicion saw themselves as courageous enlighteners of the ignorant and superstitious. Although they are associated with cynicism it is important to see that they were not cynical about all knowledge. Each of them was in fact supremely confident that he had at last got it right after centuries of human groping in ignorance and superstition. Each felt he had unmasked the most fundamental illusions that had dogged human existence. Even Nietzsche, the most skeptical of them all about human knowing, nevertheless wrote with the certainty of one who was passionately prosecuting error.

It is not as if these men were the first to ever attack another's ideas by unmasking their motivations. In fact the classical Greek cynicism of Diogenes and Crates used this weapon freely. But with them it was with laughter, satire, street theater, from society's outsiders. What is different is that the modern ideology critiques no longer come from outsiders. They come from the centers of respectability and higher education, and often claim the authority of science. Ideology critique has, to use Sloterdijk's words, "put on a suit and tie."[9] They also lay down cynical doctrines in intellectual structures that all subsequent enlightened people must follow if they are to be part of the modern discussion.

Peter Sloterdijk offers a helpful metaphor to describe this ideology critique emerging from the Enlightenment:

> Ideology critique, having become respectable, imitates surgical procedure: Cut open the patient with the critical scalpel and operate under impeccably sterile conditions. The opponent is cut open in front of everyone, until the mechanism of his error is laid bare. The outer skin of delusion and the nerve endings of "actual" motives are hygienically separated and prepared. . . . Ideology critique is now interested not in winning over the vivisected opponent but in focusing on the "corpse," the critical extract of its ideas, which lie in the libraries of enlighteners and in which one can easily read about their grave falsity.[10]

But the enlightened surgeons of suspicion, Feuerbach, Marx, Nietzsche and Freud, exposed themselves to a certain vulnerability. Who licensed *them* to do surgery? Where did their ideas of anatomy and pathology come from? Was their "operating room" really antiseptic? Had they taken the Hippocratic oath that they would "do no harm"?

There has arisen from the ranks another loosely held-together response with all these questions and more. It has cast suspicion on the masters of suspicion themselves. It has also exposed and publicized the medical disasters of their surgery. They want to keep us all on the operating table, but with different rules. This brings us to postmodern cynicism.

SEEING THROUGH MEANING TO POWER
Postmodern Cynicism

*Two contrasting interpretations of interpretation now compete
for the soul of Western culture. . . . The one seeks understanding; the other tries to avoid being taken in.*

KEVIN VANHOOZER

*Everyone is in it for the money or the political power which is too
easily translatable into money, and which money easily buys.
People do not necessarily think all this is for the good, but their
mocking cynicism tells them that this is the way things are, and
they act accordingly.*

JEFFREY GOLDFARB

POSTMODERNISM IS A DIFFUSE SET OF TRENDS, having grown in the academic community in the 1980s and into the wider culture in the 1990s.
It represents both a rebellion against our enlightened surgeons and also
an extension of their ideas. The rebellion was especially against the
therapeutic results of the surgeons of the Enlightenment. To extend the
analogy, postmodern surgeons still wanted to do surgery but had different theories of anatomy and pathology, mocked any idea that any pro-
cedures could ever be antiseptic and were cynical or indifferent about
the health benefits of their own treatments. Their basic surgical plan was
to cut open and expose the patient's overt but especially covert use of
power in a process called deconstruction. Some of the best known are
Jacques Derrida, Michel Foucault and Jean-François Lyotard (from

France), and Richard Rorty and Stanley Fish (from the United States).

The failed visions of modernism. Postmodernism has rejected modernist "treatments," that is, the positive Enlightenment strategies for building a better world. A defining moment for the public visibility of postmodernism was the tearing down of the Berlin Wall in 1989. That represented the recognition of the massive and catastrophic failure of Karl Marx's "surgical treatment" for the ills of our race. Marxism had been a grand modernist plan to end injustice and oppression through revolution and economic and political reorganization. It ended not only in economic disaster but also only after the imprisonment and slaughter of tens of millions of citizens by their own governments (far exceeding the deaths due to the two world wars). Lenin had been fond of pointing out that to make an omelet you need to break some eggs. Millions of eggs were broken, but no one ever made an omelet.

Most postmodernists also have a gloomy assessment of the track record of the modernism of Western democratic capitalism. In it they would see that the doctrine of progress has legitimized appalling slavery and crimes against indigenous peoples in general. It has sustained racism, colonialism and sexism, and has had catastrophic consequences for the environment. Progress has brought a world of prosperity for a few, but one in which just about everything is now turned into a commodity.

The Postmodern Critique: The Meaning of Language

Postmodernism wants to use a deeper ideology critique, one that deconstructs the motives of even the masters of suspicion. This, to continue the metaphor, would be the attempt to correct modernist surgeons' theories of pathology, their ideas of what is wrong with the world. They put our language itself on the operating table and took two steps: revealing the problematic meanings of words and then our hidden motivations for using them. Meanings are flexible, and our overriding motivation is winning in the struggle for power.

To start with the meaning of language, the relationship between words and the reality they refer to is much more slippery than we usually think. The objects that we find in the world do not drop down from the sky with labels on them, establishing once for all the link between each word and the thing to which it refers. People, as part of the development of human cultures have assigned not just sounds (words) to objects but they have decided on ways to classify and organize the world into groups of meanings, such as "animal," "vegetable" and "mineral," or "male" and "female," or "good" and "evil." Our words do not represent a perfect expression of the essence of things but only somewhat arbitrary and accidental conventions from our limited and changing human perspectives.

Here is a simple illustration. Think of an occasion when language is actually being constructed today on a very small scale. Imagine an entomologist who discovers a "new" beetle in the rain forest. Language is being made or changed as soon as somebody decides what to name the beetle. What will they call it?

Among the colleagues of our entomologist, there might be two groups, "lumpers" and "splitters." The lumpers are those scientists inclined to lump this beetle together with another known subspecies of beetle. It is really not a new subspecies at all, its "new" characteristics are within the normal variations of an existing, known group. But the splitters say no, these variations are outside the norm. It is a new subspecies. We need to call it by a different name. The decision will either make one classification of beetle a little wider and more inclusive (lumpers win) or it will "create" a whole new subspecies of beetle (splitters win). Whatever they decide will determine how people think of beetles.

The verdict on what name to call the beetle will be decided not because it had a label on it from God or because something in the beetle actually demanded it. It will be decided by opinions of a person or persons shaped by their different personal histories, ambitions and educational influences. Perhaps the name of the beetle was finally determined by the most dominant personality on the team or by the one who got the grant money. And who decided there should be the category "subspecies" anyway—or "species" for that matter?

This is the story of language under construction. Postmodernism points out that all language was made this way over long time periods. There is an arbitrariness of meaning, not an objective or necessary correspondence between our words and the way the world is. This is what they mean when they say that all language is "socially constructed." What is more, the meanings of words do not stay still over time or as they pass between people.

Needless to say, postmodernism is less interested in naming beetles than in words that have more significance to our power relationships. The same questions have to be raised about the "fixed meanings" of some of our most important words and ideas. Isn't the word *God* subject to the same problem we had over the beetle?

Shirley MacLaine, actress and New Age guru, made news some years ago by declaring, "I am God." Here too we have lumpers and splitters. Who gets to say if there is enough room in the word *God* to include Shirley MacLaine? A Hindu would be likely to be a lumper and say "Of course Shirley MacLaine is God." A Christian would be a splitter and would say "Of course not. She is a creature of God." With the plurality of religions and conceptions of God in the world, who gets to say what the boundaries are to the meaning of the word *God*?

Of particular concern to postmodernism is to question the distinctions between, for example, male and female, history and fiction, sanity and madness, human and animal, high and low culture, true and false, good and evil. It is these distinctions that, they say, enforce authority in power relationships by establishing privilege. But this brings us to the next step, the relationship between words and power.

The Postmodern Critique: Motive as Power

Postmodernism follows Nietzsche in seeing the most basic human motivation as the will to power. The dynamics of human power are the major force controlling the construction of language. Postmodern cynicism claims that the meanings of the words we use to think and speak with come to us having been shaped over the years by hundreds of power struggles. This of course includes the terms of political discourse, such as *justice*, *freedom* and *democracy*, as well as the words of the Bible, theology, ethics, and the creeds of the church. These words have no objective confirmation of their meanings. Their meanings have come down to us filtered through centuries of accidents, prejudices, squabbles and power plays.

This uncertainty about meanings leads postmodernism to look with condescension on not only the serious, committed believer in God but also the serious, committed atheist in the same way. Both are naive to think that they can have any certainty about God—his presence or absence. Why? Because the words and ideas they use to think with are a product of such an arbitrary process. The conventional meanings of the words we use offer us no certain grasp of reality. They only reflect the interests of the cultural winners, the dominant groups that managed to gain and maintain power through history—in the rain forest, academia, the legislature, the church or in general culture.

So, postmodern cynicism has two steps. First, the postmodern surgeon has laid bare the fluidity of the meaning of our language itself. Second, he or she has claimed that the major factor that has controlled the shaping of language (and therefore our whole thinking process) is the desire for social power. As a result, postmodern jargon is filled with deep cynicism about the meaning of words and texts, and the process of their interpretation and communication.

We hear that "every text is a pretext," a smokescreen for some hidden agenda. You should read a text not to find out what the author is trying to say but what he or she is trying to hide. If meanings are so flexible, who is to say which interpretation of a given text is more accurate than another? Authority shifts away from a text and its author to the reader, whose reading is as reliable as anyone else's reading.

Ideals are deodorants to hide the smell of personal or group ambition. They hide the smell of ambition from the noses of both the oppressed and the oppressor so nobody realizes what is going on—except the postmodern surgeon. A new term has emerged in postmodern discussion: *hermeneutic of suspicion.* A person's hermeneutic is his or her idea, principles and practice of how to interpret things. A hermeneutic of suspicion is a way of interpreting the world with suspicion as the primary lens through which an individual sees all that there is.

Belief in God. How does specifically postmodern cynicism affect belief in God? Many who believe in God are grateful for the way postmodernism has pressed them to think more carefully about the shaping power of culture on language, and of language and its interpretation on all that we think and do. Postmodernism, at least in theory, is not as hostile to theists, those who believe in God, as the modernist enlighteners were. After all, everyone has a cultural background, a community of discourse, personal beliefs and interpretations. There is room at the table for everybody, including believers in God—as long as they remember the conditions of their welcome.

What are the conditions of welcome? I can believe in God, but I must be aware that my faith is only my own private way of interpreting my experience, my culture and the world. I must never think that God exists independently of my thoughts about him or try to get anyone else to pay any attention to those thoughts. So I can believe in God, but I should not get confused into thinking that my ideas about him correspond to anything beyond my skin, or at most beyond the social experience of my community.

Postmodernism celebrates the diversity of religious beliefs. But the spirit of celebration depends on each person or group keeping the rules—faith must remain contained within private experience. My religious *preferences* are OK, but my religious *convictions* are not. A valedictorian at a Harvard commencement ceremony pointed out that "the freedom of our day is the freedom to devote ourselves to any values we please, on the mere condition that we do not believe them to be true."[1]

It makes sense that the criterion of final evaluation in postmodernism does not have to do with "what is true?" but with the pragmatic "what are the consequences of believing it to be true?" Jonathan Culler, a professor of English and comparative literature, encouraged people to read the Bible. But he instructed them to read it "not as poetry or narrative but as a powerfully influential racist and sexist text."[2]

In popular culture, modern knowledge has become "postmodern knowingness."[3] Earnestness and seriousness are out. Frank Gannon wrote:

> Something in the human mind says it's hopeless: The existence of God is something that human beings can never entirely discount, or entirely prove. Why torture yourself trying to answer a question like that? Get a hobby. Work out regularly. Eat low fat. Forget about what Yeats called "vague immensities." . . .
>
> Yet something deep in your soul says, Go ahead. Seek the ultimate answers. Maybe the human brain can actually "know" some transcendent divinity. Yeah. Good one. Don't hurt yourself, O.K.?[4]

Postmodern cynicism about God is not apt to be despairing or heavy. It tends, rather, to be playful and ironic. Journalist Jonathan Rauch described what he considered a "major civilizational advance"—apatheism. It is a "disinclination to care all that much about one's own religion, and an even stronger disinclination to care about other people's." It has more to do with how you believe than what you believe because it includes Christian and Jewish believers as well as atheists and agnostics. Apatheism is "relaxed about religion." Its most important doctrine is that it "doesn't mind what *other* people think of God." Rauch does not see it as a lazy option. To him it is an important cultural achievement that holds the destructiveness of religious zeal in restraint.[5]

Postmodernism has cast doubt on God and all the larger systems of meaning that have given us a sense of a purpose derived from a source beyond ourselves. We are left with the sense that our lives are in the final sense without meaning or connectedness. Any meaning that I have must be generated by me, for me and from my own resources: my story is all there is.

SEEING THROUGH EVERYTHING ELSE
Boredom, Irony and Satire

Reality's a nice place to visit, but you wouldn't want to live there.

JOHN BARTH

Bit by bit . . . commercialization promises to change the character of the institution in ways that limit its freedom and sap its effectiveness. Worst of all, the financial entanglements and commercial ventures of the university lead the public to question its motives, lose confidence in the objectivity of its scholars, and place less trust in statements by professors on subjects of importance to society.

DEREK BOK

CYNICISM IS IN THE AIR WE BREATHE. An articulate, sophisticated and often humorous cynical voice is at our finger tips or behind our ear, addressing any subject. We have looked at many forms of cynicism and at cynicism in different theaters of our experience: individual people, institutions and God.

There is no necessary, linear track leading to cynicism. Its promiscuity means that it can come and go or take up residence anywhere. Cynicism can stay where it is, or it can move from individual people to the church and to God, from God to the church, from marriage to both God and the church, and so on. If there is a "domino effect," we have to speak of dominoes falling potentially in all directions.

UToPIANISM
CYNICISM

Having said that, there is a special importance to cynicism about God or ultimate meanings in life. From there cynicism can cast its shadow over wide areas. The hermeneutic of suspicion can interpret everything. Real faith in, for example, the God of the Bible, provides a certain check or limit to cynicism about self, others and institutions, just as it also provides a check or limit to utopian optimism or sentimentality in each of those areas. If someone turns from faith in God to cynicism about him, those restraints on other forms of cynicism (and utopianism) are removed, making it easier to go there.

We are living in a time that is cynical not just about God, but about all claims to ultimate meaning, religious or secular. We are told that although the snow and ice of winter is replaced by the spring with its flowers, we should not let this fool us. This world, for all its beauty and mystery, is mindless, meaningless, numb, dumb and amoral. Human life raises countless expectations and hopes that are never realized but only mock us. Existentialism found this a cause for despair; postmodernism finds it a good joke—but both begin with a cynicism about our ability to know ultimate meaning.

Cynicism and the Shape of Modern Life

Modern life is profoundly shaped by the advanced industrial society of which we are a part. Its role in the cynicism of today's world is too extensive to describe here. We will touch only on the phenomenon of widespread boredom among young people and their disconnection from the meanings offered to them.

Boredom. Many scholars search for reasons for the widespread cynicism and boredom among young people today.[1] Richard Stivers in *The Culture of Cynicism* puts it this way:"Boredom and unhappiness punctuate the lives of everyone from time to time; they are universal experiences. What is unusual is the extent to which boredom and unhappiness today can be attributed to the decline of common meaning."[2]

He uses the term *hyperboredom* to refer not just to boredom as a passing mood but to what accompanies the sustained experience of meaninglessness. Young people complain that even meaninglessness is not what it used to be. It is no longer able to shock or even get anybody's attention. He goes on to ask,"If life is typically (historically speaking) experienced as overflowing with meaning, how does a society reach the point in which the experience of meaninglessness is widespread and longstanding?"[3]

If you think of how this overflowing meaning was experienced historically, it did not come out of thin air. It was seen as coming from beyond our immediate, visible world, from some transcendent or unseen source. Ultimate meaning in much of Western culture has been related to a personal God. When that God is abandoned as a personal presence of authority and redemption, the *need* for meaning does not go away or evaporate with him. Whatever is handy rushes in to fill the vacuum.

A youth worker in high school asked some students what was the most serious problem that they experienced, expecting a full litany of grievances about parents, money, stress and identity. They responded, "Boredom." In amazement he asked, "How? When there is so much to do, and you are always busy?" They all agreed, "It's not so much that we're bored, it's just that we're doing a lot of meaningless things."[4]

Our advanced industrial society has made it possible to be both busy and bored. It makes high demands for technique and efficiency—quicker, cheaper, for power and profit. These are the ascendant meanings in modern life, fulfilled for most people in the shopping mall in the form of more consumer goods. But what sort of meanings can this offer? Valuing persons is inefficient and unprofitable; the new ascendant values devalue or crush the valuing of people. Valuing people *can* lead to power and profit, but only accidentally. To cite Stivers again:

> Moreover, we have all become specialists who at best make a small contribution to our own survival. . . . But even more importantly, we make no contribution to the creation and sustenance of common meaning. What meaning there is, is reified in consumption. Edward Sapir puts if well:
>
>> Here lies the grimmest joke of our present American civilization. . . . Part of the time we are dray horses; the rest of the time we are listless consumers of goods which have received no least impress of our own personality. In other words, our spiritual selves go hungry, for the most part, pretty much all of the time.[5]

His claim is that the way our society is structured, none of us makes a significant direct contribution either to our physical survival or to a common meaning. What then is the payoff of modernity? What does it offer in return for all the long hours, hard work and high stress? It offers consumption, buying things—basically, the freedom to go shopping. Douglas Coupland brings this from the abstract to the concrete as he gives us his take on the "American dream."

> My friends are all either married, boring, and depressed; single, bored, and depressed; or moved out of town to avoid boredom and depression. And some of them have bought houses, which has to be kiss of death, personality-wise. When someone tells you they've just bought a house, they might as well tell you they no longer have a personality. You can immediately assume so many things: that they're locked into jobs they hate; that they're broke; that they spend every night watching videos; that they're fifteen pounds overweight; that they no longer listen to new ideas. It's profoundly depressing. And the *worst* part of it is that people in their houses don't even *like* where they're living. What few happy moments they possess are those gleaned from dreams of *upgrading*.[6]

Irony

The word *irony* is closely associated with the breadth and depth of cynicism in our culture. Irony has a glorious history. It is a way of speaking in which the "face value" or literal meaning of our words hides a different, often opposite, meaning, which is clear to the listener. The listener or reader is meant to "see through" the face value meaning of words to the real meaning intended. People speak ironically when they "play dumb," pretending ignorance or astonishment. Understatements are ironic; a plane crash could "ruin your weekend." Socrates was known for his irony in seeming to praise an opponent while actually making fun of him.

In the beginning of Jesus' Sermon on the Mount is a passage called the Beatitudes. They start with:

> Blessed are the poor in spirit, for theirs is the kingdom of heaven.
> Blessed are those who mourn, for they will be comforted.
> Blessed are the meek, for they will inherit the earth. (Mt 5:3-5)

The promises of these beatitudes takes you by surprise—they are ironic. The power of irony is in the tension or incongruity built between the expected or surface meaning and the intended final force of the statement. Jesus often used irony to jar his listeners, catching them off balance to open their ears and lead them into fresh ways of thinking. "Those who love their life lose it, and those who hate their life in this world will keep it for eternal life" (Jn 12:25). What in the world did he mean? Well, you have to think about it and maybe ask some questions yourself.

Irony and cynicism. How then is irony associated with cynicism? Why is irony a part of the cynical air we breathe? It is because irony now functions in a different way. The irony that I have just described is a rhetorical device that gives power to the intended meaning of a statement. Remember that Stephen Crane complained of the indifference of nature to an individual's safety by saying that "she feels she would not maim the universe by disposing of him."[7] By this understatement he captured his bitterness far more sharply than in a blandly factual complaint of nature's indifference to him. In this way irony does not undermine or neutralize an author's meaning but sharpens it and forces us to hear it.

But irony built on a foundation of cynicism works differently. It sees through the face value not just of the literal meaning of certain words. It sees through the seriousness, virtue and integrity of *everything*—persons, institutions as well as their words. What is seen lying beneath the surface is not a different meaning now sharpened, but meaninglessness, stupidity, cluelessness or the corrupt motivations of greed, lust, or power. That is, irony has come to be the way pervasive cynicism is expressed.

To use irony in this sense is to speak in such a way that your hearers know that you do not take that person, those words, that event, that institution, seriously. You are not naive. You can see through it all. We saw this in Frank Ganon's quip about being able to know about the existence of God: "Maybe the human brain can actually 'know' some transcendent divinity. Yeah. Good one. Don't hurt yourself, O.K.?"[8]

Think of the way the word *whatever* is used today. Literally, it refers to a limitless range of possibilities: "no matter what." "You can have *whatever* you want." What it has now come to mean is a complete disengagement from *caring* about any of those possibilities. When a person responds with "Whatever," no one will suspect him or her of being earnest. It serves in settings where social success is measured in competitive illusionlessness.

To the extent that someone is being cynical, that person will not want to take any apparent values seriously. He or she will not want to be caught seeming to have convictions, being earnest or serious—otherwise friends will think he or she is either naive, anal or both. People who speak with ironic cynicism send the signal that whatever they are talking about is said with a wink. Therefore they cannot be accused of being a throwback from a sentimental or dedicated past. They have maintained their detachment from all the things that less sophisticated people take seriously.

Richard Rorty has embraced irony in its postmodern philosophical form. In his book *Contingency, Irony and Solidarity* he calls himself an ironist. By this he means that he holds his deepest beliefs, desires and commitments (his "final vocabulary") with irony. That is, he has faced up to the fact that he can see through all his own deepest beliefs and commitments, that they are groundless and refer to nothing beyond time and chance. An ironist has radical and continuing doubts about his or her own "final vocabulary" and does not believe that it is closer to reality than anybody else's views, which might entirely contradict it. There exists no criterion to judge between them.[9]

At a very different level, Stanley Cohen and Laurie Taylor describe a more common example of irony in their study of the styles of psychic survival in the modern world. They write of life within suburban conformity of regulation houses, gardens, furniture and regulation books on their regulation coffee tables:

> But when the door is shut against the night, and two children are safely in bed, husband and wife turn to each other and laugh. They are subscribers to the new self-consciousness, apostles of awareness. Cynically they deride those who share bourgeois arrangements with them, but who do not see the joke. Looking around the room they declare their awareness of their apparent suburbanity, and then with a delicious sense of their own distinctive identities, record their distance from such artifacts. "We may look as suburban as those next door, but both of us know that we view so much of this life with detachment, with irony, even cynicism." . . . For them it is only others who are truly suburban, who play their roles with a routine orienta-

tion, whilst they "see through" the relativity of the setting, they live against it as much as within it, and thereby preserve their individuality in a conformist world.[10]

Living with an ironic perspective is a way we can be part of the herd, experience its benefits and securities but also see through it and detach ourselves from it by standing above it. It is one of the ways that cynical attitudes are expressed and distance is achieved. It is, after all, "only a game." This ironic attitude is also one of the ways that cynicism is carried, with wit and sophistication, into all corners of our conversation and society.

Satire and Cynicism

Satire has used irony with humor to expose and challenge the absurdities of life. At its best it is a literature of correction and has been just that in the hands of some of the giants of literature, from Aristophanes to Erasmus, Pascal, Swift, Moliere, Voltaire and on down to today with a popular lyricist like Randy Newman or journalist/novelist Tom Wolfe. The dynamic of satire is not amoral, though it might appear to be on the surface. It uses humor, deliberate misunderstanding and caricature to try to lever people away from their moral idiocies and in the direction of the author's own moral convictions.

You can find satire in concentrated doses in the Bible. With irony, Job satirizes his friends' attempts to counsel him with their glib moral theology:

> How you have helped one who has no power!
>   How you have assisted the arm that has no strength!
> How you have counseled one who has no wisdom,
>   and given much good advice!
> With whose help have you uttered words,
>   and whose spirit has come forth from you? (Job 26:2-4)

Think also of Jesus' rebuke to the Pharisees of his time, "You blind guides! You strain out a gnat but swallow a camel!" (Mt 23:24).

Satire has been a strategy for criticism and correction to expose what an author or speaker believes is hypocrisy, unacknowledged evil or failure. But what if a pervasive cynicism has made ideals themselves suspect and included in the satire? Remember that we noted the postmodern notion that all ideals are only deodorants to hide the smell of self-interest. In this view ideals themselves lose any moral authority and become manipulative tools in the hands of the powerful. They think they have, or claim to give us, a God's-eye view of reality. But everything that purports to be for the public good is really only done for private interest—maintaining the status quo as well as any plans to change it. This reverses the force of the critical impulse usually associated with satire, producing a de facto resignation.

We began by asking three questions of cynicism: What is it? How is it justified? What does it deliver? We have looked at the nature of cynicism in different areas of its influence. As yet we have done very little to question or evaluate its authority or the validity of the results that it delivers. Is it the last stopping place of the honest mind? Does it deliver a more true and human engagement with the world? It is to these questions that we now move.

Part Two

RAISING QUESTIONS

SUSPECTING OUR SUSPICIONS

I hate a thoroughgoing cynic. I don't want anyone to be more cynical than I am.

REINHOLD NIEBUHR

Suspicion is dangerous, but that does not mean that we should suspend our suspicions. It means, rather, that we should suspect our suspicions, knowing of their danger.

MEROLD WESTPHAL

I WANT TO RAISE SOME QUESTIONS, to have a critical look at the status of cynicism today. There may be some of you who will march on with your confidence in cynicism unshaken, maybe even strengthened. Then there may be others who will develop some doubts about cynicism's dependability.

In this chapter I will be arguing not for or against the truth of cynical judgments as much as looking at the justification for cynicism on its own terms. The idea that cynicism is the last stopping place of the honest mind is, ironically, a high and confident claim. It puts the cynic in the place of the surgeons mentioned when we were describing the "ideology critique." The surgeons remove the diseased tissue of error and of naive thinking. They straighten up at the end of the operation and say, "We got it all, we got all the diseased tissue out. The patient may not survive, but at least the cancer is removed." Likewise, the cynic concludes, life may not be all that happy a business—that is why the cynic must be fearless—but illusions have been stripped away, hypocrisies exposed, ideologies unmasked. The courageous honesty of the hermeneutic of suspicion has led to a bedrock stopping place, free from illusion.

A sophisticated cynicism backed, it would say, by truth and honesty is on a head-on collision course with the credibility of virtues such as faith, hope and love, which are made to appear hypocritical and naive. Is the only alternative to cynicism to be *less* sophisticated and honest? The cynic would say so, but there is quite a lot to be said from the other side. Is it conceivable that there could be a deeper honesty than cynicism offers? Perhaps we should take Merold Westphal's advice to "suspect our suspicions," and see where that leads us.[1]

Cynic as Closet Idealist

Diogenes was cynical about just about everything in the Athens of his time. But not quite everything. He was not cynical about nature or behaving in a way that he considered "natural." This was because nature and naturalness were his ideals. Nature was the platform he stood on and from which he could throw rocks at what he thought were false ideals, traditions, pretensions and artificiality around him. Every rock thrower needs something to stand on in order to have any accuracy or do any damage.

Modern cynicism is less "up front" than Diogenes about the platform it throws rocks from. Most cynical criticism today leaves its own ideals hidden, and gets on with cynicism without acknowledging them.

Ideals in the closet: Sheep in wolves' clothing. Cynics in fact are unable to reject all ideals. If they had no ideals at all they would just sit down in resigned silence—a condition we do not usually associate with cynicism. Cynics will inevitably hold at least one ideal against ideas and practices of conventional society. But the cynic will rarely articulate his or her own ideals out loud. They are kept in the closet but are still used to see through and unmask those who fall short of them. For example, much modern cynicism stands on the platforms of honesty, freedom or authenticity. These are the platform ideals from which rocks are thrown at all forms of dishonesty, oppression and hypocrisy. But the style of cynicism is such that its ideals are seldom mentioned, let alone justified as important ideals or defended as actually true.

The film *M*A*S*H*, a story of surgeons in a field medical unit in the Korean War, was seen as an archetypal cynical film of the late 1960s—mocking everything. It is true that it mocked the military and the war itself; it also mocked marriage, medicine, rules in general and religion—with mockery ecumenically distributed between Protestant and Catholic. But it really didn't mock everything—just the conventional values and institutions of respectable society—the Establishment of the late 1960s. The cynicism was coming from the platform ideals of personal freedom, friendship and coolness, which were presented as highly attractive but not stated, recognized or defended, and certainly never mocked.

There is a popular narrative pattern of the cynical person who seems just out for him- or herself, seeing through all ideals. But at the end of the story, with the cynic's back to the wall morally, he or she behaves with higher idealism than all those with more conventional moral attitudes in the story. You can think of Dickens's Sidney Carton, who goes voluntarily to the guillotine to save the life of another in *A Tale of Two Cities*. In the classic Bogart film *Casablanca*, Bogart's character, Rick, has a refrain, "I stick my neck out for nobody," and "The problems of this world are not my account." But he acts at the end with moral commitment to a cause far bigger than himself. Han Solo in the first Star Wars film had made it clear that he was only interested in money, not in any higher causes, principles or heroic rescues. Yet at the end he came to the rescue for a higher cause at great risk.

Theologian Edmond La B. Cherbonnier wrote that cynicism is "the attempt to avoid entanglement with the fickle gods of idealism by espousing none at all."[2] But Cherbonnier went on:

> Every cynic turns out to be a covert idealist, in the sense that he does gravitate toward some standard outside himself as the criterion of his decision. . . . In fact, the real motive of his apparent lawlessness is generally some hidden virtue. Most often it is the virtue of honesty. Perceiving the hypocrisy of the idealist, he fancies his own disillusioned outlook to be truer to the facts of life. . . . Despite his effort at concealment, this kind of cynic turns out to be sheep in wolf's clothing.[3]

The question of honesty. My questions are about the honesty of cynicism itself. If the ideals of cynicism were acknowledged, that would open the cynic to all kinds of questions and criticism, maybe even to the cynicism of others."Where do these ideals come from? How are they justified? Aren't they naive? Sentimental?"

In finding fault with other people or institutions, the cynic must be appealing to some implicit standard above his or her own private preference or opinion. The cynic, in mocking, let us say, the lying and self-interest of the hypocrite, makes an *implicit* appeal to a moral order in the universe (by which people *ought not* lie, be selfish or hypocritical). Where does this moral order come from? Most cynics keep that implicit appeal in the closet.

G. K. Chesterton wrote at the start of the last century that "the cause which is blocking all progress today is the subtle skepticism which whispers in a million ears that things are not good enough to be worth improving."[4] What was he talking about? He was describing the work of cynicism. Cynicism is a subtle skepticism, whispered to millions, that drains away their motivation for trying to improve their part of the world.

Why "whispering"? Certainly not because cynicism is always heard at low volume. But just as the platform ideals of the cynic are kept in the closet, so the full force of the cynical judgment with its implications is also kept in the closet. Except where cynicism is self-consciously and openly grounded in doctrines about human nature, such as in Freudian theories or evolutionary psychology, cynicism is usually expressed in innuendoes, passing remarks, moods, cartoons, glancing blows, hints, insinuations, unacknowledged assumptions and jokes. The full self-confidence of its suspicions, enabling it to unmask all things in its vision, are whispered, kept muffled in the closet along with its ideals.

The genius of cynicism is that it is a voice in your ear which does not usually hang around long enough to be interviewed, much less interrogated. It can move on, leaving an insinuation, a slur, a humiliation, an intimation and then changes the subject to start on something else. When questioned about cynicism, a cynic might sincerely respond, "Who, me?" Or when pressed, might back off a little bit, "Oh, I didn't mean that she had *no* integrity," or "Well, of course not *all* politicians are corrupt."These can be tactical retreats but with no real change of cynical conviction or habit. But they can keep the cynic and the cynic's listeners from seeing the full reach of his or her own claims.

I will be encouraging cynicism to come out of its closet, to stop whispering and to speak out loud about both its ideals and the full implications of its claims to see through people, institutions and God. This may mean pushing cynicism harder to come out of hiding than what we are used to, but it seems that is required if we are serious about honesty.

THE VULNERABILITY OF CYNICISM

We need to get more sophisticated about cynicism.

WILLIAM CHALOUPKA

All men have a natural fear of making a mistake—by believing too well of a person. However, the error of believing too ill of a person is perhaps not feared, at least not in the same degree as the other.

SØREN KIERKEGAARD

We cultivate a cynicism that does not despair, because it serves to destroy the charms of truth and beauty that might corrupt our inner peace. We enjoy an irony that does not seek resolution, because it supports our desire to be invulnerable observers rather than participants at risk. We are spectators of our own lives, free from the strain of drama and the uncertainty of a story in which our souls are at stake. We conform because nothing finally matters except the superiority of knowing it to be so.

R. R. RENO

WHAT MIGHT HAPPEN IF WE WERE TO FEED CYNICISM its own medicine? Why not give an ideology critique of cynicism itself? Could it be, for example, that a person's cynicism is motivated not *only* by a fearless and honest pursuit of the truth but by other not-so-noble motivations as well?

If so, is it possible that those other motivations could actually skew or distort the cynic's cynical perspective or judgment?

If an ideology critique is *not* allowed, then we are being asked to give the cynic's own viewpoint some special status. It would be to grant that the cynic has a unique, direct access to truth, an immaculate perception of the world. This would include an accurate understanding of the hidden workings of individual persons, society and ultimate truth, uncorrupted by sexism, ethnocentrism, social pressures, psychological distortions, or the desire for autonomy, power, money or tenure. It does not seem to me that we owe the cynic this sort of preferential treatment, nor—when it is put this way—would most cynical people expect it.

The Medicine of Cynicism

Actually there a number of payoffs for cynicism that supply incentives to be cynical. In fact these payoffs may sound familiar because they are the same as those used to discredit faith in God by the masters of suspicion. They are the incentives of consolation and an alibi for the pursuit of self-interest: crutch and smokescreen.

Cynicism and self-protection. There are a number of ways that cynicism gives consolation by supplying self-protection for the cynic. Perhaps the most obvious is that cynicism is protection against having our hopes destroyed. This is because cynicism does not allow us to hope in the first place. If we do not hope, we are not disappointed. Cynicism can seem very safe and also very enlightened and sophisticated. In a world filled with disillusionment, this is no small consolation.

To illustrate, let me misquote Nietzsche. But first I will quote him accurately. He wrote in *Twilight of the Idols:* "When it is trodden on a worm will curl up. That is prudent. It thereby reduces the chance of being trodden on again. In the language of morals: *humility.*"[1] Nietzsche has described a twisted misunderstanding of humility and its psychological function, but that is not my concern here. My purpose is to *mis*quote him to use his wonderful image to say something that he might *not* have said but which I think is both true and helpful. "When it is trodden on a worm will curl up. That is prudent. It thereby reduces the chance of being trodden on again. In the language of survival: *cynicism.*"

Cynicism is a curling up of the soul in self-protection to guard an individual from the pain of disappointment. Just as the worm, by curling up, offers a smaller target for the next boot, so cynicism is prudent and reduces the surface area of emotional vulnerability to the many muddy boots of the world. Believing in the integrity of another person, the validity of an institution or the goodness of God are all high-risk convictions. They are potential setups for disappointment. If you are concerned first and last for emotional safety and survival, cynicism is going to look quite attractive, a helpful crutch.

Douglas Coupland illustrates the role of ironic cynicism in promising to ensure emotional and interpersonal safety. He defines two terms, *knee-jerk irony* and *derision preemption:*

> Knee-jerk irony: The tendency to make flippant ironic comments as a reflexive matter of course in everyday conversation.

> Derision preemption: A life-style tactic; the refusal to go out on any sort of emotional limb so as to avoid mockery from peers. *Derision Preemption* is the main goal of *Knee-Jerk Irony.*[2]

Cynicism is an armor plate defensive strategy that can offer protection to many areas of potential scorn. Derision preemption is such a self-protective strategy. It suggests that if we make no commitments or if we express cynicism about something we are committed to, that will preempt or disarm the sting of being mocked by somebody who thought we were being serious, naive or earnest. Those who can laugh at themselves preemptively can be seen not as ridiculous but as so sophisticated that they are self-ironists.

Another kind of consolation that cynicism offers is protection from being humiliated in front of ourselves. We live in a success-dominated society and are exposed constantly to human icons of success who are completely out of reach. Every day we are shown places we can't go, things we can't have, people we can't be like and things we can't do. It is impossible to keep up. But we can turn cynicism loose on the icons themselves. They are not *really* that bright, honest, beautiful or good at what they do. We can say, "In that world, the system is so corrupt that all you have to do is know the right people." Cynicism provides damage control consolation for my experience of myself as an underachiever or as one whose talent has still not been recognized. It reduces the painful distance between me and my icons.[3]

Media are very cooperative in this kind of cynicism, especially the tabloids. They feed our vanity by showing us the beautiful people, touched up for us to identify with and envy. But then they also feed our cynicism by exposing the same people as they get old, disgraced, divorced, addicted or busted. They nurture our insecurities with these inflation-deflation cycles of the imagination. We can identify with them in their fame and beauty, so we feel important sharing a little bit of their glitter. But when we see them fall we are reassured that we are actually superior to the supersuccessful when it comes to the things that a really matter. That makes us feel better.

Søren Kierkegaard reflected on the great and solemn fear people have of making a mistake in their judgments of other people. But he then proceeded to make ironic observations about this fear—an asymmetrical fear. It is more afraid of being mistaken by believing too well of a person than of being mistaken by believing too badly of him. He went on, "Yet should it not occur to us, to speak mildly, that it is just as stupid to have believed ill or mistrustfully to have believed nothing where there was good?"[4] Because it is one-sided and not a balanced, two-sided fear—of being in error in either direction—suggests that it is motivated not by honesty or concern for truth but by self-protection or vanity.

Cynicism and moral apathy. Another variant of the consolation of self-protection is cynicism as a justification for moral apathy. If any one is looking for a respectable excuse for not getting involved working against the suffering, injustice and falsehood in this world, cynicism is ideal. If you see urgent needs and you would like to help, but you really don't feel like going beyond your comfort zone to destabilize your life or the life or your family in this messy situation, then cynicism can seem attractive. A cynical perspective allows you to see through morally challenging ideas, movements, causes, people or organizations and conclude that they are all too shallow, too compromised, too idealistic or somehow just not quite on the right track. In fact there is no cause that is quite worthy of the investment of your moral energy, time or resources. You can see through them all.

In short, cynicism enables you to do nothing but feel morally superior to those who are doing something good but imperfect in an imperfect world. You are ready for high moral commitment when the right cause of-

fers itself at the right moment—some time in the future. You are still waiting. It would be very unfair to imply that this is true of all cynicism, but put
bluntly, cynicism *can* function as a respectable alibi for those who don't
want to get their hands dirty.

Cynicism then works as a protection against the uncomfortable challenge that moral excellence is an actual possibility. There is a certain relief
in having removed all heroes from the landscape and all the top rungs
from the ladder—in case more might be expected of us than mediocrity.

R. R. Reno points to a new spirit in contemporary society. He argues that
"the confident humanism of modernity has given way to an anxious desire
to escape moral demand and the pressure it puts on us to change."[5] He sees
a moral and religious relativism that functions as a protective dogma, effectively fending off anything that might claim serious loyalty or suggest expectations that change is not only possible but could be required.[6]

Cynicism and elitism. Cynicism can also be motivated by wanting to
disguise our pursuit of elite status by a smokescreen. Looking down with
cynicism on others can lift a us up in the eyes of our hearers. Søren Kierkegaard contrasted the meager social payoffs of positively evaluating
other people with the far greater rewards of cynicism.

> When one discloses that he has discovered how basically shabby
> every human being is, how envious, how selfish, how unreliable,
> and what abominations can reside hidden in the purest people, that
> is, those regarded as the purest by simpletons, silly geese, and small-
> town beauties, then he conceitedly knows that he is welcome, that a
> premium is placed on his observation, his knowledge, and his dis
> course, which the world longs to hear.[7]

Cynicism can be a way to power and approval—from the school playground to the locker room to the bar room to the board room to the news
room or the faculty room—especially when cynicism comes with humor.
In biblical terms the cynic is known as the *mocker,* the *scoffer* or the *scorner,*
terms that mean looking down on others from a privileged position of superiority. The cynic is above the herd, which is, after all, filled with "simpletons, silly geese and small town beauties." Cynicism holds the seductive attraction of elitism. It is one means by which the sophisticated
separate themselves from the herd.

Stanley Cohen and Laurie Taylor studied people who do jobs and live in environments with high levels of conformity but try to retain a sense of their own individuality. These people detached themselves with cynicism and irony from their roles and activities, putting themselves above their neighbors who took all this suburban life seriously. Cynicism comforted them in the belief that they were not like others who were captured in their social roles. But the solution was not so simple.

Although our happy couple may not know it, the trap of routine is not so easily sprung. For meanwhile, next door, in the other half of the semi-detached house, another couple of identity workers are sitting down to start a similar distancing game.

Throughout the land previously disenchanted individuals are busily assuring others that they are more than they do; "I'm not really a social worker," they confide, "not like the others are. . . . I see the whole thing as rather a game." Dentists, doctors, shop assistants whisper similar self-distancing remarks to appropriate colleagues, unaware that down the corridor their co-workers are busily at work with the same transcending strategy.[8]

Although cynicism can seem to offer the incentive of social transcendence through a strategy of elitism, that superiority becomes dubious as more people join the ranks of the cynical. Cynicism sets us apart from the herd when the herd is earnest, but it provides no such social advantage when the herd has become cynical.

Cynicism Requires Virtual Omniscience

Cynicism is often associated with the loss of confidence that we can know anything with certainty. But cynicism has not so clearly rejected the idea of truth as we may think. Cynics see through the illusory truths of others to get down to the "real truth" beneath, which they have discovered themselves. Far from losing confidence in truth, cynicism has put enormous trust in a different set of truths—its own tools of cynical inquiry, which have enabled it to do surgery, and the results achieved by it.

This brings us to one of the places of high vulnerability for cynicism. The basic problem is very simple: How does the cynic know enough to be able to see through all that he or she claims to be able to see through? It would take prodigious intellectual power and moral integrity to see through all possible nobility in people, potential for goodness in institutions and trustworthiness of God.

Take the example that we considered in chapter one from the book of Ecclesiastes: "I saw that all toil and all skill in work come from one person's envy of another" (Eccles 4:4). How did the author know that? The statement has the aura of sophistication. But how could anyone know, short of omniscience, that all the toil and all the skill of all people is motivated by envy?

We could even lower the bar dramatically for the cynic and ask how we could know that all the toil of even one other person is driven entirely by envy? We couldn't. We couldn't be sure of it even if that person were to tell us. Plenty of depressed people are incapable of seeing anything but the worst of their own motivations.

The basic problem here is that to justify the cynical judgment, we must be virtually omniscient, or at least to know a great deal more than any of us can know about the motivations of other people. This is the overbite of cynicism.

Preempting the Last Judgment. German theologian Helmut Thielicke addressed this issue in an interesting way. He wrote: "What do people really know of each other? What do we know about how you and I will look at the last judgment? What did the Pharisee really know about the publican? We live between the false judgments we make now and the surprises which the last judgment will bring."[9]

Of course many cynics would not believe in a last judgment, but the point still remains. Your cynical verdict on another person presumes that you have the knowledge that only the last judgment of an omniscient God could reveal. It is as if the cynic expects that even if there were to be a day when the secrets of the hearts of all men and women were disclosed, for them there would be no surprises. They can see it all, right now.

In his deeply disturbing story *Benito Cereno,* Herman Melville used an innocent and naive American sea captain as his narrator. The captain is trying to figure out what kind of catastrophe has happened on board another ship in a series of mystifying conversations with second ship's captain, Don Benito Cereno. All sorts of conflicting suspicions arise in his mind from evidence of tragic and mysterious prior events. At the end the truth becomes clear, and Don Benito Cereno remarked on how thoroughly he had been misunderstood by the American captain:

> You were with me all day; stood with me, sat with me, talked with me, looked at me, ate with me, drank with me; and yet, your last act was to clutch for a monster, not only an innocent man, but the most pitiable of all men. To such degree may malign machinations and deceptions impose. So far may even the best man err in judging the conduct of one with the recesses of whose condition he is not acquainted.[10]

Melville has stated the vulnerability of cynical judgment. Sometimes even the naive are easily caught in "malign machinations and deceptions," that is, in misguided cynical judgments. Anyone can be spectacularly wrong in judging "the conduct of one with the recesses of whose condition he is not acquainted." The issue is clear. We don't know enough. It is that the cynic presumes precisely to *be* acquainted with the *inner* recesses of the conditions of other peoples' lives. Although, of course, cynics can be right in specific cases, we must admit having cynical insights in which we were entirely mistaken.

I can remember a time some years ago when I was hitchhiking in Germany. The driver who picked me up was very nice, much too nice. He seemed overconcerned that I not get out of his car. All my alarm bells went off, and memory kicked in with stories of everything from robberies to sexual assault to kidnapping. It was late at night in his country, not mine. We didn't understand each other very well, but everything he said and did increased my suspicions. Just as I was thinking about what sort of physical resistance it would take to get free, he came to a stop, wished me well, let me out of the car just where he had said he would and drove off leaving me scratching my head.

In Nick Hornby's novel *How to Be Good*, David, one of the main characters becomes disillusioned with his own deep cynicism. He was in a discussion about the president of the United States with one of his usual partners in cynical demolition, and created shock and astonishment when he said, "I no longer want to condemn people whose lives I know nothing about." The response of his friend was incredulous, "But . . . that's the basis for all conversation!" David replies, "I'm tired of it. We don't know anything about him."[11] An honest acknowledgment of our ignorance can debunk cynicism and threaten the social relationships dependent on it.

The irony of cynical knowing. Cynical self-confidence is particularly ironic since so much of the message of today's cynicism is about the unreliability of human knowing. The cynic, especially the cynic with postmodern leanings, is a prophet of the fallibility of all knowledge and even the language used to form and express it. It is difficult to see why such a cynic's perspective would remain uncorrupted by the sorts of misinterpretations that afflict everybody else. How do we know that the cynic's cynicism is not controlled by conscious or unconscious desires for money, self-protection, admiration, tenure, acceptance or power? We don't.

I have tried to question the automatic link between cynicism and honesty. If we have doubts about cynicism ourselves, we should not feel daunted or intimidated by cynicism's claim to scientific objectivity, academic status or its ability to humiliate its detractors. We must feel free to reverse the flow of suspicion.

When the flow of suspicion is reversed the vulnerability of cynicism is clear. The attraction of cynicism to us might just have to do with our internal needs for consolation (self-protection) or the desire to mask self-interest (cynical elitism). Cynicism seldom admits its own platform ideals. Just as it is fair to say that cynicism has no monopoly on honesty, so its promise of sophistication is waning as the herd becomes ever more cynical. There is reason to be underwhelmed by cynicism.

SUSPECTING CONTEMPORARY SUSPICION ABOUT GOD

In the early days of the culture of uncertainty, epistemological doubt was a way of deepening an encounter with the world, not of evading one. But eventually, in our time, the situation flipped. As doubt settled into a default setting, reality became "reality."

JACKSON LEARS

It's an interesting view of atheism, as a sort of crutch for those who can't bear the reality of God.

TOM STOPPARD

IS GOD THERE, OR IS HE THE GREATEST-EVER construct of the human imagination? How do we get at the question itself without begging it from one side or the other? What is honesty? The problem is that there is no neutral, objective or unbiased place to stand while we are trying to figure this out. There is no "default" position to revert to when all other options seem uncertain to us. Nor is there any viewpoint that must automatically assume a burden of proof that others do not. If we believe what the majority of people around us happen to believe, we are likely to feel as if our beliefs can be taken for granted because they are somehow self-evidently true. They aren't.

We all have faith at many different levels. We have faith in a chair every time we sit down, in a car every time we drive. But we also have a more complex faith in far deeper levels of reality, all the way down to having faith in some sort of a picture of the world as a whole that we believe is right. That picture might be known only in the form of some unarticulated hunches. It might even be in the form of negations, what we believe the world is *not* like, or it might be expressed in volumes of philosophical, scientific or religious writing.

The believer in God knows God's existence by faith. But the atheist also knows by faith that God is absent. Even the agnostic knows by faith that God is unknowable. When the questions are as vast as the existence of God, we fool ourselves when we think they can be resolved by the sorts of proofs and demonstrations that have been so fruitful in the hard sciences, mathematics and geometry. Even within the sciences there are many different ways of knowing. Yet this is not at all to say that faith is arbitrary, irrational or purely subjective.

Faith in ultimate things is personal, meaning that it involves us as whole persons. Our ideas about God's presence, absence or unknowability are all self-involving ideas. That is, they necessarily implicate us or make claims on us, our priorities and our futures. A dispassionate neutrality is impossible when so much is personally at stake. Neither are we able to make rational deductions from some given, reliable and universally accepted starting point. There is no universally accepted starting point. But we make moral choices: we fear, we hope, we tell stories, we experience beauty, we search, we criticize, we argue, we reflect, we analyze, we create, we love. All these activities may be engaged as we determine what we believe is true in the big picture of things. This means that our faith-held view of the world should not be less than rational but it will more than what is reducible to a set of rational deductions or inductions, because it is so deeply personal.[1]

We will arrive at different conclusions about these vast questions. This is because we look with different motivations at different issues and find different sorts of ideas, experiences and arguments to be persuasive. There is no use trying to pretend that all motivations are equally legitimate, all issues equally important or all arguments equally valid. That is why faith commitments are not just arbitrary choices. That is also why discussion, argument and critical thinking are not only worthwhile but necessary. Let's begin by looking again at the arguments of the masters of suspicion.

Suspicion and Honesty

In our quest for knowledge of God, how do we assess the powerful cynicism of the masters of suspicion? Feuerbach, Marx, Nietzsche and Freud claimed to expose the inner motivations that gave rise to the knowledge and experience of God. These motives were not the honest and courageous pursuit of truth, but psychological, social, and material needs and desires. Christian belief, when completely unmasked, is not a relationship with a transcendent God who actually existed. It is only a believer's unconscious means to achieve his or her personal ends, with the *idea* of God providing a needed crutch, smokescreen or both. It is religion as an instrument.

When we reversed the flow of suspicion, we saw that it is possible to also see through cynicism and explain it by motivations other than the honest pursuit of truth. In fact we found that we can see both crutch and smokescreen as possible motivators for cynicism. Ideology critique cuts both ways.

These two arguments leave us in a stalemate, each explaining the other by motivations that seem to discredit its claims. Since motivations for believing an idea have no necessary relationship to the truth of that idea, the real issue is what is true, whatever somebody's motivations might be for believing it. We must keep in view the variety and power of motivations that are active in our own lives but also aim to go beyond motivations to the more basic question of what is true.

The masters of suspicion themselves never spent much time taking the possibility seriously that the God of the Bible might actually exist, or allowing themselves to be challenged by the claims of Christ. They were able to identify and discredit instrumental faith so persuasively that they did not feel the need to engage questions about the possible truth of a faith that went beyond instrumentality.

The importance of their argument is not that instrumental faith exists. Of course it does. Examples are not hard to find within the Bible itself. But the cynic's claim is much more audacious and far-reaching. It claims that *all* faith in God is intrinsically and essentially instrumental. Faith is all a human projection serving one need or another. This is a much more difficult claim to defend.

Does the Need for Consolation Explain Belief in God?

The Bible and observation teach that there is a human ambivalence about knowing God. God is both a powerful attraction and a dreaded threat. Some people certainly desire that God exists, but the apostle Paul seemed more impressed by the widespread human desire that he does not. He argued that people tend to turn what they do know of God into some miniaturized, less-intrusive, user-friendly god for their own purpose (Rom 1:18-25). There is a deep human predisposition to have an instrumental God, which he called an idol. Certainly belief in Christ offers many extraordinary benefits and consolations. But many experience God's presence and Jesus' claims as something to run from, looking for consolation not in them but *from* them.

An intriguing story is found in the fourth chapter of Mark's Gospel (Mk 4:35-41). At the end of a long day, Jesus and his disciples set out at night in a boat to cross the Sea of Galilee. Jesus was exhausted and immediately fell asleep. A fierce storm arose and the boat started to swamp. Although experienced fishermen, the disciples panicked and were afraid that they were going to drown as the waves swept into the boat faster than they could bail it out. Stephen Crane's story in *The Open Boat* is remarkably similar.[2] Like the disciples, he also was rowing an open boat in such a storm that he was afraid of drowning—all within tantalizing sight of land. Crane was outraged at nature's indifference, before which he felt completely disposable. The disciples, faced with the same threat, accused Jesus of indifference. He was still sound asleep in the stern of the boat. They woke him up and cried out, "Don't you care that we are perishing?"

In both accounts we see the dread of painful death and the anguish and anger that all potential help seemed indifferent. As the masters of suspicion have pointed out, the world is a threatening place where disaster and death are everywhere. Nature in all its beauty and grandeur offers no comfort when we are in danger. Helplessness before the overwhelming power of impersonal nature is itself the problem. This is exactly why the masters of suspicion say people create God—to provide an illusion of a consoling, personal face of warmth on the cold impersonality of nature's indifferent, crushing power.

In Mark's account Jesus woke up and spoke to the wind and sea. The wind stopped and the sea became calm. The threat of death was suddenly gone. You might have thought that they would have relaxed and said, "Whew! That was a close call. Thank you Jesus, that we're safe." But when they were safe from drowning, they were actually *more afraid* than when they had thought they were going to die.[3] Mark wrote that they were then filled with great fear. The Greek word he used is *megaphobia*.

They said to each other, "Who then is this, that even the wind and the sea obey him?" God in this situation did not only bring consolation and rescue, although he certainly did that. But the disciples were suddenly aware in a new way that they had someone with the power of God at very close quarters, even in the same boat with them. That was *more* terrifying to them than the prospect of drowning. The fear that Feuerbach and Freud wrote about is very real, but this is an even greater fear, which throws their explanation of belief in God into confusion.

We often hear that there are no atheists in foxholes. This is usually followed by a joke about how few of the survivors of foxholes pay any attention to God after they can get out of the foxhole and go home. That may be true, but this account shows something quite different. It was not the fear of death that made them suddenly very interested in God. The actual presence of God and his power made them suddenly more afraid of him than they had been of death.

What does this story have to do with our discussion of cynicism about God? I am suggesting that it tells of an experience of God that does not fit the cynical explanation. In fact there is a great deal of faith that cynical explanation does not account for. God does not exist in human experience just as a projection to ensure safety and comfort when nature is coldly impersonal. If people were only after comfort, they would have devised a far more comfortable god than the God of the Bible. It would have been more like the user-friendly gods of instrumental faith. God enters human experience as a player in his own right, bringing all kinds of challenges, crises and interruptions but also unexpected gifts into our lives.

The disciples experienced a God who is a person and who is holy. This was the reason for their very great fear. As a person, he knew and understood them, and saw through them as we see through glass. As a holy God, he is other, beyond, transcendent, able to stop wind and sea with a word. They felt megaphobia because they felt utterly exposed and vulnerable, finding themselves overwhelmed by the awesome power of One at

close range who transcended the very powers of nature that had so terri-
fied them. They would have understood the character in Tom Stoppard's
play *Jumpers* who suggested that atheism is"a sort of crutch for those who
can't bear the reality of God."[4]

Jesus offered extraordinary benefits and blessings to those who would
follow him. These include promises of radical meaningfulness through relationship with him in this life. They extend all the way to passing through
death as if it were a door to a new life beyond, which is forever. Of course
these promises correspond to human desires and needs. It is understandable that such ideas raise suspicions that the whole package is a wish fulfillment. But it is also a perverse and masochistic logic which holds that
what people desire cannot be true simply because they desire it.

There is too much faith that the cynical dismissal of God cannot explain. W. H. Auden described his own reasons for belief in Christ in an intriguing way. He wrote, "I believe because He fulfills none of my dreams,
because He is in every respect the opposite of what He would be if I could
have made Him in my own image."[5]

There are certainly incentives to belief, but they are also opposed by
great and uncomfortable disincentives. Jesus warned would-be disciples
of the costs and dangers of following him. If we take him at his word, he
invades the orderliness of our well-planned lives; he demolishes precious
illusions of our self-sufficiency and self-righteousness, and he unsettles
our complacency. He challenges our autonomy in his world and commits
us to following his way, which led him to persecution and crucifixion. This
does not sound like consolation or comfort. But consolation critique is not
the only form that modern suspicion takes.

Does Justification of Self-Interest Explain Belief in God?

The other strand of suspicion holds that people believe in God not because he really exists but because they want the smokescreen that belief
in him provides. They find that believing in God enables them to better
pursue and sanctify their own self-interest. Belief in God is then unmasked by cynicism to be a cover for self-satisfaction and selfishness.
Marx explained the plausibility of the Christianity of his day by its service
to the economic ambitions of the bourgeoisie. Nietzsche saw it as a way
devised by the weak, from their status as sheep, to deviously control and

take revenge on the strong in the universal struggle for power. Postmodern cynicism takes Nietzsche's vision and focuses it on the power relationships, not just of economic class but also of race, sex and cultural dominance. The Christian faith is now particularly targeted as serving the needs of the empowered and therefore attracting their loyalty and faith. *atheist*

It is perfectly true that Christian ideas have sometimes been used to *ideas too* make the oppression of people seem justified to perpetrators and sometimes even to victims. But we will have to decide in each instance whether those ideas represent the true character of Christian thought and life or whether they had been perverted in the service of some form of instrumental faith hiding behind idols such as racism or nationalism.

The other side of the discussion is that faith built around the full breadth of the teaching of the Bible has been one of the most important forces to put limitations on power and to motivate sustained and costly work for freedom, reconciliation, peace and justice. Biblical faith promises not just individual comfort in the face of suffering and death. It includes also a powerful prophetic challenge that does not allow resignation to that brokenness. It calls for change, for justice, for peace, for compassion, and promises that God will be at work with us toward these ends. This call has been an enormous force for change in world history. The movement for the abolition of slavery was inspired by and solidly grounded in Christian theology and ethics. As slaves read the Bible they discovered the book of Exodus in which the Jewish people were enslaved in Egypt. It gave them a sense of their value before God and also a reason for spiritual resistance and hope. God himself had been on the side of the slaves against their masters and worked in momentous ways to free them.[6]

Individuals whose faith went beyond self-interest. Some of the giants who changed the shape of the world for the better in the last half of the twentieth century have done it in response to that prophetic call. They cannot be typecast either as Nietzsche's sheep or as Marx's bourgeois fat cats using religious authority to maintain economic comfort or political advantage. In the name of God and at great risk to themselves, they worked to change society in the direction of justice.

Dr. Martin Luther King Jr. led the Civil Rights Movement in the United States in the 1960s in the name of God and the application of the biblical principles of justice, love and human dignity before God. His challenge was for people to turn away from an instrumental faith that had let itself be deafened to the full force of Jesus' teaching. Beaten, imprisoned and threatened with death many times, he kept on with nonviolent protests, marches, and clear articulation of biblical principles of justice and love. When he was assassinated in Memphis in 1968, he had led the country through a profound transformation of race relations that is still going on today.

Nelson Mandela also stands out as a man who brought great change to his nation and to the world. Although he was held as a political prisoner for twenty-seven years, he emerged from prison to take leadership of South Africa. The predicted bloodbath of racial hatred was averted in his call for reconciliation and forgiveness. Those close to him described his unequivocal Christian faith and how he had grown in strength to forgive through prayer while in prison.[7]

Another long-term prisoner was Alexandr Solzhenitsyn. He may have had as much to do with the fall of Russian and Eastern European communism as any other person. Having come to believe in Christ during his eight years in the Soviet prison system, he came out not to direct political activity but to write what he had seen and heard. With extraordinary commitment and focused vision he set out to expose the corruption and brutality of Soviet communism for people who he knew were starved for hearing the truth. The correspondent David Aikman summarized Solzhenitsyn's achievement: "By turns sardonically funny, anguished, or burning in slow fury, Solzhenitsyn accomplished something truly rare in all literature, the moral impaling of an entire political system with sustained literary power."[8]

Given the history of those who have taken the prophetic voice of the Christian faith seriously and lived it out with enormous risk and loss to themselves, it is impossible to honestly account for their faith as only a means for believers to maintain power and privilege. The prophetic message of the Bible has been a powerful force to work against injustice from Roman slavery and exposure of infants all the way down to the injustices of today.

Power and the cross. But the Christian relationship to power is highly nuanced. The main symbol of the Christian faith is also its theological core. It is the cross of Jesus. The cross casts it shadow over the entire Christian vision of life and death. Not a call to personal or collective power as the highest achievement, the cross is a call to love even when that includes self-sacrifice for the good of others. That is, the Christian faith at its center does not offer a means for the satisfaction of our own desires, but a call to put aside our desires for the sake of others and so to follow Christ wherever he leads. The historian G. G. Coulton describes the impact of the teaching of the crucifixion of Christ:

> The belief in a crucified carpenter—the conviction that the highest triumph may be gotten of the completest earthly failure—did, as a matter of fact, take more men out of themselves, and took them further out of themselves than anything else since the dawn of history.[9]

As followers of Christ have faithfully lived out his teachings, they have not withdrawn from public life because their hope was only in the next world; nor have they scrambled for personal or group power in this world. An intriguing study is provided by Douglas Johnston and Cynthia Sampson in their book *Religion, the Missing Dimension of Statecraft.*[10] In it they chart the recent history of the largely untold role of the Christian faith, as well as other religious traditions, in working to bring reconciliation between hostile groups of people. Of particular note were the roles of followers of Christ in the peaceful collapse of the Iron Curtain in Eastern Europe, the undoing of apartheid in South Africa, and the People Power revolution overthrowing the Marcos regime in the Philippines, all without major violence.

Remember where our discussion has come. The Christian faith has sometimes been sadly compromised and reduced to instrumental faith. This is undeniable. But it is much more difficult to claim that all faith in Christ is instrumental or that it is instrumental in its origin or essence. The masters of suspicion fairly expose and discredit some of the idols of the human mind. So does the Bible. What they do not show is the truth of their basic assumption—that all faith in God is instrumental faith. In fact, there is a great deal of faith that is very hard to account for in this way.

Part Three

AN HONEST ALTERNATIVE TO CYNICISM

THE PROVIDENCE OF GOD
A Theology of Brokenness

The professional pessimist sees one half the picture, the professional optimist the other. The former calls the latter superficial and is in turn pronounced defeatist. Each possesses a distorted fragment of the Christian truth. The Bible's realism exceeds that of the worst cynic, for it knows what man has done to God. At the same time its hope surpasses the wildest utopian fantasy, for it has concrete experience of what this same God will do for man.

EDMOND LA B. CHERBONNIER

There was one question which I never dreamed of raising. I never noticed that the very strength and facility of the pessimists' case at once poses us a problem. If the universe is so bad, or even half so bad, how on earth did human beings ever come to attribute it to the activity of a wise and good Creator? Men are fools, perhaps; but hardly so foolish as that.

C. S. LEWIS

HOW COULD GOD POSSIBLY BE BOTH POWERFUL AND GOOD in a world where there is so much suffering? For some, their faith survived and even strengthened under the battering of this question. Others came to believe that God was malevolent, indifferent, unknowable or absent. How can we understand these grievances with providence?

A Theology of Brokenness

The Christian faith shares at least part of a common diagnosis with many cynical judgments. There is something profoundly and desperately wrong here. There are no hidden corners of innocence in the world—neither in the human head nor on some South Pacific island. There is what seems to be mindless, purposeless suffering, and cruelty and waste in this world; there is hatred, chaos, poverty and death mixed with love, beauty, peace, prosperity and vitality. Those realities are not distributed according to any apparent equality or fairness. Most honest observers of this world can see the point of the Preacher of Ecclesiastes when he wrote, "Again I saw that under the sun the race is not to the swift, nor the battle to the strong, nor bread to the wise, nor riches to the intelligent, nor favor to the skillful; but time and chance happen to them all" (Eccles 9:11).

Creation and Fall: Two primal events. But how do we understand this? Is it evidence of randomness and mindlessness at the origin and heart of all things? The Bible tells a different story in its first chapters, that even before the beginning there was a Person. In the early chapters of the book of Genesis it tells of this Person creating a good world out of nothing. This included the creation of human beings, uniquely made in his image, that they might then image him as subcreators, multiplying and being stewards of God's garden. But it also tells of our first parents' rebellion against him, bringing down on their own heads the wreckage and brokenness of this good creation, and dragging alienation into every area of existence. This is called the Fall of the human race. Subsequent human history is filtered through this initial alienation. We are still images of God by creation, but now we are bent and twisted by sin. As theologian Francis Schaeffer has said, each of us, being marked by these two events, is a "glorious ruin."[1]

The rebellion itself was at the instigation of Satan, who suggested that God had lied about death and that if the first humans ate of the tree of the knowledge of good and evil, they would take a step up in the world and be "like God, knowing good and evil" (Gen 3:5). It was not an innocent offer of greater self-awareness or further moral education. It was the temptation to determine good and evil by themselves, without God's counsel or authority. The lure was to be *like God,* over good and evil, as architect and governor of all moral order and enforcer of praise and blame, punishment and reprieve.

HUMAN CHOICES
NATURAL PROCESSES
GRAVITY, WEATHER, CONTINENTAL DRIFT

After rebelling they immediately felt the need to hide from God. He had suddenly become a threat to them—a challenge to their pride and a threat to expose the guilt of their betrayal. They experienced shame. Ever since, people have made moral rules for themselves, but they have broken their own rules. Human nature is skewed and twisted. We are so enmeshed in its brokenness that we cannot remove our predisposition to evil. If it is true that human nature is so profoundly flawed, it is easy to see that this could be the raw material for cynicism of all kinds.

But in the biblical story this alienation is not the last word. God is not finished with us. The entire Bible is the story of God's not giving up on his people. They know that they have earned God's anger and rejection, but they have received his mercy. They are not entitled to his approval, but they are given his blessing. They are forgiven, and he is at work in their lives to transform them in wonderful ways, but they are still broken people living in a broken world. They do not have charmed lives of immunity to serious sin, wars, cancer or car accidents.

The Struggle with Providence

If God is in control, why is there suffering, injustice, genocide? While giving a neat and tidy answer to this question would be overwhelmingly arrogant, the question nevertheless needs to be addressed. The world is broken and twisted after the Fall. It is not as God made it or as he wanted it. The world itself is a glorious ruin.

Jesus taught us to pray in the Lord's Prayer, "Your will be done, on earth as it is in heaven" (Mt 6:10). This means that although God is in ultimate control, his will is not being done on earth *in the same sense* that it is in heaven. What is happening on earth is under the shadow of the Fall; it is bent and spoiled here, yet God still reigns. He has not given up on us and is doing his will through us. He has the power to make earth more like heaven and will one day do that fully.

God's relation to blessing and suffering is asymmetrical. We must begin by admitting that there is a profound mystery with the way the power of God relates to both human choices and natural processes such as gravity, the weather or continental drift. But there is a distinction that is important—God's relationship to blessing and to suffering is asymmetrical.[2] That is, he stands behind or is more directly involved in causing blessing in this fallen world than in causing suffering. Blessing and suffering do not come to us in the same way as simple "effects" of divine causes. Blessing and goodness are described as coming directly from the hand of God. Suffering occurs within God's overall sovereignty, but it is not described as coming directly from him, unless it is specifically in his judgment or discipline.

God did not directly inflict Job with sores on his body; Satan did. Lazarus, a friend of Jesus, died. When Jesus saw the impact of that death on Lazarus's family he was both upset and angry at what had happened, but he was *not* angry at something that he had done himself (Jn 11:33). While Francis Schaeffer suffered from the cancer that eventually took his life, he believed fully in the sovereignty of God. But he often said, "God did not give me this cancer." God's will was not being done on earth *in the same sense* that it was in heaven.

"Reading" providence. If a loving God is in ultimate control of events on earth, that is a great source of confidence. Even when we cannot figure out what is going on and why, somebody who is both powerful and good can. But with belief in providence comes the temptation to try to "read" it, in the sense of figuring out what God is intending through the events of our experience, looking for a play-by-play running commentary on God's purposes. This temptation has led many people into terrible folly—as if they could determine whether God is for or against them and their efforts by observing their circumstances. If we think we can read providence, we are likely to think God is on our side when things seem to be going well, and that he is against us when events do not go as we had hoped. Perhaps neither is true.

Often interpretations of God's providence have been notoriously self-serving. After the great fire of London, all seemed to agree that it was the result of the judgment of God on Londoners. Protestants knew that it was because of the sins of the Catholics; Catholics could tell that it was because of the heresies of the Protestants; and the Dutch (who were at war with England) saw clearly that it was because the sin of England as a nation.[3]

By contrast, the apostle Paul wrote to the Romans:

O the depth of the riches and wisdom and knowledge of God! How unsearchable are his judgments and how inscrutable his ways!

> For who has known the mind of the Lord?
>
> Or who has been his counselor? (Rom 11:33-34)

Did you notice the words *unsearchable* and *inscrutable?* It seems that real faith in God does not need to interpret providence but allows God to be God and admits that his providence may include things completely outside of our understanding. Faith often requires that we obey God while having very little idea of what God intends for our future or what part we may be playing in the larger story.

The apostle wrote a letter to a Christian friend of his called Philemon. A slave owned by Philemon had run away and became a follower of Christ with Paul. Paul wrote a powerful letter to persuade Philemon to release the runaway from the bondage of slavery and welcome him back as a brother in Christ. He then said, "Perhaps this is the reason he was separated from you for a while, so that you might have him back forever" (Philem 15). Notice that he said "perhaps" this is why things happened as they did. He did not know, so he did not pretend, though it would have sounded more impressive and persuasive if he had said, "God did this so that you would release Philemon!" God might have had quite different intentions.

What we can see of God's intentions is like the back side of a tapestry, where the pattern is difficult to discern. It is actually more like seeing a *small piece* of the back side of a tapestry of such vast size that it goes well beyond our field of vision. Therefore, we must approach "reading" providence with profound humility.

LIVING WITH THE PROVIDENCE OF GOD

We are not honest and open-minded explorers of reality; we are alienated from reality because we have made ourselves the center of the universe.

LESSLIE NEWBIGIN

My hosanna has passed through the purgatory of doubt.

FYODOR DOSTOYEVSKY

I believe that God can and will bring good out of evil. For that purpose he needs men who make the best use of everything. I believe God will give us all the power we need to resist in all time of distress. But he never gives it in advance, lest we should rely upon ourselves and not on him alone.

DIETRICH BONHOEFFER

LET'S RETURN NOW TO THE BIBLICAL CHARACTERS Job and Asaph, whose complaints against the providence of God were actually resolved into deeper faith. How did they manage to hold together their beliefs in God's power and goodness and in the reality of evil in the world?

Job: Instrumental Faith or Something More?

The book of Job is a deep reflection on cynicism in two of our three theaters (people, institutions and God). It began with God's assertion that

Job was "my servant," a "blameless and upright man." Satan immediately countered this with one of the standard cynical challenges to faith in God, now familiar to us from our discussion of the masters of suspicion and the ideology critique. He said, "Does Job fear God for nothing?" (Job 1:9), followed with the argument that *of course* Job "serves" God—Job's faith was just opportunism, self-interest in disguise, clearly instrumental religion. God has given him everything anyone could ever want—big house, large family, possessions, successful businesses and social prestige. But if some of those things were taken away from him, then the true Job would stand up, show his real self-centeredness and curse God to his face. The whole book of Job is about the question, Who is right about Job: God or Satan? Is God only an instrument for achieving Job's agenda, or is God the Lord?

Two theaters of cynicism. First, would Job show himself to be a servant of God or an opportunist and hypocrite? Was his faith real or only a veneer hiding selfishness, better understood cynically by Satan than at face value by God? As the story develops the answer to that question depends on another cynical challenge in a different theater.

The second question raised is the subject of this chapter, Would Job end up cynical about God? If cynicism about God becomes Job's final conviction, then Satan's cynicism about Job will be vindicated, a giant feedback loop of cynicism.

Job suffers one of the ultimate nightmares that all of us dread: loss of all his property, all his children and all public respect.

> Then Job arose, tore his robe, shaved his head, and fell on the ground and worshipped. He said, "Naked I came from my mother's womb, and naked shall I return there; the LORD gave, and the LORD has taken away; blessed be the name of the LORD."
>
> In all this Job did not sin or charge God with wrongdoing. (Job 1:20-22)

Job then lost his health and the support of his wife, and then, making matters worse, friends from his philosophy club came to help. They might have been some comfort to him for the first few days, when they had the sense to be speechless as they looked on his suffering, but soon a long and heated argument began.

His friends had no doubts about how to read providence: Why do the righteous suffer? That's easy. They don't. God does not make mistakes. Job must have done something terrible to have caused these awful things to happen to him all at once. God was disciplining Job. The world runs in moral harmony and balance. Couldn't Job see that as a theological necessity?

Job could not see that, but he could not figure out what he *could* see either. From the intensity of his own suffering together with the cruelly misguided advice of his friends, Job began to justify himself and challenge his friends with cynical charges against God's intentions. He could see through the idea of a loving and caring God. God must be his enemy, a sadist or at least indifferent to his suffering and his prayers for relief. God had deserted, abandoned and forsaken him.

Job's question. Job had accepted his status as a creature of God when it was a matter of his recent catastrophe. He had relinquished his losses to his Creator. "The LORD gave and the LORD has taken away; Blessed be the name of the LORD." But when it came to the question why, he would not relinquish it. Why does the world runs as it does? Why is it so unfair?

> Why is light given to one in misery,
>   and life to the bitter in soul,
> who long for death, but it does not come? (Job 3:20-21)

> Why have you made me your target? (Job 7:20)

> Why do the wicked live on,
>   reach old age, and grow mighty in power? (Job 21:7)

Job held on to this question for a thirty-six-chapter argument, escalating his complaints about God's character. The answer to this question itself became an entitlement before God in Job's mind and a condition of his submission and service. He insisted on seeing the whole tapestry from the front side so he could be satisfied that everything was just and fair according to Job. Job was not confident enough about all of this to curse God, but his demand stood between him and submitting to God.

God's questions. When God finally entered the story again, it was not to answer Job's question but to ask over sixty questions of his own. The first two give an idea of the rest.

Then the LORD answered Job out of the whirlwind:
> "Who is this that darkens counsel by words without
> knowledge? . . .
> "Where were you when I laid the foundation of the earth?
> Tell me, if you have understanding." (Job 38:1-2, 4)

Job was questioned mainly about what he knew about the natural world, but he could give no answers at all. Somehow, through the long process of the questioning, he began to develop a different picture of himself in his ignorance and dependency and of God in his transcendence. He had been given a glimpse of God so immense that his own questions seemed to dissolve before it. He repented and worshiped God as God's servant, knowing God in a radically new way:

> I had heard of you by the hearing of the ear,
>> but now my eye sees you;
> therefore I despise myself,
>> and repent in dust and ashes. (Job 42:5-6)

Job turned from his experiment with cynicism about God. God's questions had been a reality check. His renewed faith centered in a willingness • to allow God's ways to be "unsearchable" and "inscrutable," to let God be God. It meant recognizing his own finiteness—lowering his expectations of what he could demand to understand in his own terms. It seemed reasonable, as a person with a finite mind, to admit such mystery in God's dealing with the world.

The story of Job was a test case for instrumental religion. Would Job worship God because God was the Lord, or only on the condition that God produced a satisfactory, mystery-free explanation of the moral workings of the universe? Between Job's suffering and the "help" of his friends, he had drifted toward an instrumental faith that rested not on a demand for health, wealth and popularity but on the insistence that God supply him with the answer to the deepest questions of moral philosophy.

Job abandoned cynicism toward God, not because cynicism was not nice, nor out of a fear of punishment, but because he no longer believed it to be true. In that response he also refuted Satan's cynical accusation that his faith was just opportunistic. He had been willing to serve God "for nothing."The book of Job ends with the cynicism of Job about God, and Satan about Job, defeated.

Through the ages, people in times of suffering and tragedy have turned to the book of Job. As we face grief, loss and bewilderment, perhaps leading to cynicism about God, it offers a vitally important perspective. It gives us permission to fully express our complaints and anguish. It also turns our complaints away from looking for satisfaction or comfort in facile, watertight "answers." The book actually warns us that if we insist on such answers, that insistence could walk us backward into a more instrumental, entitled faith than we realize. The hope is that we might be able to stand in a new way before our transcendent Creator, willing to admit mystery that is appropriate to our finiteness.

Asaph: Faith Seeing Through Cynicism

Asaph was a writer of psalms in ancient Israel. In chapter five we looked at his grievances written in Psalm 73 (see pp. 46-47). He also was cynical about the way God runs the world. He envied those who mocked God and who seemed to have such an easy and prosperous time of their lives. But for him, serving God seemed to be in vain. His whole life was like a plague. Getting up in the morning was punishment.

When Asaph went to the house of God to worship he began to see a wider picture than the narrow focus of his cynicism. He began to realize that he really did not envy God's enemies at all, because they were in "slippery places," close to ruin, and that they would be "destroyed in a moment, / swept away utterly by terrors" (Ps 73:18-19). He looked back on his cynicism as a terrible mistake that he had almost committed himself to by teaching it publicly and spreading it to others.

> When my soul was embittered,
> 　　when I was pricked in heart,
> I was stupid and ignorant;
> 　　I was like a brute beast toward you.
> Nevertheless I am continually with you;
> 　　you hold my right hand. (Ps 73:21-23)

Think of the contrast here with the idea of cynicism as honest, sophisticated and enlightened. His experience was the opposite. Asaph reversed the flow of suspicion. He looked critically at it from a wider picture of life. He saw that cynicism was not the result of honest insight but of the clouded misunderstandings that had come with being deeply embittered. This bitterness had not led him not into enlightenment or any sharper perspective but into ignorance and shortsightedness, even to the point of being as insensitive toward God as an animal. Psalm 73 is a reversal of the direction of cynicism. It is faith's suspicion seeing through cynicism.

As he became free from cynicism, he realized that God had not forgotten or abandoned him at all. God had actually been with him the whole time, even through the cynical episode, holding him by his right hand.

Where can peace of mind come from if we are honest with these tormenting questions? There are many arguments that promise to be logically satisfying but which in the end miniaturize both God's transcendence and the seriousness of human agonies in the interest of somebody's idea philosophical neatness. It is intriguing that the Bible itself never leads us down this road. It pictures the mystery of evil in the world not as an intellectual riddle to be solved but as a reality of inexhaustible depth that deepens even as we reflect on it.

We can see a pattern in people of faith in the Old Testament of approaching God with their agonies, questions and complaints. As they were able to understand, engage or experience something of God's transcendence and love, their grievances changed shape and were replaced with humility. It is not as if they had received a three-point answer to memorize. It is more that they somehow saw themselves and their Creator in a different light. As we move forward to the New Testament and into our own era, human grievances and questions have not changed. But momentous events have happened in the intervening time.

PROVIDENCE EXPERIENCED
Does Jesus Make Any Difference?

> *We are treated as imposters, and yet are true; as unknown, and yet are well known; as dying, and see—we are alive; as punished, and yet not killed; as sorrowful, yet always rejoicing; as poor, yet making many rich; as having nothing, and yet possessing everything.*
>
> THE APOSTLE PAUL

> *For God so loved the world that he gave his only Son, so that everyone who believes in him may not perish but may have eternal life.*
>
> THE APOSTLE JOHN

JOB AND ASAPH WRESTLED WITH THE ISSUES of how God could be good and all powerful, and yet evil could be real in his world. They did not stop at cynicism but went beyond it to renewed faith. But we have more to think about than they did as we struggle with the same questions. A great intervention has taken place from God's side.

An event within God's providence on earth has transformed our perspective on providence itself. The Christian claim is that eternity has intersected time. The author personally entered his own story. The Lord of lords and King of kings has joined the human race in the person of Jesus of Nazareth. Astonishingly, he lived in obscurity, taught for three years, but never did the things we normally associate with leadership. Nevertheless, he offended the local authorities and was tortured to death by crucifixion. But that did not end it.

The Crucified God

The meaning of Jesus' death was so significant to those who followed him that the cross itself became the main visual symbol of the Christian faith. I suspect that we have lost our perspective about how strange this is. The cross is a means of execution and torture. It is instructive to compare this central Christian symbol with the central symbol of Buddhism: the Buddha sitting cross-legged, meditating. Buddhist scholar D. T. Suzuki puts it this way: "Christian symbolism has much to do with the suffering of man. The crucifixion is the climax of all suffering. Buddhists also speak much about suffering and its climax is the Buddha serenely sitting under the Bodhi tree by the river Niranjana."[1]

This image of the Buddha shows his experience of harmony and peacefulness, having transcended all the suffering and conflicts of human experience. In his enlightened state, moral conflict—the struggle between good and evil, which is central to the Christian faith—is illusory to him because the human self and therefore human suffering do not ultimately exist. Suzuki points out, "Buddhism declares that there is from the very beginning no self to crucify. . . . As there is no self, no crucifixion is needed."[2]

The contrast is stark. Jesus on the cross is the incarnate God in agony, nailed through his hands and feet to timbers of wood. He cried out, "My God, my God, why have you forsaken me?" (Mt 27:46), reminding us of Job's complaint. The symbol of the cross represents the core of the Christian faith, as God's involvement in human suffering and sin—a suffering God. It does not show God peacefully transcending the conflict between good and evil, but God engaged in the battle on the side of good and against evil at enormous cost to himself. His victory in that battle was assured on the first Easter as he rose from the dead to new life, but the battle is not over.

God has not simply allowed suffering to be part of this world order. He has himself entered into our suffering in an extreme way, not only as a gesture of solidarity with us but as a means of eventually breaking the power of suffering and evil over us. So the crucifixion is not a metaphor or illustration of any higher truth. There is no higher truth. It was the historical reality from which Christian metaphors and illustrations came and to which they point.

Of all the historical events recounted in the Bible the crucifixion is the most thoroughly described and carefully interpreted. This humiliation was the only major happening of Jesus' life that was a totally public event for all to see. God allowed all the world to see him captured, tortured and executed as an impostor on his own planet, helplessly defeated by human cruelty and corruption.

The meaning of the crucifixion. The Bible describes God restraining evil, opposing evil, defeating evil, freeing people from the power of evil and sometimes permitting evil for his inscrutable purposes. But on Good Friday (the day Jesus was crucified), the Bible tells of God judging, cursing and condemning evil, and destroying its power—all on the back of his own Son as he hung on the cross. Jesus himself gave a clear interpretation of his death before it happened. "For the Son of Man came not to be served but to serve, and to give his life as a ransom for many" (Mk 10:45). He was forsaken by his Father, for the sake of those who would trust in him. He was forsaken that we might not be forsaken. Martin Luther described the significance of what Jesus did on Good Friday.

> [Christ] says to me, "You are no longer a sinner, but I am. I am your substitute. You have not sinned, but I have. . . . All your sins are to rest on Me and not on you." . . . The Son of Man performs the basest and filthiest work. He does not don some beggar's torn garment or old trousers, nor does he wash us as a mother washes a child, but He bears our sin, death, and hell, our misery of body and soul.[3]

The death of Christ confused people at the time it happened, just as it still confuses people today. Most people did not and still do not realize that something so radical was needed for their own salvation—simply that they would need that much saving. The cross has never made sense to those who see themselves as decent, respectable, confident people who simply want to add a spiritual dimension to their lives. They are apt to feel insulted by its implications. But it has made very good sense to those who realize that they fall hopelessly short of what God requires and so need his costly forgiveness.

You may ask, Well, what difference does all this make to the questions of Job and Asaph? In the life and death of Jesus God put his own love and goodness on the line. This is part of the meaning of the familiar verse, "For God so loved the world that he gave his only Son, so that everyone who believes in him may not perish but may have eternal life" (Jn 3:16). This giving of God's Son may be where God wants us to look when we feel cynical about his love. If God was *not* loving, he would not have sent his Son to save anybody—why bother with us? On the other hand, if God was *not* just, why would he have sent his Son to die as a substitute for his people? He could have, like a corrupt judge, ignored our sin and evil rather than satisfying his own justice at such great cost to himself.

I remember a professor saying that his brother had just died in his late twenties, leaving a wife and several children. My professor asked, "How can I look at that and say that God is good?" He continued, "I can't. But that is not all that God has given me to look at." He went on to say that he looked not to his own limited evaluation of the fairness of history for his assurance of God's character, but to the death and resurrection of Jesus. Everything else is seen in that light.

C .S. Lewis's grievance. In chapter five, we saw C. S. Lewis's searing judgment on God's character after his wife's death from bone cancer. In his pain his mind heaped up cynical explanations for God's involvement in the course of her sickness. But this was not the attitude to God that he took with him to his grave. There was a change, which he described in his book *A Grief Observed.* In the midst of his complaint against God, he wrote:

> Yet this is unendurable. And then one babbles—"If only I could bear it, or the worst of it, or any of it, instead of her." But one can't tell how serious that bid is, for nothing is staked on it. If it suddenly became a real possibility, then, for the first time, we should discover how seriously we had meant it. But is it ever allowed?
>
> It was allowed to One, we are told, and I find I can now believe again, that He has done vicariously whatever can be so done. He replies to our babble, "You cannot and you dare not. I could and dared."
>
> Something quite unexpected has happened. It came this morning early. For various reasons, not in themselves at all mysterious, my heart was lighter than it had been for many weeks.[4]

Many people struggling with the problem of evil and suffering in their own lives or in the lives of others have found a new perspective as the suffering and death of Jesus becomes part of their picture. He could and dared to lay down his life. It is not as if Lewis had forgotten about the crucifixion of Christ and suddenly remembered it just then. Nor was it some sort of quick, automatic fix. It was that at that point in his own suffering he was somehow able to see what Jesus came to do in a fresh way—"I find I can now believe again"—a way that cast different light on his own and his wife's agony.

Understanding Our Own Suffering

In a society so dedicated to youth, pleasure, beauty and material success, suffering is not meant to happen. If it does, it is the great indignity. It is pathetic. Don't think about it.

The biblical viewpoint is very different. The world is not a pain-free or frustration-free place. In it we are warned that events will not seem fair—especially if we compare ourselves with others. God's people are not spared suffering. Yet even terrible suffering does not destroy meaning in our lives or even meaning in the suffering itself. The apostle Paul wrote of his own experience: "We are afflicted in every way, but not crushed; perplexed, but not driven to despair; persecuted, but not forsaken; struck down, but not destroyed; always carrying in the body the death of Jesus, so that the life of Jesus may also be made visible in our bodies" (2 Cor 4:8-10).

He was reflecting on a certain limit to his suffering—up to a point but not beyond, "struck down, but not destroyed." We know from later in the same letter that he had been beaten, imprisoned, abandoned, stoned and left for dead, shipwrecked, sick and flogged countless times, often almost to death. Three times he received a beating with rods, five times the judicial Jewish thirty-nine lashes (2 Cor 11:23-27). Given the amount of his body that must have been covered with scar tissue, it is unlikely that he meant that there was a limit to the simple quantity of pain that he endured. The limit seems to be in the quality of his suffering. It was not meaningless, mindless or random. Even if we cannot understand it, Someone does. Someone cares. Suffering is part of the journey spent serving that One and his people.

When suffering seems to drive us from God. The New Testament teaches that suffering can strengthen our faith and can be walking in the footsteps of Jesus himself. I can go through very heavy times when any trust that I have in God is severely strained—through illness, accident, betrayal, abandonment, poverty, loneliness, bereavement. The faith of Psalm 23 that "The LORD is my shepherd" may seem far away and beyond recovery. It can feel as if the growth that is meant to happen through suffering is working in reverse, that my faith is being shredded, undone, destroyed. I may feel that I am failing God's test, losing the battle and becoming more cynical every day.

If you feel this way and read the Bible carefully, you find yourself in good company. This was the experience of many of God's greatest servants. For King David this struggle lasted for quite a while. He prayed, "How long, O LORD? Will you forget me forever?" (Ps 13:1). The prophet Jeremiah was resigned that God would "out argue" him but protested anyway.

> You will be in the right, O LORD,
>   when I lay charges against you;
>   but let me put my case to you.
> Why does the way of the guilty prosper?
>   Why do all who are treacherous thrive? (Jer 12:1).

These men of God did not always feel peaceful and secure in their faith. Their complaints, anguish and doubts were real and heartfelt. They did not feel the way the Buddha looks. God did not seem to expect them to. Suffering and conflict were real.

It is intriguing that at the end of the book of Job, God addressed Job's three friends who had been so self-confident that moral harmony existed on earth. He spoke to Eliphaz, "My wrath is kindled against you and against your two friends; for you have not spoken of me what is right, as my servant Job has" (Job 42:7). He then instructed them to offer sacrifices and to get Job to pray for them, "for I will accept his prayer not to deal with you according to your folly; for you have not spoken of me what is right, as my servant Job has done" (Job 42:8).

Job's friends were rebuked twice for their too-neat moral theology where everything was in order and the books of cosmic justice were already balanced for all to see. For them, goodness was rewarded, evil was punished, all in this life. The world showed moral harmony, perfect justice. There was no "problem of evil" because the righteous do not suffer. But God rejected this theology of moral harmony as foolish and untrue.

This same objection would actually apply to the doctrines of karma, of Eastern religious traditions. These teachings hold that the moral books are balanced in this life for deeds done in past lives so that, similarly, what we see now in this world represents moral harmony, perfect justice being done. From this perspective Job would have done such evil in previous lives that his present sufferings were fully deserved and appropriate.

The extraordinary thing is that God called Job's views "what is right." Of course God refers primarily to Job's repentance and faith after he was questioned, but there is approval also of Job's refusal to go along with his friends' falsehoods, which they held in order to maintain a "nicer and neater" picture of the world.

Job had called God a sadist and an enemy, indifferent to his prayers. While God certainly did not agree with these characterizations, it turned out that God was not shocked or disturbed by them either. In fact he far preferred Job's angry protests to the seemingly more respectable views of Job's friends, which were comfortable lies.

Sometimes when believers in God's goodness think they are failing God's test, they may not be doing so badly. Perhaps God is teaching them deeper things about humility, about being honest in their own vulnerability and fragility, dependence on him in a broken world. Maybe they are dealing with radical disappointment and the collapse of long-held dreams. Perhaps they have peace in the midst of all the chaos, but perhaps they don't. I have concluded that sometimes God only gets our attention to teach us what he wants us to learn when we have to live without peace for a time.

What Became of Providence?

For all of us, one of the deepest and most far-reaching questions is whether there is an Author of the whole human project, or if we are in a random world with no mind or authority higher than our own. I have described part of the biblical worldview about God's providence in a fallen world as a way of understanding the world that holds the strengths of cynicism without its weaknesses and liabilities. The Bible honestly recognizes evil in us and in the world yet maintains hope because we reflect God's image in *progress / pessimism*

a world where God is at work and for which God has a future.

But the idea of the providence of God has fallen on hard times in the popular understanding of our society. It is now a forlorn and quaint sounding word, having been displaced by belief in progress in the nineteenth and early twentieth centuries, and by pessimism in the late twentieth century and into the twenty-first.

How did the providence of God suffer this fate in the popular understanding of the developed world? For most people the answer is "the Holocaust," "the Killing Fields," "Rwanda" or some reference to the extraordinary scale of organized death and suffering within the life time of many of us. There has been just too much suffering and cruelty for the idea of a powerful and caring God to make sense. Under the sheer weight of human tragedy the providence of God buckled and was crushed into implausibility. In the shadow of the Nazi horror soon after World War II, Dutch theologian G. C. Berkouwer wrote: "The crisis of the Providence doctrine brings a new task to the Church in her preaching of the Gospel. She must now preach to men for whom experience has made it obvious that God does not rule."[5]

While the scale of human cruelty and suffering is appalling, humbling and utterly tragic, I am not sure that it is the most important reason for the loss of belief in providence today. This is because belief in a good and powerful God began millennia before the invention of anesthesia, antibiotics or pain-killing drugs, and continued through the great bubonic plagues that killed a quarter to a third of the population of Europe. The point is that large-scale suffering from both natural disasters and human cruelty were not new developments in the nineteenth and twentieth centuries. For a very long time nature has sometimes behaved with terrifying disorder, and people have been inflicting cruelties on each other in proportion to their political power and technological inventions.

Providence with a miniaturized God. There is another possible factor to help to account for the popular repudiation of providence. It is the view of God, the director of providence himself. The eighteenth-century thinkers of the Enlightenment and their followers shaped their doctrines of God to fit their ideas of an orderly, benign natural world and of a morally benevolent human nature. Human authority replaced God's authority as expressed through his revelation. Most important was the human authority to determine the nature of God—whether he was allowed to define himself or whether his nature could be established by the speculations of philosophers.

The results, of course, were different views of God. Generally, God became more polite, genteel and removed. He was a master designer and general philanthropist. He encouraged cultural progress and good will among people in their attempts to build a better society. More recently God has also become a cosmic therapist. God's grace was not strictly necessary for Enlightenment thinkers because sin was not serious. God merely sent Jesus to be a good moral teacher and example. Nobody needed a Savior.

C. S. Lewis often pointed out that one of the defining features of modern society is a profound absence of the sense of sin. This was not always so, but it had to be so, given the changes in the idea of God.

> The ancient man approached God (or even the gods) as the accused person approaches his judge. For the modern man the roles are reversed. He is the judge: God is in the dock. He is quite a kindly judge: if God should have a reasonable defence for being the god who permits war, poverty and disease, he is ready to listen to it. The trial may even end in God's acquittal. But the important thing is that Man is on the Bench and God is in the Dock.[6]

It was not so much the dimensions of extreme human tragedy itself that turned a society away from belief in God's providence. Instead, belief in providence did not survive because its Author's stature was shrunk to the dimensions of human speculation and *then* this miniature God had to confront desperate tragedy. Ultimate authority had shifted from God to human moral sensibilities. A "straw God" was asked to account for extreme suffering, and he collapsed. People then were pressed into the false choice between belief in a God who might have meant well but was powerless before human evil and natural disorder, an evil God, or no God at all.

This brings us to an unpopular and countercultural idea: God is not so far off and remote as we might suppose. He can actually be angry with what happens on this planet. It is not as if anger is an attribute of God, like love, holiness and justice are. But precisely because love, holiness and justice are attributes of God, he can become justly angry with cruelty, betrayal and injustice when he finds them on his earth.

This may sound primitive, crude or horrifying. But it is interesting to ask some questions. Have you ever been angry because of moral wrongs done to other people? If so, don't you think God can be angry at moral wrongs as well? If not, is it because he is less morally sensitive than you are to injustice? Or is it because he is too transcendent and far away to care about cruelty and oppression on earth? The biblical assertion is that things occur on earth that are an affront to God. His displeasure is as much of a reality as the brokenness and twistedness of the world itself.

Even for the person who believes in the biblical (unminiaturized) God and is sensitive to human suffering, understanding God's providence can still be a great struggle. We saw this in the experience of Job, David, Asaph, Jeremiah and our relative contemporary C. S. Lewis. The Bible does not give us a quick and easy answer to why God allows evil to continue in his world. But if we think back about how God involved himself in such a costly way in the ultimate defeat of sin and death (crucifixion), then whatever reason he may have, it is not that he is indifferent to the human race.

Despite their open doubts, complaints and questions, the biblical authors' response to God's providence was not a faith that just barely survived the ordeals of their suffering, but a faith that included doxology—praise and thanksgiving to God. The prophet Habakkuk began his prophecy with the lament about the nation he loved:

> O LORD, how long shall I cry for help,
>   and you will not listen?
> Or cry to you, "Violence!"
>   and you will not save? (Hab 1:2)

But he ended his prophecy on a very different note.

> Though the fig tree does not blossom,
>   and no fruit is on the vines;
> though the produce of the olive fails
>   and the fields yield no food;
> though the flock is cut off from the fold
>   and there is no herd in the stalls,
> yet will I rejoice in the LORD;

I will exult in the God of my salvation.
GOD, the Lord, is my strength;
>> he makes my feet like the feet of a deer,
>> and makes me tread upon the heights. (Hab 3:17-19)

We will revisit the status of cynicism's charge against God's providence in chapter fifteen. The existence of evil in the world is a reality that cuts in unexpected directions.

15

A POINTER TO TRANSCENDENCE

In a sense, it [Christianity] creates, rather than solves, the problem of pain, for pain would be no problem unless, side by side with our daily experience of this painful world, we had received what we think a good assurance that ultimate reality is righteous and loving.

C. S. LEWIS

The great masquerade of evil has wrought havoc with all our ethical preconceptions. This appearance of evil in the guise of light, beneficence and historical necessity is utterly bewildering to anyone nurtured in our traditional ethical systems. But for the Christian who frames his life on the Bible it simply confirms the radical evilness of evil.

DIETRICH BONHOEFFER

Only those conscious that the world is transcended, and that our lives in the world lead beyond the world, can say that a human being is morally perverse yet of measureless value, fallen yet sacred.

GLENN TINDER

IN *THE QUESTION OF GOD*, HARVARD PSYCHIATRIST Armand Nicholi has written a comparison of ideas about God in the lives of Sigmund Freud and C. S. Lewis. He summarizes Freud's rallying call to cynicism as "Grow up!" You must see through the fairy tales of religion to the truth that the world is not a nursery but a harsh, bleak place where we are all alone.

C. S. Lewis, who had once agreed with Freud's view, changed and came to the opposite conclusion. He saw a world filled with signposts pointing to a transcendent God as its Creator and Sustainer. His call to us was "Wake up!" Look around and understand what you see.[1] This chapter will look around to try to understand a few things that are there to see.

We cannot survey all the possibilities that faith has found in this world, although there are fewer ultimate options than you might suppose. I grew up without any experience of organized religious faith, the Christian faith or any other. But my final year in university coincided with the tightening of the draft for the Vietnam war. For me, this meant an atmosphere of high voltage discussion about the moral legitimacy of that war. Surrounded by passion on both sides of the debate, I was painfully aware of having no moral perspective of my own to bring to my decisions about military service. This anxiety soon expanded into the largest questions of all—what in the world do I want to do with my life, and why? Over the next two years, by a long and circuitous route and with a great deal of help from other people, I came to believe that the transcendent God of the Bible is really there, that Jesus of Nazareth was and is his Son.

Some of the most important issues for me in this journey were the very issues of these chapters. Is there any author to history? Where does morality come from? How can we know good from evil? Does it make any difference if good and evil are only human constructions or fictions? I finally concluded that God was real, that Jesus was who he claimed to be and that the ability to go beyond both cynicism and sentimentality was found in his teachings.

I will deal with two quite separate issues about belief in a transcendent God. The first, in this chapter, is a pointer to a transcendent God from within the ordinary, everyday experience of the cynical person. The second, in chapter sixteen, is the incarnation—that we have actually been visited by this transcendent God, present in this finite, material world.

Inescapable Moral Convictions: Three Thresholds

The landscape of cynical discussion is littered with accusations of what is wrong with the world—its brokenness, hypocrisy and corruption. Moral grievances are a central core of cynicism, so let us begin with these grievances and with issues raised by them. Not only cynics but everyone in everyday life has grievances that point to a transcendent reality beyond our immediate world.[2] Peter Berger called them "signals of transcendence."[3]

The first threshold of morality: The strange idea of obligation. What does it mean to have moral values or convictions? We might say "I like to do this," "I prefer that" or "Things will work out better if I do it this way." These are not moral statements. But we say something different if we say, "I ought to do this or that." We have crossed a threshold by using the word *ought* and introduced the strange new idea of moral obligation, which was not there when we were only talking about our likes, opinions, preferences and pragmatic judgments. Saying "I ought to pay for my groceries when I leave the store," or "I must (or ought) not be cruel to helpless children," submits me to the obligations of a moral order—even if it is only one that I know I have made up for myself.

The second threshold of morality: Other people. But we are likely to cross a second threshold. This is when we think or speak as if our own moral obligations extend to the way other people ought to live as well. For example, we might say "*You too* ought to pay for your groceries, and *you too* must (or ought) not be cruel to helpless children." Here the plot thickens. Before, we were just making these strange "oughts" for ourselves. Now we are submitting other people to obligations that limit their freedom. What right do we have to do this?

If we have any right to do it, it must be because we are appealing to a moral order or some level of obligation that is higher than both us and those other people. Otherwise, our own rules might be interesting, but they could never carry any moral force. Why should anyone else pay any attention to our private ideas of "ought" any more than to our tastes in films or ice cream? So, when we think or speak of obligations that are morally binding on others (and none of us seem to be able to keep *from* doing that), the only way those obligations can refer to anything beyond the sound of our words is if they refer to a *moral order* that is somehow authoritative for both us and the individuals we addressed.

The third threshold of morality: Cultural ideals. There is still a third threshold that we cross, even though we may be unaware of it. Most of us extend our moral obligations even farther—over the ideals of other cultures. Though we may resist admitting it because it seems arrogant and ethnocentric, we habitually distinguish between good and bad ideals beyond our own cultural boundaries. For example, many of us believe that what took place in the Holocaust under Nazism, in the starvation of the Ukraine under Stalin's communism, in the genocide in Rwanda under tribalism, in the raping and ethnic cleansing in Bosnia under nationalism, and in the slavery of the American South under racism was morally wrong, even evil.

Although there was dissent in each of these societies, nevertheless *these atrocities were consistent expressions of the stated ideals or "isms" of the societies where they took place.* They were done in pursuit of what were considered to be the loftiest standards of human excellence. Although those particular barbarities have now ended, they did not end because of repentance or reform from within the various "isms" named. They ended only as a result of internal corruption and collapse or because they were challenged by different, external ideals, some of which were backed by military interventions.

It may seem preposterous to stand over the ideals of other cultures and judge them to be evil. Who in the world are we to do that? We are *not* "anybody" ourselves to have such a right. But those judgments do have meaning and truthfulness if they correspond to some authority that stands above or beyond us all.

Making any moral judgment of these atrocities, even in our own minds, presumes that we are calling for or appealing to a *moral order* by which all people and cultures should be held accountable. If we complain about these nightmares of cruelty and injustice, we sign our signature to the demand that these people *ought* to have behaved differently than they did. The Nuremberg trials of Nazi war criminals felt the need to hold those men responsible to a higher moral order than their Nazi ideals. Were they right?

Where Does Morality Come From?

The assertion of a moral order that stands above cultures raises enormous questions (as it did in Nuremberg)—especially if we are cynical about God. If there is no transcendent person who is good and who has also made this goodness known to us, to what do our moral convictions refer?

Moral alchemy. If there is no such transcendent person, and a morally indifferent nature is our final reality, what way is there to differentiate good from evil, with the enormous gravity we attach to our use of those words? Would it not mean that our most precious moral ideals are just the wistful and pleading efforts of human sentimentality? It seems that even the cynic's favorite platform ideals of freedom, honesty and integrity become inventions of intellectual and moral alchemy the minute we expect them to exert moral leverage or obligation on anyone. Yet this is just what we daily expect them to do.

We are not talking about the difficulty of doing fine-tuned moral decision-making in a highly complex and sophisticated society. The real question is much more basic and crude. Is the distinction between good and evil valid at all or just sentimental and imaginary? Remember Robert Wright's words of unusual candor, from the perspective of evolutionary psychology: "The question may be whether, after the new Darwinism takes root, the word *moral* can be anything but a joke."[4] It seems that he has a point, but it is much more chilling than he wants to concede.

Nature has no purposes. Only persons have purposes. The sun might warm you and give you a tan, or it might kill you through dehydration or skin cancer. The sun does not care. The water in the sea can refresh you, cool you or drown you. The sea does not care. To the universe you are not unique, important or in any sense valuable. It does not care how it treats you, how other people treat you or how you treat them. As far as the universe is concerned, you can be as cruel as you like.

The moral convictions necessary for creating or sustaining civilization apparently call for a moral order that nature or the universe cannot give us. I am fully aware that there are many theories that try to account for the source of moral experience from within nature or society: the theories of Marx, Nietzsche and Freud all the way down to today's evolutionary psychology.

The real problem comes after we have accepted one of these theories and still want to be honest with ourself and others about how to live. If human existence began as the result of a mind-numbing number of infinitesimally unlikely accidents and will end in accidental annihilation by heat or cold, what is the intellectual status of any moral order that our minds could fabricate? If we believe that all moral convictions are only the products of human brains resulting from amoral power struggles or social needs in the late hunter-gatherer society, or that they originated in psychological defense and compensation mechanisms or are only the demands of electrical impulses or selfish genes—then what sort of *moral* obligations are we talking about? Wouldn't it be more accurate and honest to speak of them as the *illusions* of moral obligations? If not, then ask yourself, What *is* an illusory moral obligation?

Yet we are still not able to live without appealing to our convictions as distinctly *moral* convictions, imposing obligations on others even in different cultures. We are stuck as irrepressible moralizers in an amoral world.

What is an illusory moral conviction? I think of the famous passage in Mark Twain's *Adventures of Huckleberry Finn:* the battle fought by Huck inside his own head as he floats down the Mississippi River on a raft with his friend Jim, an escaped slave. The battle is between Huck's moral obligation and "Christian duty" to turn Jim in as a runaway slave who "rightfully belongs" to his owner and, on the other hand, his intuitive self-hatred at the very idea of betraying Jim, who has been his faithful friend.

He agonizes and abuses himself in guilt and self-recrimination. He argues back and forth and finally resigns himself that he will do wrong, because he just can't bring himself to do the "right thing" and betray Jim. Mark Twain hammers the reader with the full force of his irony. He can assume that most of his readers would see that Huck's conscience, for all the force of its guilt, was exactly backward. His moral convictions were illusory moral convictions, upside down and laid on him from no real moral reality at all but only by the prejudices of his upbringing in a slave-owning society.[5]

If nature is all there is, then Huck's morals were certainly groundless, but *no less so* are the moral convictions by which we determined that his were upside down and backward, equally groundless. Whatever he does with Jim is not really a moral issue. It just is.

The Problem That Will Not Go Away

We can't stop making moral judgments, because we don't want to. We are helplessly drawn into moral commitments because they are basic to the intelligibility of life and the possibility of civilization. As we have seen, the survival of cynicism itself depends on morally solid platform ideals from which the cynic can throw rocks.

One of cynicism's most well-worn arguments against God's character and existence is the "problem of evil," which we touched on while discussing God's providence. The Christian faith claims three things: God is good, he is powerful, and yet pain and evil are real. The problem is that evil is still here in God's world even though a powerful and good God hates it. It is perfectly true that there is no fully logically or psychologically satisfying explanation to the problem of pain and evil, although there is good reason for it to be a mystery that is beyond our understanding. C. S. Lewis even suggested that the Christian faith creates the problem rather than solves it.[6] But the cynic's charge includes a strange irony.

If we try to argue from the existence of evil in the world to the absence or indifference of God, it is fair to ask us some questions. The problem of evil really is a serious problem for the Christian—but *only* for the Christian or any theist who believes God to be powerful and good. If there is no good God and the universe is all that exists, what is the ground for the cynic's complaint? The evil we see in the world is just nature being natural, which is being indifferent to human pleasure and pain. If our own highest and final truth is the existence of the universe, what reason do we have for a grievance when the universe produces suffering?

This raises a greater problem than the Christian problem of evil. As we are standing on indifferent nature, there is no honest way to complain about either nature or human nature, tsunamis or genocides—it is all just nature behaving naturally. Ideas of both evil and good, vaporize.

So we are asking, if morally indifferent nature is our final backdrop, how can we ever judge nature to be unnatural or in any sense wrong? There might be one way: Impersonal nature has mindlessly produced unlikely beings with high moral convictions and a sense of tragedy. In such a scenario, tsunamis and genocides are not unnatural, but human horror and objection to them are. Moral sensibilities, in this case, must only exist because of a series of freak accidents in an amoral process. Perhaps believing them might have caused some reproductive advantage to our distant ancestors so they became encoded in our DNA, but as *moral* principles they are illusory since there is no moral reality to which they correspond or appeal. This process has made us misfits with our morality, at odds with our origin, our present existence and our destiny, the only unnatural things in the world.

With no bricks and no temple. These issues are not just abstractions but get worked out in the agonies of real-life situations. Think of how they apply in two of the stories I have mentioned. Remember Stephen Crane's true story "The Open Boat" and his cry of frustration and bitterness:

> When it occurs to a man that nature does not regard him as important, and that she feels she would not maim the universe by disposing of him, he at first wishes to throw bricks at the temple, and he hates deeply the fact that there are no bricks and no temples.[7]

In what seemed senseless suffering and almost certain death, Stephen Crane wanted to cry out against God because of his moral outrage at being disposable. He wanted to "throw bricks at the temple." That is, he wanted to lodge a protest of real and solid grievances (bricks) against someone who was the authority responsible (who lived in the temple) for such a poorly managed world in which valuable people routinely get treated like trash.

Stephen Crane was a deeply sensitive man with profound moral commitments in his life and writing. He wrote that he "hates deeply" that there are neither bricks to throw nor temples to throw them at. Having dismissed God, he could see that his moral passion corresponded to no moral reality outside of his head. "No bricks" meant that he could get his hands on no solid, grounded moral realities that he could throw at whomever was responsible. "No temple" meant that there was no God or moral order responsible against which to throw his grievances. He was frustrated by the "fact" that even his anger was groundless on his own terms.

Why should nature care for him? Nature never promised to be anything but indifferent to his existence. Nature did not care that he was a valuable human being or even that he was a great writer. The cynic about God becomes stranded from his or her own deepest moral feelings, convictions and experience. One of the great and often unacknowledged costs of cynicism about God is that it makes what is most important in human experience—our highest longing as well as our deepest anger—groundless.

With many bricks and a temple. Think of the contrast with the sufferings of Job, who also struggled with cynicism about God but did not surrender to it. Job had bitter grievances, but he had both bricks to throw and a temple to throw them at. He threw bricks at the temple for the best part of thirty-six chapters of the Bible. His bricks were made from moral principles that he knew to be true because they were rooted in the character of God. He knew that he and his family were not disposable trash but were valued by God. The temple was God himself. Job felt that God was not walking his talk, that he was not being true to his own character and promises, so Job told him so.

It turned out that God could handle Job's bricks. He was not shocked or bruised. He asked Job a lot of questions that eventually led him to see things very differently. Finally, God commended Job as his servant. Even in Job's pain and confusion, his honesty led him to resist the facile moral theology of his friends, who had claimed that they could make clear and easy moral sense of Job's troubles. His honesty also enabled him to resist giving in to the cynicism about God that had threatened to overwhelm him.

Some Good Questions

There are many good questions and objections to be raised here. I will mention only three of them. We may say, "We are relativists. Our moral values are only for ourselves and we never judge others," or "We don't make distinctly moral judgments at all, only judgments of preference or prudence." Both of these objections claim that we are not calling for a higher moral order at all. Neither of them is convincing. There are real moral convictions hiding in the closets behind the claims of preference or prudence. There are always hidden assumptions, such as that it is some-how "better" to maximize pleasure and minimize pain or to have social order rather than chaos. In fact nature knows no such preference for plea- ￫ sure or order.

If we think this way, we may find that our own complaints and grievances will surprise us when we confront radical evil in the world or in our personal lives. Few people can look at mass murder, whether the Holocaust or September 11, 2001, and brush aside the distinctively moral issues. Can we tell *ourselves* the relativist's doctrine with a straight face: "Mass murder was OK *for them.* I can't say they were wrong, though it wouldn't have been right for me"?

Of the people who do disapprove of those actions—and not everybody does—my hunch is that it is not a judgment of mere preference or prudence but overwhelmingly a moral disapproval. It is a recognition of failure of basic obligation to our fellow human beings. They *ought not* to have done it. It was evil.

Another question invited by this discussion is, "Human moral norms in different societies are so diverse, how can they point to a single source, let alone a divine one?" Actually, the basic moral axioms held by all people are not as different as we might think. I would suggest that there is agreement over basic moral axioms like the value of human life, love of neighbor, fairness and truth telling. The objection is right that the differences between cultures turn out to be enormous in practice, but these moral differences do not come from differences in the most basic moral convictions. They come in large part from the way each culture filters those moral axioms through its own worldview and practices. For example, one of the most important differences is in the way each society defines *neighbor.* How much of the human race is "my neighbor" and therefore within my circle of obligation to value and love? How much of it is *not* "my neighbor" and therefore *outside* my circle of obligation and who might therefore even be expendable?

Even cannibals do not kill and eat their family members. The over-the-top barbarity of the twentieth century did not come from a rejection of the ethic of "love your neighbor" or from a celebration of amorality. It came from different worldviews maintaining the "love your neighbor" axiom but reducing (from the biblical norm) who was defined as the neighbor I am obliged to love. Nazism restricted neighbor to race; Marxism restricts neighbor to class; nationalism restricts neighbor to ethnicity. The different moral practices still point to a single transcendent source. It was the same moral axioms that were there before they were filtered, distorted and radically limited by diverse worldviews and cultural applications.

Still another question might be, "Are we in danger of anthropomorphizing God, that is, painting a comfortable conception of him that reminds us of ourselves?" Let's say we have a psychological need for a God who is basically like us, only on a much larger scale. It helps us to feel important and to orient ourselves in a confusing and hostile world if we can scale God down to our level of experience and concern for goodness and badness. This way he will love us and our friends but conveniently hate our enemies.

Although this is a danger that calls for suspicion of each theistic commitment, the greater call today is for suspicion from the other direction. In our fear of dragging God down to our level we may distort and misunderstand his transcendence by emptying it. We make him so high and remote that he ends up being morally lower than we are ourselves. He becomes so removed from this world that he is beyond engaging in the petty business of human moral concerns. In doing this, we actually tame God to be even less than we are—perhaps even insensitive to the distinction between good and evil altogether, all because of his greatness. The prophets confronted this as they saw the people of Israel imagining that God was so transcendent that he was deaf and blind to human activity on earth and dumb in his response to it. The prophets called it idolatry.

Morality as a Pointer to God's Reality

Let me be clear about what I am *not* saying. I am not saying that only people who believe in God can do things that are good or that they are somehow necessarily better than those who do not believe in God. In biblical faith, we should never place our hope in human moral achievement or stature, much less in being more moral than anyone else. The Christian's hope is that through Christ, his followers can be forgiven for their *failure* to live morally. It was because of our immorality that Jesus came in the first place.

God's character is the foundation of our moral convictions, even if his commands are sometimes ignored, denied or corrupted. A sense of moral atrocity, tragedy and outrage against evil is not strange or unnatural to the biblical world. Evil is real. On the other hand, if an indifferent nature is all that exists, the inescapable categories of good and evil stick out as strange and absurd anomalies.

I am suggesting that the moral sensibility of the cynical and noncynical alike points to a transcendent God. Otherwise, taking our own moral convictions seriously requires an enormous leap, not so much a leap of faith but of intellectual alchemy. It would be to believe that our moral convictions refer to meaningful *moral* obligations although we believe that those obligations correspond to nothing beyond our skin.

WHAT IF THE TRANSCENDENT HAS COME TO EARTH?

We are not honest and open-minded explorers of reality; we are alienated from reality because we have made ourselves the center of the universe.

LESSLIE NEWBIGIN

If I am saved from cynicism at all it is by some sense of personal loyalty to the spirit and genius of Jesus.

REINHOLD NIEBUHR

And the Word became flesh and lived among us, and we have seen his glory, the glory as of a father's only son, full of grace and truth.

APOSTLE JOHN

THE QUESTION OF THE IDENTITY OF JESUS of Nazareth is an entirely different line of inquiry into the transcendent. The extraordinary Christian claim is that Jesus was God himself, but he also came into the material world and was fully human. The vast implications of his teaching about himself and his mission have understandably made him a lightning rod for cynicism from the start of his public ministry down to today. The religious leadership of his time never tired of trying to expose him as a charlatan, imposter and blasphemer. There had to be a way to see through and unmask such arrogance. But this did not seem to surprise him, nor should it surprise us. But the honest evaluation of Jesus' life and teaching introduces unique questions and challenges.

We admire many of the great men and women in history for their abilities and also for their character. We respect their courage, brilliance, strength, realism, honesty and sometimes their humility. Most of them would not have dreamed of claiming to be God. Had they made this claim, we would conclude that they had become deranged, and the claim itself would immediately and completely discredit any of their other apparent virtues. The strange thing is that Jesus has been so widely recognized—even outside the Christian tradition—not as a lunatic or hopeless egotist, but as the high water mark of humility, love, sanity, moral integrity, excellence.

He is the one who gave us the Sermon on the Mount, the ultimate teaching and example of forgiveness and love, the parables of the good Samaritan and prodigal son. Yet he claimed to be God and the Savior of the world. Those closest to him, although strict monotheists, were persuaded that his claim to divinity was entirely believable. This extreme paradox puts him in a category by himself. What would have been hideously inappropriate for someone such as Abraham Lincoln to claim for himself seems to have been quite natural for Jesus. How then should we think of him?

Where to Begin?

Evaluating Jesus is not a question that can be handled at arm's length by philosophers without deep personal self-involvement in the question itself and its consequences. But neither is it only an inner and subjective intuition having no bearing on arguments or anything outside of our heads. We must pay attention both to the world "out there" and how to interpret it, but also to ourselves as human interpreters, with diverse motivations and ambitions that can potentially either skew or enlighten our search.

We must not be afraid of using all our critical faculties in this investigation. Otherwise how can we avoid the con-artistry that is so openly part of our religious landscape? Our search cannot be less than rational. But we must also be prepared for the search to involve ourselves as whole persons. So it will be more than rational simply because it engages so many aspects of who we are.

This means that the search for the truth about God is not like the search for a chemical in a test tube that we can study in a detached way. We are not talking about knowing an object but a person, so that person's self-disclosure will be a critical part of our investigation. But we are talking not only of a person but a transcendent person, in no way our equal. The claim is that he is so much not our equal that we are under his authority and dependent on him for every beat of our heart. If we find him to be there and true, that could result in changes in how we relate to ourselves and every aspect of our lives—our family, sexuality, money, politics. It is a search for a truth that promises to change us even as we begin to approach it.

So we must not expect to be able to reduce such large questions to neat proofs for propositions that we could write on a blackboard. Some attempts to prove God's existence are doomed to be as effective as using a microscope as the only way to know about the stars. If the microscope is powerful enough, we are liable to be quite satisfied that the stars do not exist.

A feedback loop. There was a very influential book written in the sixteenth century by the French Reformer John Calvin. It was called the *Institutes of the Christian Religion.* The tome of well over a thousand pages starts out in this way:

> Our wisdom, in so far as it ought to be deemed true and solid wisdom, consists almost entirely of two parts: the knowledge of God and of ourselves. But as these are connected together by many ties, it is not easy to determine which of the two precedes, and gives birth to the other . . . indeed, we cannot aspire to Him in earnest until we have begun to be displeased with ourselves. . . .
>
> On the other hand, it is evident that man never attains to a true self knowledge until he have previously contemplated the face of God, and come down after such contemplation to look into himself.[1]

What he described was a theological-psychological feedback loop in which true understanding is found. Knowledge of God and knowledge of ourselves are inextricably tied together. We cannot know God truly without crucial self-understanding, yet we cannot understand ourselves truly without seeing ourselves before God. These two are so interdependent that it is impossible to say "which of the two precedes, and gives birth to the other." But it is not a closed circle. In fact, we can break into the feedback loop at any point. Then we are in a loop that can take us well beyond our starting point. If we look at the way Jesus himself spoke to people who were cynical about him, we find a deep sensitivity to this interdependence.

A Step Back

But before we go there, we must take a step back. Almost all the information we have about Jesus comes from the documents of the New Testament, and particularly from the four Gospels: Matthew, Mark, Luke and John. For the last several hundred years, in the intellectual atmosphere following the Enlightenment, there has been a profound suspicion about the reliability of those Gospels as a record of who Jesus was and what he said and did. Cynicism about God was brought to the study of the Bible, and that led to cynicism about the biblical record itself. From this perspective it seemed much more believable that in those accounts we do not have accurate records written by eyewitnesses and those who were close to them. It seemed more likely that they were stories written well after the events by unknown leaders in the early church, functioning as spin doctors for their particular causes or conflicts.

This basic project of seeing through the text of the four Gospels to the real story beneath them has taken too many shapes to chronicle here. But the common theme has been to strip away the distortions and additions of later writers to get back to the actual historical Jesus who walked the hills of Palestine. For all their differences, there has been a consistent bias against the authenticity of miraculous events and divine claims.

One difficulty with this method throughout its history has been that scholars have never been able to agree about who the real, historical Jesus was as opposed to the supposed nonhistorical veneer added by the early church. Each group used the sophisticated scholarship of its time to determine the Jesus of history as distinguished from the imaginative, ideological and superstitious overlays in the Gospel accounts. But each group ended up with a Jesus who was suspiciously like a partisan for their own particular modern worldview and moral perspective, whether it was Hegelianism, rationalism, existentialism, Marxism or postmodernism. What was rejected as nonhistorical was any theological or narrative material that conflicted with the Jesus of their choice.

The claim has always been that, with the benefit of their specialized insight, we can clean the dust and dirt of superstition and ignorance off the window of the text of the New Testament to better see through it to the Jesus who was really there in history, outside the window. But it seems that this window had actually been a mirror, in which each school had seen mainly its own reflection. Jesus became an incarnation of their own values, his story a projection of their idealized autobiography. The danger of this project is that it has permitted scholars to simply exclude and omit anything from the life and teaching of Jesus that did not fit their particular paradigm—arguing that it was not original to the historical Jesus.

Ironically for this study, one of the more recent attempts to discover the Jesus of history behind the Gospel records has been the idea that the real, historical Jesus was actually an itinerant Cynic in the tradition of Diogenes.[2] He was probably influenced by the first-century revival of Cynicism that was linked to the Stoics and which might have found its way to Palestine. Jesus embraced the simple nomadic life, was critical of authority structures of his time and was a master of short, pithy and bold repartee.

Certainly we can find parallels between Jesus and Diogenes. But there is no reason to assume that where Jesus' life and teaching might remind us of Diogenes that is because he was actually influenced by first-century pagan Cynics. It is far more likely that in his partly Cynic-like lifestyle he was simply continuing in the tradition of the Jewish prophets from whom he regularly quoted and whose words he fulfilled. Some of the prophets of the Old Testament could have taught even Diogenes quite a lot about bold language and street theater.

Another problem with this reconstruction is that it follows the pattern of removing all those parts of Jesus' life and teaching that do not fit the model of an itinerant Cynic teacher. So, those in search of the historical Jesus explain that Jesus' teaching about his cosmic mission as a savior, divine identity and future return are not original, so it can be dismissed. The Jesus that emerges is, not surprisingly, a radical social egalitarian and a theological relativist, a pretty good reflection of the postmodern academic climate in the early twenty-first century.

I cannot pretend to give this long and diverse movement a fair evaluation in the scope of this book. But the quest for the historical Jesus has had a track record of dubious reliability and of slavery to academic fashion. While we can learn from it, we do not need to let it keep us from reading the four Gospels as a historical narrative of the life and teachings of Jesus.[3]

You Can Believe, Look at the Evidence

In looking at Jesus as his life is recorded in the Gospels, how did he expect people to believe him when he claimed to be able to forgive sins, to be one with the Father, to be the bread of life or to claim that he would return to end history as we know it? He looked more or less like everybody else. How could he expect diehard Jewish monotheists (of all people) to believe that he was the transcendent God in human flesh? He knew they would be horrified and cynical about his claims to divinity. Such statements could not be proved, and those who followed him were not easily convinced. But Jesus walked on water, stopped a storm's wind and waves by his command, gave sight to the blind, healed every kind of disease and deformity, and raised people to life who were dead. He did things so extraordinary that those who were with him day and night for three years were unable to deny the claims that he made about his own identity and mission. They started to persuade others by simply telling the story of what they had seen and heard by being with him. The apostle John wrote:

> We declare to you what was from the beginning, what we have heard, what we have seen with our eyes, what we have looked at and touched with our hands, concerning the word of life—this life was revealed, and we . . . testify to it. (1 Jn 1:1-2)

Notice that the appeal was to the evidence of what the disciples had actually seen and heard of Jesus themselves. Jesus was the "word of life." John was not talking about a vision or an idea, much less about his own personal needs getting satisfied, but about his own concrete experience of sight, sound and touch. The transcendent God was making himself known in the very tangible, material world. Jesus himself encouraged faith based on what was open to their observation. When some onlookers were outraged that he claimed to be able to do what only God had authority to do—to forgive sins—he said:

"But so that you may know that the Son of Man has authority on earth to forgive sins"—he said to the paralytic—"I say to you, stand up, take your mat and go to your home." And he stood up, and immediately took the mat and went out before all of them; so that they were all amazed and glorified God. (Mk 2:10-12)

So he did not just tell people to have faith in him. He pressed them to be honest to what they had just seen with their eyes, letting them make the connections between his words and their own experience.

If I am not doing the works of my Father, then do not believe me. But if I do them, even though you do not believe me, believe the works, so that you may know and understand that the Father is in me and I am in the Father. (Jn 10:37-38)

His disciples would often speak of witnessing or testifying to the truth of what they had seen and heard. These were not terms suggesting the kind of scientific proof that came into currency so much later. They were the legal terms of a courtroom, dealing with forensic evidence. They treated their hearers as jurors who would have to reach their own verdict about the claims of Jesus.

The apostles' first message was that after Jesus' death, the tomb Jesus had been buried in was empty. Jesus had risen from the dead with a new body after his crucifixion, and they had seen him—alive! He had appeared to them in Jerusalem, outside of Jerusalem and in Galilee, even to five hundred people at one time. The apostle Paul would later claim as part of his own legal defense before King Agrippa that the death and resurrection of Jesus "was not done in a corner" (Acts 26:26).

The disciples' testimony was persuasive both because it was from eyewitnesses, and also because the integrity of the eyewitnesses was immediately put to the test. They were persecuted for it, and many were killed for speaking publicly of the resurrection they had seen. But they kept on talking about it. In fact our English word *martyr* comes from the Greek word for "witness" because so many Christians were "martyred" as a result of their witness to this event.

An idea is not true just because someone is willing to die for it. Many people have given their lives for crazy causes. The most obvious objection of cynicism has always been that the resurrection account must have been a deception, a public-relations hoax. But it was not a political utopia, a hope, a vision, a prophecy or a dream that these first Christians were willing to die for. They were willing to die for events that they had all actually seen and heard a few days earlier. More importantly, if it was a deception, why would they have done it? Of all people, they were the ones with most to lose by such a lie—if it was a lie.

The argument that they lied asks us to believe that they were willing to die for a story that they did *not* believe in, since the resurrection account must have been their own collective invention. Jesus' disciples had fled for their lives in disarray and panic when he was arrested but was still alive. It is too much to ask us to believe that a few days later the same men were willing to risk their lives for their own fabrication after he was dead.

The whole tenor of Jesus' ministry was to challenge cynics to step out of suspicion and to observe, investigate, listen, think, remember, question, and study the Scriptures to figure out for themselves who he was. He seemed confident that anyone who wanted to know the truth about him would be able to find it. He promised, "Ask, and it will be given you; search, and you will find; knock, and the door will be opened for you. For everyone who asks receives, and everyone who searches finds, and for everyone who knocks, the door will be opened" (Mt 7:7-8).

But there was also the other part of the feedback loop of knowledge of God, connecting to self-knowledge. The wildcard of self-understanding introduces a significant complication into the courtroom of the human mind.

You Can't Believe, Look at What You Do to the Evidence

Jesus, who encouraged some people to believe by pointing to the evidence said, "even though you do not believe in me, believe the works, so that you may know and understand that the Father is in me and I am in the Father" (Jn 10:38). But he also gave different people a very different message. He asked others with a deeper cynicism about him the rhetorical question, "How can you believe when you accept glory from one another and do not seek the glory that comes from the one who alone is God?" (Jn 5:44). Here he seemed to make the opposite point. Not, "There are good grounds for faith in me, believe," but "You can't possibly believe when your desire for your own glory is your ultimate commitment."

If they were looking for glory from each other and not from God, they would never take the claims of Christ seriously or be convinced by any evidence for them. They already had another god to whom they were loyal. God's glory, taken seriously, would threaten their own. Jesus was not pushing them away or trying to insult them but rather helping them to understand where they stood. It was not about the quality or quantity of evidence. Their own commitment would work as a primary interpretive filter, making any evidence for him seem irrelevant in the courtrooms of their minds. A desire for personal glory from our contemporaries remains a roadblock to faith down to today.

On another occasion Jesus taught, "Truly I tell you, unless you change and become like children, you will never enter the kingdom of heaven. Whoever becomes humble like this child is the greatest in the kingdom of heaven" (Mt 18:3-4). Again we find Jesus predicting the failure of the cynics' search for God and his kingdom. Again the failure did not have to do with the quantity or quality of the evidence. It was because of a lack of self-knowledge on the part of the searchers—to be specific, it was their lack of humility. Unless a person is capable of humility, the search for ultimate truth is a waste of time.

Evidence can never compel belief, because evidence is always interpreted. Our interpretation of any evidence allows us to consciously and unconsciously filter and sift what we come to accept and know. One of the most astonishing miracles that Jesus did was to raise his friend Lazarus from the grave. Lazarus had been dead for four days, and onlookers were worried about the smell when they opened the grave. At the word of Jesus, Lazarus walked out of the grave and was unwrapped from his grave clothes. No one who was there at the time seems to have disputed either the factuality of this event or its miraculous character.

But that did not mean that all the onlookers interpreted it as evidence of God's power and presence among them. In fact some of the religious leadership saw it as the final argument—not that he was God or was from God—but that they would have to kill him. They had other "gods" to whom they were loyal. He was too much of a threat to their power structure, too unpredictable, too uncontrollable, too dangerous. He might destabilize their delicate relationship with the occupying Roman government. The evidential force of what they had all just seen was lost on them, eclipsed by their overwhelming anxiety. They called a special council and concluded, "If we let him go on like this, everyone will believe in him, and the Romans will come and destroy both our holy place and our nation" (Jn 11:48). They immediately began plans to kill Jesus, but not only Jesus. They decided to kill Lazarus also, "since it was on account of him that many Jews were deserting and were believing in Jesus" (Jn 12:11).

What was the problem here? Was raising a man who was dead for four days not enough evidence to convince them that Jesus was the Son of God? In one sense the problem was the reverse. There was too much evidence. Had the evidence been weak, they would have scoffed and left him alone. They might have even been willing to let Jesus live to old age. It was only because the evidence was so strong that Jesus was such a threat to them. They decided to kill both Jesus and the evidence. Then they would not have to endure the existence of Lazarus, alive, as a challenge to their own authority. What they saw in Jesus was not a revealer of God but only a threat to their power and security.

When Jesus confronted people who were locked into a deep cynicism about him, he did not just give them more evidence or arguments shouted in a louder voice; he pointed them to ways they could break into the feedback loop of self-knowledge and God-knowledge. Sometimes this was by a direct call to repent of self-deception.

Perhaps his most direct challenge to self-deception was in his letter to the church in Laodicea. He said, "For you say, 'I am rich, I have prospered, and I need nothing.' You do not realize that you are wretched, pitiable, poor, blind, and naked" (Rev 3:17). Illusions of self-sufficiency and self-righteousness left them far from God. He offered them hope of reconciliation, but not without a radical change of self-understanding.

More often Jesus told cynical inquirers searching stories and gave them demanding homework. He asked them many questions about themselves: "Why do you see the speck in your neighbor's eye, but do not notice the log in your own eye?" (Mt 7:3). "Why do you break the commandment of God for the sake of your tradition?" (Mt 15:3). "What will it profit them if they gain the whole world but forfeit their life?" (Mt 16:26). These questions aimed at helping them understand themselves and their own commitments, and to then better understand their position before God and their need for his mercy.

The reason for the two sides of Jesus' teaching (you can believe; you can't believe) was his understanding of the deep ambivalence in human attitudes to God. We are created in his image and for relationship with him. Augustine wrote, "O Lord, you have made us for yourself, and our heart is restless until it rests in you."[4] Part of us longs for a relationship with God. But we are also fallen—rebels on his planet—so there is another part of us that raises our closed fist against him as one who would interfere with our freedom. This ambivalence brings a motivated distortion of the whole process of our knowing. C. S. Lewis described his own pre-Christian attitude:"Amiable agnostics will talk cheerfully about'man's search for God.'To me, as I then was, they might as well have talked about the mouse's search for the cat." God was "Him whom I so earnestly desired not to meet."[5]

When Jesus taught"You can't believe," challenging the pride and self-centeredness of his cynical detractors, he was following in the footsteps of the prophets of the Old Testament in an early form of the ideology critique. Jesus looked behind cynical challengers, not assuming their honest pursuit of truth but pointing out their less-than-honest motives for rejecting him. It was their lack of humility that distorted their interpretation of claims and events. But because Jesus was not speaking from cynicism, he did not reduce them to those motivations and leave them there. He challenged the motivations but also encouraged them to look at the evidence that he presented:"You can believe."

Jesus asked his disciples,"Who do people say that I am?"After they replied with a list of the usual suspects, he asked them,"But who do you say that I am?" (Mk 8:27-29). This is a question that confronts each one of us. If we take our lead from Jesus himself, we will be challenged to look at the evidence and arguments in any area where it is relevant. But we will also be challenged to question ourselves and the baggage that we bring on the journey.

QUESTIONS ABOUT A TRANSCENDENT MESSAGE

The history of human thought demonstrates rather clearly . . . that it is possible to go some way in asking questions of truth while disregarding the spirit of an age, and even to arrive at answers that contradict this spirit. Genuine timeliness means sensitivity to one's socio-historical starting point, not fatalism about one's possible destination.

PETER BERGER

From a Christian perspective, God is first and foremost a communicative agent, one who relates to humankind through words and the Word.

KEVIN VANHOOZER

IF THE TRANSCENDENT CLAIMS OF JESUS ARE TRUE, how can those truths be passed on in the words of finite, fallible human beings? How could they ever get all the way to us in any reliable form? We will look briefly at two of the questions raised here: first, can transcendent truth be expressed at all in human words? and second (a question raised by postmodernism), are the intended meanings of words so uncertain, corrupted and skewed by their interpretation that coherent communication of any message between people over time and across cultures is impossible?

Revelation and the Limitations of Words

How can transcendent truths be carried at all in the finite and fallible medium of human language? It is one thing to say that some sort of God exists. It is quite another to say that you know something about him that you could put into words. We might ask, Isn't knowledge of God himself beyond all human thoughts and the words used to express them? Some claim that anything which can be expressed in words necessarily and by definition cannot have any universal meaning or application. Because it is mere words, it is completely immersed in the perspective and interpretation of the writer or speaker, bound to his or her psychological state, culture and moment in history. We are told that perhaps language about God can carry suggestive or symbolic truths about God to us, but never truths about him that are *true for him* also. Is it not arrogant for us—finite, fallible people—to presume that we can use words about God that are true also for God himself?

In answer to this, we must say overwhelmingly, yes, it certainly is arrogant—*unless* that transcendent reality is a Person who has chosen to disclose himself to us in words and equipped us to understand them. If this has happened, the charge of arrogance does not stick. It could even go the other way. If a transcendent God has actually spoken, might it not be arrogant to refuse to acknowledge his words to us because, as we know, we sophisticated people somehow know better? The claim of the Bible for itself is exactly that. God was able to use fallible people, embedded in their cultural settings, to reveal truths in words about a transcendent order.

There is a conversation between Moses and God recorded in the book of Exodus when God called to Moses to go back to Egypt and confront Pharaoh to tell him to release the Jewish people from slavery. Moses, who had been enjoying a peaceful retirement, dragged his feet as hard and long as he could. He used all the arguments he could think of to disqualify himself. One of the last of these was that he was a poor speaker. God's response was to that specific point, but it had far wider philosophical implications.

> Moses said to the Lord, "O LORD, I have never been eloquent, neither in the past nor since you have spoken to your servant. I am slow of speech and tongue."
>
> The LORD said to him, "Who gave man his mouth? Who makes him deaf or mute? Who gives him sight or makes him blind? Is it not

I, the LORD? Now go; I will help you speak and will teach you what to say." (Ex 4:10-12 NIV)

There are many obstacles to human beings actually being able to use their words to think and communicate transcendent meanings. People tell lies, they are deceived, they are confused, they are mistaken, they are limited in the reach of their understanding. But the biblical emphasis was that God, who gave us the gift of language, used it himself to communicate with us by using fallible, limited people such as prophets and apostles in that process. He had promised, "I will help you speak and will teach you what to say." The limitation of human language itself was not the roadblock. Language was the exalted gift of a communicating God in whose image we are made.

God does not reveal exhaustive truth about himself so that we could know him in the complete way that he knows himself. But what he has revealed is adequate for us to know true things about him, his actions and his intentions so that we can respond to him. To deny this possibility is not so much a mark of humility as a denial of the resources of God has provided and, ultimately, his status as our Creator.

The Problem of Meaning

How can a transcendent message reliably come to us in a text passed on by generations of fallible people? To unpack this issue, we must back up to remember postmodern cynicism about meaning in language. The postmodern claim is that the struggle for power has been such a basic dynamic in history that it has shaped the meanings of our words. For this reason they say that we cannot trust the meanings of our own words about the world. Words do not correspond to the way the world really is, since their meanings are only the constructions of powerful people who shaped those meanings for their own advantage.

In chapter seven, we looked at language construction in the problem of naming a beetle in the rain forest, and we also looked the far greater question of how to understand the word *God* in the light of Shirley MacLaine's claim. Is language so malleable in the hands of conscious and unconscious motivations that the reliability of its meanings are forever out of our reach? Is the reading of a text only like looking at our own reflection in a mirror, or is reading a text like seeing through a window to meanings beyond us in the world?

Postmodernism is right to point out that the meanings of words exert power. It is easy to see, for example that national, racial and sexual prejudices and oppression have sometimes been served by the accepted meanings of words—used by both oppressors and oppressed.

But it is not as if language itself was the problem. The story of oppression has another side. Words have also been used to clarify, challenge and motivate people to overcome prejudice, oppression and injustice. What movements to reform any institution, social structure or practice have ever been accomplished without the vast power of words to bring about that positive change?

The reason everyone has not given up on language and lapsed into silence is because real (but not perfect) communication is possible when we are patient, care for each other and are willing to work hard to understand each other. We may not finally agree with each other about how to define either a beetle or God (see pp. 59-60), but if we invest time and energy in the discussion, we can at least become better able to understand our disagreements and subsequent attempts to communicate.

Written texts and language in any form need not be so intrinsically unclear that real communication on difficult topics is impossible, even when there are great cultural barriers or power inequalities between the people in a conversation. It is with words that the meaning of other words can be clarified. Our own experience shows us that with patience, love and determination this process need not be the endless regress into uncertainty envisaged by some postmodernists. It can be a process of clarification and greater mutual understanding.

In *Is There a Meaning in This Text?* Kevin Vanhoozer has given us a helpful exploration of these issues. He raises the central question of how we can have confidence as we interpret texts, such as the Bible. Can we know that we have discovered its meaning, and not just our own projections into it? His book argues that our knowledge must be tempered with humility and our skepticism countered by conviction.

The interpreter has two kinds of responsibilities. There is the negative responsibility, to humility, that we do not *exceed* the grasp of what we actually can know. Humility will counter overconfident suspicion. But there is also the positive responsibility, to conviction, that we make every effort to know what *can* be known.[1] When readers respect the text of the Bible they are not limited to looking at their own reflections in a religious mirror. Not only can they come to knowledge about God and the world, but they can learn things about themselves that they had not previously seen in their own mirrors. Vanhoozer concludes that "postmodern theories have *not* succeeded in showing that interpretation is impossible. For while our knowledge of textual meaning may never be absolute, it may nevertheless be adequate."[2] We need a hermeneutic of suspicion, but to maintain contact with the real world we also need a hermeneutic of trust and the wisdom to fulfill both responsibilities well.

An important example of crosscultural communication is when the apostle Paul went to Athens. Paul was a Jew, born in Tarsus (now eastern Turkey), and his first language was Hebrew. As he traveled and preached in the Greco-Roman world, he spoke Greek. He went to Athens and spoke to the philosophers there about the God of Israel and the Messiah, Jesus (Acts 17:16-34). He had studied their thinking already and knew that although they used the Greek word *theos* for "God," their idea of God was very different from his own. In fact, the difference was so great that with their view of God they would never understand what he had come to tell them about the life and death of Jesus.

Paul did not give up and go home, nor did he resort to shouting. He carefully challenged their definition of God in a series of observations, negations and assertions as well as quotations from their own inscriptions and literature. Some scoffed at him, not because they could *not* understand the meaning of his words but because they understood him *all too well* and did not like what they heard. Others were persuaded that he was right, and still others wanted to continue the discussion. It is a good example, within the Bible itself, of real communication across vast linguistic, cultural and religious differences.

Paul, along with many other biblical writers, was intensely aware of the slipperiness of the meanings of words and how they were culturally shaped. As Paul wrestled to clarify the meaning of the word *God* to his hearers, he was continuing the long tradition of prophets. They had repeatedly described who God was, then contrasted that with who God was not—the peoples' ideas of false gods or idols—and then came back to speak of the true God from many different angles and metaphors, with street theater and theological argument. With contradiction, contrast, metaphor, illustration, comparison and assertion they pressed toward clarification and mutual understanding.

Because our society is religiously pluralistic in its demographics and postmodern in its sensibilities, Paul's example provides an intriguing challenge for Christian people today. In the book of Acts we observe Paul in an even more radically pluralistic setting than our own. If you read this book of the New Testament you will notice that he preached in city after city. He also *dialogued, argued, persuaded* or *debated* with Jews and Greeks alike. These words are about conversation, two-way communication. Preaching never will be obsolete. But in his pluralistic setting, Paul did much more than only one-way communication. Otherwise how could he hope to clarify the meanings of words of transcendent importance that had powerfully different cultural histories behind them? My suspicion is that as a society becomes more pluralistic, effective Christian communication will have to include more two-way communication.

We have considered three separate questions raised by the possibility that there is a transcendent reality we can know. In chapters fifteen and sixteen I suggested that we should be able to see pointers to the existence of a transcendent God in our everyday moral convictions. We should also be able to understand the reasons why Jesus' contemporaries came to believe that in him they saw the presence of God himself. If such a God is involved in human history, it should not seem strange to us that he is able to communicate truths about himself to us in words that we can then pass on to other people, assuming we relate to them in love, humility and patience.

Part Four

REDEEMING SUSPICION
A God's-Eye View

WHAT IF GOD IS NOT A CYNIC?

It is dangerous to make man see too clearly his equality with the brutes without showing him his greatness. It is also dangerous to make him see his greatness too clearly, apart from his vileness. It is still more dangerous to leave him in ignorance of both.

BLAISE PASCAL

We're all bastards, but God loves us anyway.

WILL CAMPBELL

HAVING RESPONDED TO SOME OF THE ARGUMENTS surrounding cynicism about God, it is time to allow God into the discussion of cynicism. I have suggested that cynicism can be maintained only if the cynic has extraordinary access to accurate and unbiased information about the inner lives of his or her neighbors—to the point of requiring near omniscience. Cynicism is vulnerable at this point, especially because it has often "seen through" and discredited the reliability of human knowing in general. If all human knowing has been so corrupted by self-serving motivations, how is it that the cynic's own knowledge can be superhuman in its reliability? Although the assumption of near omniscience is essential to cynical knowing, this assumption is usually kept in the back of the closet, away from public view. The strange twist is that as we bring the God of biblical faith into the discussion, we include One who makes open, never-in-the-closet claims to omniscience.

What's Right About Cynicism?

Is suspicion really such a bad thing? Cynicism at its best dares to recognize

therapeutic overhaul — psychology
utopian overhaul   politics   political ideology
154   SEEING THROUGH CYNICISM
                                economics — economic ideology

that things are not as they should be, as they pretend to be or as we might like them to be. Cynicism is willing to see through pomp, hypocrisy and self-righteousness. It is suspicious of spin and plastic smiles. It does not shield its eyes from the dark side of human motivation—at least in principle. Cynicism at its best has a refreshing aversion to naiveté, sentimentality, hypocrisy and blind optimism. It can often speak to these problems with clarity and wit. We need more of this.

The attempt to be unfailingly positive and nice does not always lead to peace, truth, justice or growth. It is dangerous to have false hopes, self-deceiving visions and naive dreams or to follow those who do. We should be thankful for those who can see through virtuous appearances to selfishness, lust, greed and hunger for power—when those vices are really present. It would seem then that cynicism performs a useful function.

The need for suspicion. One of the reasons that I was initially attracted to the Christian faith was that it encouraged a brutal realism about people. There seemed to be no inclination among the biblical writers or Christian theologians to make therapeutic or utopian overhauls of human nature, sacrificing truth to political ideology or delicate self-esteem. In fact there are some cynical observations the Christian should not try to oppose. Christian hope is not built on the assumption that the human race is in pretty good shape or that we only have minor flaws that can be cleared up by the right adjustments or engineering, whether spiritual, psychological, political, educational, biological or economic.

We can see human brokenness everywhere. There is no aspect of life or experience that can be trusted as pure and reliably good—our reasoning, our imagining, our sexuality, our family life, our artistic gifts, our science, our technological and economic life, our politics or our religion. A twisted and self-serving dynamic can corrupt them all to be used against our fellow creatures, ourselves and our Creator. We can see people—including ourselves if we are honest—who are both actively cruel to others and also passively tolerant of their suffering. We express this brokenness individually and also live it out collectively in wider groups and institutions.

The biblical story casts considerable light into this darkness. We could say that the Bible does not so much permit suspicion as it mandates suspicion, given our identity as fallen human beings. We have passed through a primal alienation—from God the Creator but also from ourselves, each other and nature. We were created to image God, but now we are not able to image him in the way we live. The apostle Paul expressed his own frustration at being unable to live as he wanted, and to be unable to stop doing the very things he tried to resist (Rom 7:15-25).

No person you see walking down the street or sitting in a restaurant will show you a good reflection of the character of God. We sin because we are sinners. Something is twisted in our natures, and we cannot untwist it. Along with lives of external decency and respectability, we discover that we can be cruel, lie and have enormous investments in covering our tracks by damage control, hiding our motivations from each other and from ourselves. We then instinctively disapprove of others who do the same thing.

All of this points to the need for suspecting others and ourselves. Suspicion itself should not be seen as some sort of moral failing but as an honest and realistic precaution for broken people functioning in a broken world.

Suspicion limited. The destruction that people can wreak on themselves and others is all around us, but it is not the whole story. I have described a human being as a "glorious ruin." So far we have only looked at the ruin. The whole biblical story can be summarized as creation, Fall and redemption. We are gloriously created and ruinously fallen. Yet that fallenness has not erased all marks of our createdness, nor has it put us beyond the reach of redemption.

If we are going to be honest, we have to admit that there is glory as well as ruin in human lives. We may have suspicions. Sometimes our suspicions will be justified and should be maintained, but at other times they will not be justified and should be dropped. Take, for example, the cynic's line "everybody has their price." I know too many people who show a marvelous freedom from the love of money for that "everybody" to be actually true. I was intrigued to learn of a TV reality show that tried to pit wilderness survival instructors against each other by putting them in crisis situations in exotic places, the winner to get a million dollars. The first one they asked refused but gave them other names to try. They all refused. To compete against each other was antithetical to all that they believed and all they had been teaching about the need for cooperation in their wilderness survival schools. Not one would do it, even for the chance of a million dollars.[1]

Likewise, there are too many marriage relationships that are not dominated by sexual exploitation or patriarchal hierarchy for marriage to be reduced to those motivations. There are too many people whose commitment to justice is too genuine and sacrificial to be explained as veiled exercise of power for themselves.

The cynic might be committed to seeing through all claims to heroism. But I was intrigued that the cynics were strangely quiet after September 11, 2001, for a short time. I heard no cynical voices debunking the heroism of the New York fire and police departments. I do not think this was only because cynicism would have been socially tasteless at a time of shock and bereavement. I suspect that most of us realize that such cynicism simply would not have been true. Perhaps cynical perspectives built for invulnerable superpowers in comfortable and prosperous times simply would not support the weight of that much reality. My hunch was that cynicism was momentarily embarrassed.

The same honesty that sometimes drives us into suspicion will at other times lead us to qualify that suspicion or to drop it altogether, or if we have grounds to do so, even allow it to become admiration. There is a mandate for suspicion rooted in the Fall. But there is also a mandate rooted in creation and redemption to moderate or sometimes abandon suspicion. Pascal's words are to the point:

> It is dangerous to make man see too clearly his equality with the brutes without showing him his greatness. It is also dangerous to make him see his greatness too clearly, apart from his vileness. It is still more dangerous to leave him in ignorance of both.[2]

Messy, complicated and unclear though it may be, it is impossible to honestly understand human nature and experience unless we have plenty of room for the extremes of greatness and vileness. While we will sometimes be grateful for the cynic's unmasking vision, we will also have to admit that there are people and actions that we cannot unmask. They defy cynical scrutiny. What we see on the surface may be the same all the way through. They may command our admiration and be worthy of our aspiration. They might even be heroic.

A God's-Eye View

If God himself is omniscient, what does he see? The Bible is very clear that

God knows us better than we know ourselves. Israel's king David wrote:

> O LORD, you have searched me and known me.
> You know when I sit down and when I rise up;
> you discern my thoughts from far away. (Ps 139:1-2)

A contrast is also made to human seeing and knowing: "the LORD does not see as mortals see; they look on the outward appearance, but the LORD looks on the heart" (1 Sam 16:7). In the New Testament letter to the Hebrews, the writer says that the Word of God "is able to judge the thoughts and intentions of the heart. And before him no creature is hidden, but all are naked and laid bare to the eyes of the one to whom we must render an account" (Heb 4:12-13).

God can see the human heart, the inner seat of motivation and of life direction. Inner motivation is the home turf of the cynic's area of operation.

God sees through us. The Bible gives many examples of God seeing through individuals to the heart of their convictions and sensibilities, often using his prophets to unmask them. For example, the Lord spoke through the prophet Isaiah to a hypocritical people:

> Because these people draw near with their mouths
>   and honor me with their lips,
>   while their hearts are far from me,
> and their worship of me is a human commandment learned
>   by rote;
> so I will again do
>   amazing things with this people,
>   shocking and amazing.
> The wisdom of their wise shall perish,
>   and the discernment of the discerning shall be hidden.
>   (Is 29:13-14)

God saw through busy, pious appearances to the reality of their motivations, which were far from him. The prophets unmasked all forms of idolatry and instrumental faith to expose it for what it was, anticipating by thousands of years the method of the masters of suspicion.

Merold Westphal, a philosopher from Fordham University, has argued in *Suspicion and Faith* that much of the criticism made by Marx, Freud and

Nietzsche is actually similar to prophetic judgments made within the Bible itself against *corruptions* of biblical faith.[3] What they criticize is instrumental religion, that is, using God as an instrument or tool for some other more important loyalty to the believer—such as power, wealth or peace of mind. If faith is only acting as a front for some form of selfishness, of course that faith lacks spiritual and intellectual integrity at its foundation, and it will be dysfunctional in its practical expression.

The idea of the providence of God had sometimes been used in just the way Karl Marx charged—to sanctify an existing unjust social and economic order. Charlotte Brontë, for example, was attacked by church people in nineteenth century England as godless and anti-Christian because in her novel *Jane Eyre,* she had undermined the "God-given" social order. This was because at the end of the novel she had allowed a mere governess to marry the lord of the manor!

The prophecies of Isaiah, Jeremiah and Amos are filled with exposures and denunciations of those who used God's name to legitimize such traditions of injustice and idolatry. I can imagine that Karl Marx might have been shocked (as would much of the Christian church) if the prophet Amos had turned up in mid-nineteenth century Europe or North America.

There is, however, an important difference between the prophetic exposures of the biblical prophets and the cynicism of the masters of suspicion. The prophets were able to make a distinction that was impossible for the leaders of the ideology critiques. The prophets distinguished between true and false faith. True faith was real trust in and commitment to the living God. Bogus faith was using the *name* of that same God to mask all sorts of private, self-serving agendas, and in the process playing fast and loose with the person and laws of God. True faith could stand for what it was—trust in God. Bogus faith could be seen through, exposed and rebuked.

But the cynicism of the masters of suspicion made them incapable of distinguishing between true and bogus faith at all. Their worldview would not allow it. All faith was bogus by definition. It had to be since they had already presupposed that there was no God. As Nietzsche wrote, the purpose of their critique was to make a "clean sweep" of theism.[4]

So, the cynicism of the ideology critiques lay not in their perfectly valid criticisms of instrumental religion, where their message echoed the prophets. Their cynicism lay in the much more radical assumption that instrumental religion was the only religion to be considered. There never could be any other. There was no room allowed for the faith of the prophets, which had challenged, encouraged and reformed their nation.

A surprising irony. In Jesus we find the prophetic ability to see through to the inner motivations of peoples' lives, but at the same time an unwillingness to reduce them to their most selfish motivations. Suspicion was not a blanket or totalizing attitude for him. After chasing the money changers out of the temple, Jesus remained in Jerusalem for the Passover festival. John wrote in his Gospel: "But Jesus on his part would not entrust himself to them, because he knew all people and needed no one to testify about anyone; for he himself knew what was in everyone" (Jn 2:24-25).

He did not entrust himself to them because he could see through them and was rightly suspicious of what he saw.

But the great irony that we have been finding is that God, who alone has the epistemological equipment to be a cynic, is not a cynic. The same Jesus who "knew what was in everyone," called Nathaniel "an Israelite in whom there is no deceit" (Jn 1:47). The one who could see through people was not saying that Nathaniel was sinless but that he was a person of integrity; he was not trying to con anybody. Jesus later marveled at the faith of a Roman centurion whose servant he healed (Lk 7:9) and at the love of a prostitute who washed his feet with her hair, "She has shown great love" (Lk 7:47). He even seemed to take at face value that favorite target of cynicism, the death-bed conversion. It would have been hard to imagine a more unpromising life, past or future than the criminal who was dying on a cross next to Jesus. But Jesus granted his request for salvation, "Truly I tell you, today you will be with me in Paradise" (Lk 23:43).

One of Jesus' best-known stories is the parable of the prodigal son (Lk 15:11-32). It is a fascinating study in noncynicism. In a family with two brothers, the younger demands his inheritance early, goes to a far country, squanders it, gets hungry and comes home repentant. The father receives him with joy and has a banquet to celebrate his return. The older brother hears the music but is angry and refuses to come to the party because he had stayed at home and worked hard but had never been honored as much as this worthless little brother. The parable ends with the father repeating his invitation to the older brother to come and join the party.

The father clearly represents the figure of God in Jesus' story. Can you imagine how a cynical father might receive a son coming home after partying away his half of the family fortune? He might have unmasked the confession and said, "You're not repentant, you're just hungry! You haven't had a change of heart, you're just broke." He might have begun a marathon interrogation. But this is not what he did. He saw his son coming in the distance and ran to hug him as he arrived home. He joyfully forgave him, accepted him and called for the caterers and musicians.

The older brother refused his father's invitation with his own cynical view of "this son of yours." The older brother saw through him and could see nothing but irresponsibility, debauchery and now insincerity. Here again, a cynical father might have said, "Sour grapes. You only resent your brother because you never had the courage to leave home and see more of the world yourself." But this is not what he said. The father went out and repeated the invitation to the banquet, "Son, you are always with me, and all that is mine is yours. But we had to celebrate and rejoice, because this brother of yours was dead and has come to life; he was lost and has been found" (Lk 15:31-32).

Another parable that Jesus told was about a Pharisee and a tax collector who both came to the temple. The Pharisee was preoccupied with his own virtue and his superiority over the tax collector. The tax collector was overwhelmed by how far his own life fell short of what was acceptable to God. He stood far off and prayed, "God, be merciful to me, a sinner!" Jesus said that the tax collector was justified before God, not the Pharisee (Lk 18:10-14). The tax collector knew that God had seen through him. But Jesus was teaching that the eyes that had seen through him were not closed against him. He had come in honesty and humility, and the eyes that saw through him were the eyes of the God of grace. He was guilty but was not beyond redemption.

God in his omniscience sees vastly more, not less than the human cynic. He misses nothing that is there. Omniscience sees through, but in seeing through, sees that there is sometimes no mask to take off. He does not cynically force people into a mold by reducing them to the worst of their own corruption and shame. There is plenty that is wrong with us but there is more to see than only what is wrong.

It was Satan, with pretended x-ray vision, not God, who tried to establish a cynical view of Job. He charged that Job was not a servant of God at all but had only been given a good deal. He would have been a fool not to have served God since God had lined his pockets. God denied this cynical evaluation. By the end of the story Satan's cynicism was shown to be wrong—not because it was not nice but because it was simply not true.

SEEING THROUGH CYNICISM

Cynicism is the complacent confidence that suspicion reveals the whole story of human ideals and idealism. There is nothing but self-interest, self-righteousness, and self-deception.

MEROLD WESTPHAL

Frivolity, inexperience, simplicity believe everything that is said; vanity, conceit, self-satisfaction believe everything flattering that is said; envy, spite, corruption believe everything evil that is said; mistrust believes nothing at all.

SØREN KIERKEGAARD

THE REPUTATION OF THE CYNIC RIDES HIGH IN OUR SOCIETY. Cynicism is associated with sophistication, education and having greater courage, honesty, and intelligence than the herd. Given this public status, it can be a bit of a shock to look at cynicism in the wisdom literature of the Bible. The words that most closely correspond to *cynic* are translated "mocker," "scoffer" or "scorner." The scoffer is the one who sees through everyone and lets people know what he or she sees.

What Is God's Perspective?

The book of Proverbs is fertile ground for this reflection. The mocker, scorner or scoffer is the cynic. The writer asks:

How long, O simple ones, will you love being simple?
How long will scoffers delight in their scoffing
  and fools hate knowledge? (Prov 1:22)

The cynic of today is not accustomed to being associated with the simpleton or the fool. Again, "A scoffer seeks wisdom in vain, / but knowledge is easy for one who understands" (Prov 14:6). Here the point is not that the scoffer is lazy. He or she may in fact search with diligence for years. But the attitude of scoffing is a barrier to discovering the very wisdom that is the purpose of the search.

The warning, "A worthless witness mocks at justice" (Prov 19:28) refers to someone who has probably seen plenty of injustice but who cynically concludes that the very idea of justice is a travesty. As a result the witness is useless as a witness and fails to serve justice when the opportunity arises to actually make a difference.

The final word for the scorner refers directly to God's response to the cynic.

Toward the scorners he is scornful,
　　but to the humble he shows favor.
The wise will inherit honor,
　　but stubborn fools, disgrace. (Prov 3:34-35)

Here is the ultimate sting for the cynic. God sees through, unmasks and scorns the cynic's cynicism. This is the greatest irony of all—and so something that is rarely imagined—that the transcendent God laughs at cynicism, not with the laughter of glee but of pity and sadness at its grandiose pretensions. When he who knows everything is not cynical, and we who know so little claim cynical insight, we appear ridiculous in his eyes.

What Does Cynicism See?

Why is it that in the wisdom literature of the Bible the writers look at the core of cynical judgment and see it as a misleading source of folly? Not because cynicism identifies things that are wrong in the world. Those same biblical writers did that themselves. Nor is it because the cynic is always wrong in every criticism. The cynic is sometimes right in specific places and times. It is folly because cynics presume to see through those that they cannot in fact see through at all. The arrogance of the cynic—the presumption to be able to unmask everyone and everything—makes the cynic a mocker, scoffer or scorner.

C. S. Lewis concluded that high confidence in being able to see through things was one of the characteristics of the modern world. He also noted the dangers of this confidence.

You cannot go on "seeing through" things for ever. The whole point of seeing through something is to see something through it. It is good that the window should be transparent, because the street or garden beyond it is opaque. How if you saw through the garden too? It is no use trying to "see through" first principles. If you see through everything, then everything is transparent. But a wholly transparent world is an invisible world. To "see through" all things is the same as not to see.[1]

We saw that a cynical view of faith is that all faith is bogus faith. All faith is "seen through" since the cynic knows before he has examined anybody's faith that there is no God. But that means that the cynic cannot see the vast differences between true and instrumental faith, no matter how much evidence there is for integrity in the life and thinking of the believer. Seeing through all faith may be the same as not seeing any faith except the cynic's own, but without recognizing the cynic's own faith as faith in cynicism. This same observation can be made about many of the cynical views of people that we have considered.

θ   We have learned a great deal about the way different biological, psychological, social, political and economic forces shape human attitudes, motivations and choices. People are not islands, making free choices in a vacuum, uninfluenced by parents, society, unconscious forces or biochemistry. But that is not to say that human choice is eclipsed by any or all of these influences so that our choices are determined. To admit that there are many nonconscious and ignoble factors involved in our decision making is entirely different from saying that our decision-making process itself is illusory. It may seem intellectually exhilarating to discover a "theory of everything" that reduces all human choices to some known set of causes, but the cost is great. In the words of the psychotherapist Rollo May, it is "making molehills out of mountains."[2] Here are three such examples of cynicism at work:

Self-interest in popular psychology. I am always confronting a street-level cynical wisdom that says that all of our ideals, values and positive motivations are respectable smoke screens for self-interest. So whether we realize it or not, self-interest is the engine driving the full range of human choices.

It is not hard to see that self-interest must be a component in all our actions. Even choices that are extremely painful or costly can be seen to involve self-interest at some level. Take some extreme examples. Among the many things that motivate martyrs, they may know that they would hate themselves if they betrayed their faith. So, it is fair to say that there is an element of self-interest in martyrs' martyrdom. They want to avoid self-hatred. The suicide believes that whatever happens after death, it will be better than life before it. In this also we can see the element of self-interest. To recognize these examples of self-interest as components in decision making is neither surprising nor cynical.

Cynicism begins when we say that self-interest is the root or the most basic of all motivations, the motivation to which all other motivations can be reduced. Immediately that becomes a different discussion. First of all, it is impossible to establish (without omniscience). How could we ever know that it is the most basic motivation for everyone? Or even for anyone? How would we ever recognize an exception? It could always be defended by ingenious attempts to show how every choice, attitude and behavior (however diverse) could be driven by self-interest because it has some component of self-interest. But would this process really bring us closer to a real and useful understanding of people?

How does this idea—that self-interest in *the* basic motivation—help in answering the most interesting and important questions about human experience, such as, Why do people respond so very *differently* from one another? The assumption tends to level and homogenize the vast, wonderful and outrageous differences that there are between both people and their motivations for their wildly diverse actions. All differences must be reduced only to differences in the mechanisms they each use to pursue their self-interest. This street-level cynicism blinds us to the great variety of human inspirations. When we see through too much, we see less. When we see through everything, then we see nothing except the theory that we started with, but even that is misunderstood because it is not recognized as a faith commitment.

Heroism and dysfunction. We noted earlier that a test case for cynicism is how it deals with moral excellence. Cynicism does not allow a face-value understanding of morally heroic actions. It must see through them and find them driven by less-than-noble motivations. The impor-

tant question in any discussion of heroes is, What made them stand out
and behave so differently from the nonheroic people they lived among?
Why were they so exceptional? In *Rescuers: The Lives of Heroes* Michael
Lesy claimed that most of the heroes that he studied, which included winners of the congressional medal of honor, were compelled to act as they
did because of the need to compensate for some deficit, whether it was
guilt for a past failure or a loss, such as lack of love from a parent.[3] Although they were very normal people, they were somewhat more dysfunctional than average. In a cynical society we should expect that a reflex
response to heroism would be to look for the personal insecurity that
would account for a courageous action as its compensation.

Again, from this perspective we find that wildly diverse human differences are leveled and homogenized. The exceptional behavior of the hero
is explained by his or her feelings of inadequacy, inner guilt, anxiety, insecurity and frustration. But then, why is it that most of us who also experience a wide range of dysfunction, failures, frustrations and insecurities
manage to avoid heroic action so easily and consistently? There are countless nonheroic choices that are far more likely to be our responses to frustration and inadequacy. Why did the hero respond with heroism instead
of with the more normal cowardice, excuse, evasion, denial or indifference? The very *nonnormality* of the hero is what is interesting and demands explanation. Telling us that heroes experienced themselves as failures does not account for heroes at all because it does not differentiate
them from the rest of us. Again, by seeing through too much we are able
to see almost nothing.

The cynicism of evolutionary psychology. Evolutionary psychology
presents one of the most thorough forms of cynicism that we have considered. Instead of rooting motivation in self-interest or consolation, evolutionary psychology bypasses human self-awareness altogether. It finds
the driving force of human behavior to be the human genes' demands for
their own replication. That is, when rightly understood, all human motivations are gene-driven ways of enabling the bearers of those genes to live
long enough to reproduce and so to get those genes copied in the next
generation.

Evolutionary psychology is an ingenious and elegant "theory of everything" in human motivation. All forms of sexual behavior, social and po-

litical activity as well as all morality and religious faith are ultimately genetic strategies to get our DNA into the next generation. It sees through everything—except the theory itself, which is immune. It asks an enormous step of faith from us to trust the ingenuity of the evolutionary psychologist who can explain any conceivable behavior pattern by retrofitting it to the paradigm of something that must have been reproductively advantageous.

For example, if we listen to different evolutionary psychologists, the great diversity of sexual behavior is all somehow caused by the same thing—the reproductive advantages of that behavior. So, surprisingly, Victorian sexual faithfulness in marriage is genetically advantageous for men. This is because stable marriages are more likely to produce children whose paternity is not in question, who will therefore be well cared for and who will also marry and have children. But equally (and somewhat more plausibly), evolutionary logic in different hands argues that it is male promiscuity that maximizes genetic replication. Rape is genetically coded in men so that those who are social failures can still pass on their DNA. Illegitimate children also grow up and reproduce—the more the better for the success of their genes.

I suggest that the differences between the celibate male, the sexually faithful husband, the adulterer and the rapist are more fruitfully explored by investigating the many sources of motivation that are themselves not reducible to genetics. The human brain seems to have a high degree of biologically hard-wired flexibility that is open to many motivating influences from family, religion, general culture and personal choices. If we want to understand the differences between these male sexual behavior patterns, I suspect that many other sources of motivation will be more enlightening than the homogenizing doctrines of evolutionary psychology.

Evolutionary psychology seems particularly strained when trying to explain the extremes of human behavior that Pascal called "greatness" and "vileness," and which he claimed were essential for our self-understanding. Evolutionary psychologists cannot take altruism at face value. Unless the face value of altruism is seen through and unmasked, it refutes the whole theory. Altruism involves the capacity of people to choose the interests of others even when they are against their own self-interest in patterns of behavior that are crucial for the maintenance of civilization.

Great ingenuity and effort is expended to unmask altruism. Altruism is not what it appears, but only is a strategy for selfish genes to use persons as pawns in their game. The self-sacrificial act of altruism is advantageous for the genes of the altruist because they are protected and continue in the life of his or her relatives (with the same genes) even if the altruist dies as a result of the act. Ingenious theories and computer models are used to demonstrate this. For example, we are told that it is genetically worth dying for two brothers or four first cousins. But it is difficult to imagine how this explains the real-life diversity of human selfishness and altruism, vileness and greatness.

We have to account not just for animals who put themselves at risk to predators by giving an alarm, or for soldiers who fall on a hand grenade in single-act heroism. The phenomenon of European rescuers of Jews during the holocaust is a far bigger challenge to the theory. Many of these rescuers spent four to five years daily risking their lives and the lives of their own children (all the DNA of their next generation) for total strangers who were specifically defined by being of different genetic stock.[4] These actions stand evolutionary psychology on its head because the rescuers acted directly and consciously against the demands of their "selfish genes," not as single reflex actions but purposefully, for years.

The doctrine of "reciprocal altruism" offers no better explanation. It suggests that people behave altruistically out of ultimate self-interest— because they will then be more likely to be treated with kindness by those whom they have helped. But from this perspective Jewish people had no reciprocal altruism to offer. Their presence was nothing but a danger and liability to their rescuers. Without heroic intervention on their behalf, they were headed for the gas chambers. I would suggest that evolutionary psychology leaves us with very little that is helpful in understanding the vital question of what distinguished these rescuers from the rest of occupied Europe. What was it that made them different from those who cooperated in the rounding up of Jewish people, or from the majority who watched from the sidelines, wanting to know as little as possible about it?

The same thing could be said of human vileness, or what is called radical evil. If we are hard-wired for altruism and cooperation, how do we explain the presence of serial killers, the extraordinary prevalence of war throughout human history, or even the level of hatred and violence within families. (Most murders in the United States are within the family.) If human behavior really is so genetically driven to cooperation that culture has relatively little influence, how do we explain relative civility and cooperation turning into mayhem and bloodbath when cultural variables change?[5] Think of the vast butcheries of Lenin, Stalin, Mao, Hitler, Pol Pot or the nightmare in Rwanda.

Again, I find myself underwhelmed by the explanatory power of these reductive systems to explain the vast richness and extravagant diversity of both human nobility and wretchedness. They see through so much that (using C. S. Lewis's metaphor) the only thing that is not transparent and therefore invisible is the theory itself, yet the faith commitment of the theory is usually invisible to the believer.

God, who alone is omniscient and therefore capable of seeing through everything, is not a cynic. Not only is he not a cynic but he sees through cynicism itself to expose it as unwise and misleading. I have suggested that the unwisdom of cynicism, which is so emphasized in the wisdom literature of the Bible, is shown in its lack of explanatory or enlightening power in some typical modern cynical paradigms. We move next to cynicism about individuals and then to the last theater of cynicism, the institutions of society.

BEYOND CYNICISM I
Humility—A Reality Check

*If . . . we remember God's grace, then we lose the pride that
would make us a Pharisee and the despair that would make us
a cynic.*

MEROLD WESTPHAL

*To know oneself is, above all, to know what one lacks. It is to
measure oneself against Truth, and not the other way around.
The first product of self-knowledge is humility, and this is not a
virtue conspicuous in any national character.*

FLANNERY O'CONNOR

*Jesus Christ is a God whom we approach without pride, and be-
fore whom we humble ourselves without despair.*

BLAISE PASCAL

I HAVE ARGUED THAT CYNICISM DOES NOT HAVE a monopoly on honesty but that it is itself suspect for all the same reasons that it suspects
other perspectives. Having said that, suspicion seems necessary to see
through the triviality and con-artistry that surrounds us. If there is an alternative for cynicism, what is it? Friends have urged me to think of a word
to describe what to put in its place. I have tried.

Honesty is a good word, but it seems to beg the question—of what, exactly, honesty requires. *Realism* is a good word also, but it has too much philosophical baggage from its past, and it too begs the question of who gets to define what is real. *Skepticism* is too negative, as if the burden of proof rested on anyone inclined to recognize goodness or integrity in the world. *Shrewdness* is also too negative and connotes an overinvestment in self-interest. *Discernment* is a more balanced word, but it seems too weak. *Suspicion* is getting there, but I am looking for a word that includes both suspicion and also the suspicion of suspicion, a suspicion that is not as overly self-confident as cynicism. I have looked high and low and have not found the word that, standing alone, will do the job as the replacement for *cynicism.*

I have decided that it is not such a terrible thing that there is no single word to carry the burden of this alternative. It could too easily become a cliché, producing a one-word false impression of real understanding. The biblical idea of"wisdom"might come as close as any, but it still demands explanation. What I am really looking for is the lifelong determination to see the world as it really is, as much as we can, with eyes open. This means being suspicious of the deceptive filters of our culture and of our personal experience—filters both sentimental *and* cynical. I am looking for wisdom expressed in a redemptive suspicion, limited by humility and tempered by love and mercy. Suspicion is both necessary and dangerous. In a world of accelerating hype and spin the question is how to use the wisdom of suspicion without letting that suspicion extend beyond its legitimate reach to invade the equal legitimacy of, for example, faith, hope and love.

We will be looking in this and the next chapter primarily at cynicism about other individuals. We will be trying to articulate a suspicion that is preemptive in its anticipation of brokenness and redemptive in its resulting wisdom. The teaching of Jesus helps us to begin this project. He pushes us to start with large ideas. Some of the most important limitations to cynicism come in three large ideas: humility, individuality, and charity or love. We will start with humility and then go on to individuality and charity in chapter twenty-one.

Humility as a Reality Check to Suspicion

Humility is not, as Nietzsche imagined, the habit of obsequiousness and compliance by which the weak try to gain indirect control of the strong and guarantee their safety by avoiding conflict with them. It is not false modesty or groveling. Humility is not pitted against our basic humanness, creativity and all that we have called "glory" in human nature. It is pitted against pride. Pride is that self-inflation that distorts and deceives us into refusing to accept ourselves as finite and dependent creatures in need of forgiveness. The late British philosopher and novelist Iris Murdoch put it this way: "Humility is not a peculiar habit of self-effacement, rather like having an inaudible voice, it is selfless respect for reality and one of the most difficult and central of virtues."[1]

We will see that humility, in opposing pride, limits overconfident suspicion. Jesus directs us to use our God-given critical powers of suspicion first on ourselves. We will begin with two central foundations of humility: acknowledgement of our moral weakness, and of our limitation.

Suspicion and moral weakness. To understand ourselves morally is to know that we are morally frail, weak, bent out of shape. We do not just sin: we are sinners, meaning that we are predisposed to deny, betray and disobey our Creator. To realize this is to relinquish claims to righteousness within ourselves and to realize that although we are valued by God, we need his forgiveness and mercy. We will also realize that our knowledge of ourselves and others is affected by this same bentness.

The same sin that puts us in the need of mercy from God also distorts our perception and evaluation of ourselves and others. For this reason I must be careful of my suspicions, which can sometimes be simply wrong, mistaken not only because of lack of information but also because of my inclinations to jealousy, self-protection and self-interest, which twist my vision. Of course this does not only impact our perceptions of other people, it can start with our understanding of God. The writer of Proverbs warned, "One's own folly leads to ruin, / yet the heart rages against the LORD" (Prov 19:3). What better self-protection than to shift the blame for our ruins onto a cynical picture of God?

This teaching of Jesus is important. While the cynic has developed critical skills of seeing through and unmasking others in their hypocrisy, false-consciousness and phoniness, Jesus turned us back to use our suspicion on ourselves first. In a well-known section of his Sermon on the Mount, Jesus raised searching questions:

Why do you see the speck in your neighbor's eye, but do not notice the log in your own eye? Or how can you say to your neighbor, "Let me take the speck out of your eye," while the log is in your own eye? You hypocrite, first take the log out of your own eye, and then you will see clearly to take the speck out of your neighbor's eye. (Mt 7:3-5)

Peter Sloterdijk noted in his book *The Critique of Cynical Reason* that these words of Jesus taught a "revolutionary self-reflection." He writes:

Matthew 7:4 contains psychoanalysis in a nutshell. What disturbs me in others is what I myself am. However, as long as I do not see myself, I do not recognize my projections as the outward reflection of my own plank, but as the depravity of the world. . . . Even if the world really is depraved, I should be concerned about my own defects first.[2]

Sloterdijk saw this as revolutionary because the normal order is reversed. Lawgivers and teachers usually begin with critiquing others, and it is not clear that they ever get around to looking at themselves. Jesus was not encouraging us to be naive, as if to say that people are all sincere, self-aware and never pretend to be what they are not. He said that because we live in a crooked and bent world, we need to start the suspicion with ourselves. This might give us the humility to see what is actually there. It warns of the danger of hypocritical moral scrutiny of other people. Welsh preacher Dr. Martyn Lloyd-Jones called this a more dangerous situation than the blind leading the blind. It was a picture of a blind oculist.[3]

Jesus did not say, "Never under any circumstances make a moral judgment of another person." It was rather, "Take the plank out of your eye first. Then you might see enough to help the other person with their moral issues—if those moral issues are still there." After you get your plank out of your eye and have a chance to look around again, the moral issues may have disappeared.

In this passage Jesus equipped us with preemptive suspicion. That is, he was teaching us to measure ourselves by this suspicion before taking on the task of correcting our friends, neighbors and colleagues, or, for that matter, even subjecting them to our internal cynical evaluation. Sharp-edged though Jesus' teaching was, it was not as revolutionary as Sloterdijk imagined. In fact it was an extension of one of the well-worn themes of self-suspicion in biblical wisdom literature, such as, "Do not be wise in your own eyes" (Prov 3:7).

Suspicion and being limited. We are creatures, not the Creator; images of God, not gods. As creatures we are finite and our finitude poses a problem for the process of knowing. We are small, limited in space and time. We live inside our heads, in our moment of history, culture and place. We are limited in our perception in that we notice only a little bit of what is around us at any moment of time and remember even less. We are also limited in our interpretation of what we know. All that we know has been interpreted by us, for better or for worse. Humility insists that I admit these limitations and allow them to limit my confidence in what I think I know, including confidence in my suspicions. This means I will preemptively suspect my suspicions.

When we do not take into account the profound limitations of our understanding, we can make serious mistakes in our judgment. Think of Jane Austen's novel *Pride and Prejudice*. The two main characters in it are kept apart in condescension and hatred, one by his pride and the other by her prejudice. These are two styles of cynicism. It is only humility on both their parts that eventually cuts down pride by recognition of its arrogance and prejudice by learning of its ignorance—making room for love.

Let me give some examples from the Bible. When David was a teenager, he kept his father's sheep and ran errands such as taking meals to his older brothers who were in the army. He came to bring food to his brothers one day just as Goliath, the giant Philistine warrior, was taunting and scorning their army, nation and God. David started asking what was going on. His oldest brother, Eliab, was furious with him.

> "Why have you come down? With whom have you left those few sheep in the wilderness? I know your presumption and the evil of your heart; for you have come down just to see the battle." David said, "What have I done now? It was only a question." (1 Sam 17:28-29)

Here is a typical cynical put-down: power, age, experience and sophistication condescending to youth and inexperience. Eliab could "see through" David to what he supposed was the evil of his heart, unmasking the crass motivations of teenage curiosity, a voyeur hoping to see some blood and excitement. It was an insult to real men in combat.

As we know, David himself went on to kill Goliath and become an international military hero that very day. We don't hear much more from Eliab. What had Eliab really known about David and his motivations? You can see in him the overbite of cynicism. He was not thinking either of his own limited perspective and profound ignorance of his little brother, or of God's possible plans for that little brother. Perhaps it was easy to stereotype a teenager. Perhaps cynicism was especially a temptation for him as a relief from his own humiliation before the giant. Maybe putting David down let him feel better about himself. The point is not that Eliab was just not nice to or unsupportive of David. For whatever reason, he was wrong, mistaken. He did not know of what he spoke.

Then there is the example of Elijah, a prophet of God who was running away from Queen Jezebel, who had vowed to kill him. Even after a great demonstration of God's power Elijah, in the exhaustion of his flight, spoke with cynicism about his own life, God and God's work on earth. He said:

It is enough; now, O LORD, take away my life, for I am no better than my ancestors

And later he said:

The Israelites have forsaken your covenant, thrown down your altars, and killed your prophets with the sword. I alone am left, and they are seeking my life, to take it away. (1 Kings 19:4, 10)

God answered him not with wind, earthquake and fire, but in a "still small voice" and told him that he was wrong. God's work on earth was not finished; even God's work through Elijah himself was not finished. Elijah was also not as alone as he thought. There were still seven thousand who were faithful to God in Israel. In his fear, discouragement and exhaustion Elijah could only see from within his own shrunken perspective. From within these limitations he could not see the other servants of God or the future plans God had for him and the nation.

The apostle Paul, in a completely different context, seemed to have

been on the receiving end of cynical criticism from the church in Corinth.
He put their criticism in perspective.

> But with me it is a very small thing that I should be judged by you or
> by any human court. I do not even judge myself. I am not aware of
> anything against myself, but I am not thereby acquitted. It is the
> Lord who judges me. Therefore do not pronounce judgment before
> the time, before the Lord comes, who will bring to light the things
> now hidden in darkness and will disclose the purposes of the heart.
> (1 Cor 4:3-5)

Here Paul clarifies a theme we have met before. The cynic is overreaching with judgments that would be legitimate only if he or she were omniscient. Paul did not credit the Corinthians' judgments about him or even
his own judgments about himself with final reliability. The cynic's whole
agenda is to "disclose the purposes of the heart." But the cynic is not
equipped to "bring to light the things now hidden in darkness." The result
is that the cynic pronounces "judgment before the time," trying to preempt the final judgment of God but likely to remain in darkness. It is better to let God do what only God can do.

Humility is a reality check to presumption about how much any of us
can know about each others' and God's motivations. Again, humility
plants in us a preemptive suspicion of our grand and far-reaching assumptions and conclusions about ourselves, our judgment, our neighbors, our world, our future, and what God is doing.

Humility and the Big Story

Part of understanding our finitude is knowing that we are part of a larger
story, far larger than we can ever know, whose Author has plans for us far
greater than we can fully understand.

The Bible gives us the big story or metanarrative, the very God's-eye
view that postmodernism insists no one can have. They are perfectly
right that we cannot have it—unless God has actually spoken and revealed it, telling us the story of which we are a part. The story is of creation, Fall, redemption and final consummation. While the Fall mandates suspicion, creation, redemption and consummation mandate
tempering that suspicion and open the possibility for faith, hope, and

love. We live within the unfolding of this story. In it we are dependent; every beat of our heart depends on forces beyond our control. We are not self-created, self-sustained, self-sufficient or righteous ourselves. What we can see as finite, dependent creatures, limited in space and time, is only a tiny piece of the back side of a tapestry, with only the crudest inklings of what the front side of the tapestry of God's providence must look like.

These are important realizations that keep suspicion from turning to cynicism. The temptation to cynicism is powerful when we are in pain, afraid, disappointed, depressed or exhausted, because these experiences shrivel and shrink our consciousness of what matters in the world. Our awareness implodes on itself, not able to see past our disillusionment, suffering or self-pity. The *big story* is much bigger than your suffering and mine, and it is a story that contains hope, even for those at the edge of death. It also brings the possibility of meaning to the specifics of our life situations that might in themselves seem meaningless.

There is a French poem that I first heard from a missionary doctor in Haiti who had it on his wall. It is sometimes attributed in various forms to Mother Teresa, who also had it on her wall. Most sources say that its author is unknown. It is called "Anyway."

People are often unreasonable, illogical and self-centered;
Forgive them anyway.
If you are kind, people may accuse you of selfish, ulterior motives;
Be kind anyway.
If you are successful, you will win some false friends and some true enemies;
Succeed anyway.
If you are honest and frank, people may cheat you;
Be honest and frank anyway.
What you spend years building, someone could destroy overnight;
Build anyway.
If you find serenity and happiness, they may be jealous;
Be happy anyway.
The good you do today, people will often forget tomorrow;
Do good anyway.

Give the world the best you have, and it may never be enough;
  Give the world the best you've got anyway.
You see, in the final analysis, it is between you and God;
  It was never between you and them anyway.

This poem is certainly not sentimental or utopian about human nature. But nor is it resigned or cynical. It is a call to continue engagement for good against evil in a world that would drag us down with frustrations and disappointments. It is true that years of work can be destroyed overnight. But it is also true that not all of God's work will be destroyed, and the power of what remains will be enormous. Even if our visible work is destroyed, we live before a God who sees in secret what really matters at the end of the day. According to Jesus, on that day the first will be last and the last will be first. All this rests on the reality of the big story, which has resurrection from death both in the past and in our future.

It is a common notion that time is on the side of cynicism. The idea is that time is corrosive to virtue. That is, if you see faith, hope or love, just wait a while and time will tear them down and show your belief in them to be nothing but sentimentality, naiveté or wishful thinking. But if the big story of the Bible is true, time is actually not on the side of cynicism. In his picture of the final end, when everything else passes away, the apostle Paul wrote, "Faith, hope and love *abide*, these three; and the greatest of these is love" (1 Cor 13:13). This is one of the great one-sentence challenges to cynicism. The passage of time will not vindicate cynicism but will establish faith, hope and love for eternity.

This is a faith and a worldview that has sustained countless people in the face of loss, pain and frustration. If people are cynical about God or do not think there is any such big story, they will still follow gods or stories of some sort. In wealthy and technological societies, the local deities for many people are health, wealth, youth, beauty, popularity, fame, power and accumulating stuff. In the brokenness of the world it is worth noticing that if you are suffering or experiencing frustration, failure or loss, these deities spit on you and turn away.

Humility is not the only requisite for reliable understanding, but it is a necessary one. Humility about our moral and creaturely status draws limits for suspicion. It is an integral part of Christian faith. This means that the Christian faith itself contains the preemptive suspicions that we have been exploring, as essential components of faith itself. It starts us on the way to preserve what is right about cynicism, but without being drawn into its overconfident liabilities.

I have emphasized humility not as a thought experiment or psychological technique devised to avoid cynicism. Humility is a reality check, a true recognition of what is in us and around us. It *will* help us to avoid cynicism, but that is a byproduct of having our eyes opened to what is true. We turn now from humility to two other strategies of knowing that can help us understand people more truly—individuality and charity.

FAITH—
HOPE—
LOVE——→

BEYOND CYNICISM II
Individuality and Charity—Walking a Tightrope

The air we breathe is so infested with mistrust that it almost chokes us. But where we have managed to pierce through this layer of mistrust we have discovered a confidence scarce dreamed of hitherto. Where we do trust we have learnt to entrust our very lives to the hands of others. . . . Trust will always be one of the greatest, rarest and happiest blessings of social life, though it can only emerge on the dark background of a necessary mistrust. We have learnt never to trust a scoundrel an inch, but to give ourselves to the trustworthy without reserve.

DIETRICH BONHOEFFER

Now it has appeared to me unfair that humanity should be engaged perpetually in calling all those things bad which have been good enough to make other things better, in everlastingly kicking down the ladder by which it has climbed. . . . I have found that humanity is not incidentally engaged, but eternally and systematically engaged, in throwing gold into the gutter and diamonds into the sea.

G. K. CHESTERTON

HUMAN BEINGS ARE GLORIOUS RUINS. The Christian faith gives us eyes to see both glory and ruin, greatness and vileness. Of course we want to be able to recognize both of them for what they are in this world, not just to identify abstractions. We all think of ourselves as good judges of character. I don't think I have ever met a person who did not consider him- or herself above average in this ability. Most are exceptional. Yet as we live our lives, this self-perception gets battered pretty hard. Where is wisdom?

In the last chapter we saw that some of the large ideas of the Christian faith require humility and that humility works to put a check on suspicion. We need to look at two other checks that also help to keep our suspicion from the overconfidence of cynicism. They are closely related to humility but need to be considered on their own—individuality and charity.

Respecting Individuality

To respect individuality in our evaluation of people is to resist the seductive, totalizing attraction of cynicism. Cynicism generalizes about groups, races and people from a few things that it has seen them do or say. In treating people as individuals we are actually just trying to take seriously humility's awareness of our limitations. Remember the line from Ecclesiastes:"Then I saw that all toil and all skill in work come from one person's envy of another"(Eccles 4:4). The word *all* is what takes the statement from what might be substantially true of someone as an individual to being a wild, cynical exaggeration (see p. 12). In being specific we are trying to limit ourselves to what we are more likely to actually know.

The attraction of cynical totalizing is that it radically simplifies the world from its staggering complexity into packages, generalizations and clichés. It also sets the speaker or writer on a pedestal of sophistication in being able to see through appearances that deceive others. At its worst it can feed and encourage hatreds in prejudice or stereotyping, such as in the many forms of racism or sexism. If, on the other hand, we are specific in our evaluations, that will resist wholesale dismissals of individuals and groups.

It is easy to glibly categorize people so that we can evaluate them without having to pay much attention. The priest Eli saw Hannah praying and crying in great distress in the temple. He had seen this sort of thing before, so rebuked her,"How long will you make a drunken spectacle of yourself? Put away your wine"(1 Sam 1:14). But in fact she was not drunk at all. In prayer she was sincerely agonizing over her inability to have a child. God heard her prayer, and she bore a child, who became the prophet Samuel.

Think about Jesus as an evaluator of people. His conversations with people are a fascinating study because even though he was fully human, he had the power to see what was in peoples' hearts and minds in a way that we cannot. There is an account recorded in the Gospel of John that tells of an interaction between Jesus, Mary of Bethany and Judas Iscariot at a dinner party the week before the Passover when Jesus was arrested and crucified.

> Mary took a pound of costly perfume made of pure nard, anointed Jesus' feet, and wiped them with her hair. The house was filled with the fragrance of the perfume. But Judas Iscariot, one of his disciples, (the one who was about to betray him), said, "Why was this perfume not sold for three hundred denarii and the money given to the poor?" (He said this not because he cared about the poor, but because he was a thief; he kept the common purse and used to steal what was put into it.) Jesus said, "Leave her alone. She bought it so that she might keep it for the day of my burial. You always have the poor with you, but you do not always have me." (Jn 12:3-8)

Mary had acted with unexpected and shocking extravagance. It demanded some explanation. Judas quickly supplied a cynical one. He could see through and unmask the appearance of Mary's love for Jesus. Beneath her piety he claimed to see irresponsible extravagance and indifference to the poor. She was a flake. But then John, the Gospel writer, made an editorial comment that turned everything around. He took a hard, suspicious look through Judas' cynicism and saw a hypocrite and embezzler beneath the social conscience. Judas had wanted to take the money for himself and had just lost a windfall. John has given Judas some of his own medicine. But John's suspicion was not a cynicism that extended to all people or even all the other disciples. It was a very specific judgment made after observing Judas, with whom he had traveled and been living closely for three years. A cynic who had been there that evening might have agreed with John about Judas. Cynics will sometimes be right in particular judgments.

Then Jesus weighed in on the discussion. He came positively to Mary's defense and specifically rejected the cynical interpretation of what she had done. Jesus could see through her, but he did not unmask her. She was

PRAISE BEFORE GOD

not wearing a mask. A face-value understanding of Mary was the true understanding. So Jesus said, "Leave her alone." Then he praised her for her love and understanding of the occasion. Any attempt to deconstruct what she did would have simply been untrue. So, the cynic at the dinner party would have been right about Judas but wrong about Mary.

This incident gives an intriguing view of how the omniscient God sees people. He knows us through and through, better than we will ever know ourselves. But the result is not a totalizing or all-reducing cynicism. He does not reduce us to our sin. He sees us as specific individuals made in his image, each a multidimensional person who can change and be changed through time. In God's revelation, we see great differences in the way God himself evaluates individuals: Judas is unmasked, but Mary is seen at face value and praised.

Although Jesus' teaching is not usually described in this way, he clearly taught suspicion. He even began sentences with, "Beware of . . ." Remember that the main theme of the masters of suspicion—Feuerbach, Marx, Nietzsche, Freud and their followers—is exposing instrumental faith, faith that used God for some self-serving purpose. It is intriguing that hundreds of years before, Jesus also taught us to be suspicious of this very same problem, instrumental faith that used God as a tool to fulfill human agendas.

One of the clearest places to see this is in the Sermon on the Mount, where Jesus teaches his listeners to deconstruct instrumental piety.

> Beware of practicing your piety before others in order to be seen by them; for then you have no reward from your Father in heaven.
>
> So whenever you give alms, do not sound a trumpet before you, as the hypocrites do in the synagogues and in the streets, so that they may be praised by others. Truly I tell you, they have their reward. (Mt 6:1-2)

He continues with a similar unmasking of pretentious public prayers on the street corners (Mt 6:5-6), and ostentatious fasting, making sure to be seen as disfigured by it (Mt 6:16-18). Jesus taught that all this was bogus faith. It is not the real thing. Through it people use the external posturing of faith for their own self-marketing. It is not directed toward God but is a performance for a human audience.

While both Jesus and the masters of suspicion speak against instru-mental faith, notice the profound difference between them. The masters of suspicion are unable to distinguish between true and bogus faith. To them all faith is instrumental intrinsically and by definition. But Jesus moves beyond deconstructing instrumental faith to explain that true faith in a living God is possible, and he tells us what it looks like. True faith cannot be unmasked or deconstructed because it does not hide any self-serving agenda. It is a relationship of integrity with a God who is there.

This faith is shown by a very different kind of generosity, prayer and fasting. Giving to the poor is not done by blowing a horn to make sure no one misses the event, but in secret, our right hand not even knowing what the left hand is doing (Mt 6:3-4). Prayer also should be done in our own room with the door closed. Jesus even gives us a short prayer as an exam-ple: the Lord's Prayer (Mt 6:9-13). When we fast we should not indulge in competitive suffering, looking dismal, but we should clean ourselves up and behave normally. We see Jesus' suspicion of corrupted faith, but we also see that his suspicion does not extend to all faith. There is faith and piety that are real.

Notice also that Jesus' warnings are two-edged. They are addressed first to"you." "Beware of practicing *your* piety before others in order to be seen by them."Be suspicious of yourself first. But he also is training us to observe others wisely."Do not sound a trumpet before you, *as the hypo-crites do.*"So he is teaching us to be suspicious of instrumental faith in oth-ers, but with a suspicion limited by the knowledge that there is faith that is true and real.

Behind these and other examples is Jesus' respect for the differences between people. Cynicism is too simplistic in its overconfident suspicion to do justice to the diversity and complexity of human experience.

Being Charitable

We have examined suspicion limited by humility and individuality. The third limit on suspicion is charity, or love. Like the first two, this is a chal-lenge to our own character. We must see and understand each other with charity. But this is far from simple or easy.

Paul began his famous discourse on love, 1 Corinthians 13, in a way that is not designed to elicit the sentimental sighs that we sometimes associate with this passage of the Bible. He seemed more concerned to trip us up and force us to start all over again when we think that we have understood what love was about.

> If I speak in the tongues of mortals and of angels, but do not have love, I am a noisy gong or a clanging cymbal. And if I have prophetic powers, and understand all mysteries and all knowledge, and if I have all faith, so as to remove mountains, but do not have love, I am nothing. If I give away all my possessions, and if I hand over my body so that I may boast, but do not have love, I gain nothing. (1 Cor 13:1-3)

It seems that Paul wanted to begin by planting suspicions in us about whether we even know what love is. It is possible to be outwardly a spectacularly successful moral, upright, spiritual person yet have no love and therefore be a walking disaster. But notice that Paul wrote this section in the first-person stance of self-suspicion; he is not wagging a judgmental finger at us. He wrote, "If I speak . . . If I have . . . If I give away . . . "then I am nothing, I gain nothing, I just make noise.

The shocking force of Paul's suspicion here is that it is possible to do all these extraordinary heroic and spectacular things apparently for God, and yet have them all be about "me." There is ecstatic religious experience, extraordinary gifts of speech and intellect, inspiring faith and willingness for martyrdom. But these things *can* be motivated by fear, self-righteousness, self-marketing or desire for power. Such external achievements *can* be self-referential, looking for the payback themselves. Paul is not being cynical about love. He is teaching us the preemptive suspicion to see through its counterfeits so that we will know the real thing when we see it and do it. Paul warned that if people are without love, they are nothing, they gain nothing, they just make a racket.

What does love look like?

Paul described what love does and does not do:

> Love is patient; love is kind; love is not envious or boastful or arrogant or rude. It does not insist on its own way; it is not irritable or resentful; it does not rejoice in wrongdoing, but rejoices in the truth.

It bears all things, believes all things, hopes all things, endures all things. (1 Cor 13:4-7)

Love is not first about what pays me back. It is a radical self-giving to someone else, beginning with patience and kindness. Paul lists a number of things that love does not do, all of which put me at the center at another's expense: envying, boasting, insulting, stubbornness, resentment and gloating over someone's failure. These things are about the gratification of my feelings, my status, my reputation, my freedom to say what I like. They are about me getting my way and having the right to get even. They all reference my importance and my dignity. The dignity of others is disposable or at best negotiable. Every one of these behavior patterns has an enormous power to distort my vision and evaluation of other people, who, after all, exist finally to gratify me.

Suspicion about love should make us suspicious of ourselves if we enjoy seeing through other people. Catching someone in hypocrisy should not make my day. Seeing through other people may sometimes be necessary, but if we love them it will be done with reluctance, not enthusiasm.

Paul tells us that love "believes all things and hopes all things." There are some fascinating parallels here between cynicism and love. As cynicism sees through people to unmask them, love also "sees through" them, but with a very different agenda. When we believe and hope in someone, we are also looking through or beyond them, past their face-value appearance or past track record. We see their potential for growth in goodness, strength and virtue. That means that while cynicism is controlled by self-protection, love (because it includes hope) is willing to risk giving the other person the benefit of the doubt.

But love is not naive. Two other phrases form brackets around "hopes all things and believes all things." They are that love "bears all things" and "endures all things." There will be things to bear and endure because what we hope for is not always going to happen. This means that love risks disappointment. Paul anticipates this. Again, he is not saying that love calls us to be naive. There are people whom legitimate suspicion will lead us to distrust. We are not called to have blind trust in complete strangers or be helpless before the world's con artists. But we are called to give others the benefit of the doubt when that is realistic.

We could say that where cynicism sees through to unmask and expose appearances of virtue, love sees through to unbind and free from sin, suffering, ignorance and dysfunction. An interesting illustration of this work of love is seen in the film *Dead Man Walking*. Sean Penn plays a convicted rapist and murderer on death row, waiting for his lethal injection. He shows nothing that would ever encourage us to respect, like or value him. Susan Sarandon plays a nun who keeps visiting him in prison, knowing against all appearances that he has dignity because he bears the image of God. By keeping on loving him, battling against her own cynicism and the cynicism of everyone else, she sees through his despicable exterior. Her persistent love enables him to finally face himself and God. Love is not only a way of seeing—hoping and believing—but it turns out to be a great power in its own right to transform him, to bring about the very changes in him that she had dared to hope for.

Walking a Tightrope

So, the Bible gives us some tools to limit our suspicion and thus to avoid both cynicism and sentimentality. But anyone who thinks that such discernment is easy has not understood it. We are glory and we are ruin. If we were all glory, any suspicion would be wrong. If we were all ruin, all suspicion would be right. We all live in the interface between glory and ruin. This is why Jesus told his disciples, "I am sending you out like sheep into the midst of wolves; so be wise as serpents and innocent as doves" (Mt 10:16). He never said that this was going to be easy.

The apostles did not find it easy, nor did they always agree with each other about where to draw lines between cynicism and legitimate suspicion. If you read the book of Acts, you will find that after their first missionary journey, Paul and Barnabas had a disagreement about their next journey. Barnabas wanted to include his cousin, John Mark, again. Paul disagreed. John Mark had abandoned them on their previous journey, and Paul did not want this to happen again. Their disagreement became so sharp that Paul and Barnabas parted company and went separate ways (Acts 15:37-41).

We do not have a report of their discussion, but I will take the liberty of guessing how it might have gone. Barnabas might have accused Paul of cynicism by not being willing to give John Mark another chance. Maybe he had apologized. Maybe he had changed. Did Paul believe in practicing what he preached about forgiveness, or not? On the other hand, Paul might have stressed how dangerous it was to be deserted in the middle of such a trip, and how they might be putting their own lives and the work of the Lord in extreme, unnecessary risk. It was not cynicism, it was just being realistic when the stakes were so high and John Mark's behavior had been so irresponsible. Wasn't Barnabas letting family loyalties corrupt his judgment about God's work?

We have no idea who was right, but we are told that John Mark and Paul were reconciled later, when Paul spoke of being very grateful for his help.

When my wife and I lived in London, a church met in our house, and we were involved with quite a few people who had spent time on the wrong side of the law. One evening a man stole someone's rent money, which had been left in a coat pocket. The thief came back several weeks later to apologize (but had drunk all the money). We had a serious talk and had him in for a meal, during which time he excused himself to go to the bathroom and was gone for no more than two minutes. After he left we discovered that in those two minutes he had been through the whole upstairs of our house, stealing cash and everything that he could hide in his pockets that was not nailed down. Again he came back with more apologies a few weeks later. What to do? It was lunchtime. This time I sat with him on the front step of our house, and we ate some sandwiches together. I told him that I forgave him and was glad to talk to him, but that I was not going to trust him in the house.

We have to make decisions, and sometimes we will not know whether we are on the tightrope running between cynicism and sentimentality or if we have fallen off either side. Wisdom has to adjust to our setting and the culture that we are living in. It will probably not look the same in the inner city as it will in a rural village. But the Christian faith gives us a way to approach the problem raised by cynicism by anticipating with preemptive suspicions. If we want to understand others honestly, humility, individuality and charity will be the most important things we have going for us.

As we go on to consider cynicism about the institutions of society, we will find that the Christian faith again equips us with preemptive suspi-

cions that are woven into the fabric of those institutions themselves—
rightly understood. Institutions, being made up of individual people, will
of course include all the dynamics of cynicism that we have just observed,
but also many more.

CYNICISM AND MARRIAGE

Inasmuch as when taken one by one most human beings of both sexes are either rogues or neurotics, why should they turn into angels the moment they are paired?

DENIS DE ROUGEMONT

Marriage is a great institution . . . but I ain't ready for an institution yet.

MAE WEST

Nearly all marriages, even happy ones, are mistakes, in the sense that almost certainly (in a more perfect world, or even with a little more care in this very imperfect one) both partners might be found more suitable mates. But the real soul-mate is the one you are actually married to.

J. R. R. TOLKIEN

WHILE GOD SEES PEOPLE AS FALLEN BUT STILL made in his image and not beyond redemption, what about the institutions of society? Evil can be compounded when people get together and grant each other the enormous powers that institutions wield. Cynicism about institutions is very widespread. We are told not to trust institutions because although they promise life and social benefit, they are death-dealing, driven by self-interest, money or power. Is cynicism about institutions justified?

There is no Christian view of institutions in general, but there are three central institutions of which the Bible speaks and which have been vital to society—marriage/family, church and state. Many find themselves horrified at psychological destruction in families, appalled at hypocrisy in churches, shocked at corruption in political life. This shock and disappointment often becomes anger, withdrawal and cynicism. There is no question that appalling abuses, cruelty, injustice and untruth have taken place in and through these institutions, so where is the omniscient God? Does he see through them as intrinsically corrupt and corrupting?

As we think of a possible honest alternative to cynicism about institutions, two qualifications are important. There are tempting expectations that are *not* promised by the Christian faith. First, it is not promised that these institutions will thrive automatically, apart from following God's design for them and apart from the motivation for honoring God in them. If, for example, God's design for marriage is ignored or repudiated, it is not promised that marriage will be life-affirming for those who dismiss that design. Second, even if God's design is followed to the best of our ability and our motivation is to honor God, it is not promised that life in the family, the church or the state will be perfect or even live up to our expectations. There has never been a perfectly harmonious marriage, a completely faithful church or a fully just society.

Insofar as God has given us designs for family, church and state, those designs include not only broad, positive visions, but also the requirement of suspicions, guarding against the very abuses, neglect and sophisticated cruelty that human nature is prone to produce. You can think of the Bible including these suspicions as God's warnings into naive and utopian expectations of his people. Christian people are called not to cynicism but to a qualified, redemptive suspicion of themselves and others. Only on this basis is hope for these institutions realistic.

Of course it is impossible to even outline a Christian perspective on family, church and state in three short chapters. I will do something much less ambitious, which is to simply point out some of the preemptive suspicions within God's design. They show that he requires us to anticipate our own collective weaknesses with brutal realism. Hope then is neither naive nor utopian, but reliable and life-giving.

naive hope: it will all work out
utopian hope: we will make it work out

Marriage

The Christian picture of marriage and family is part of God's original creation, designed as a good gift for human fulfillment, for society to prosper and for the continuity of the race. It is not good that man or woman is alone. Marriage is not a relationship designed for angels but a realistic plan even for people bent by selfishness. But there are now many alternatives to marriage that seem less demanding. They are increasingly socially acceptable. So, why get married?

Modern cynicism about marriage sounds familiar to the reader of the New Testament. In answer to a question designed to trap him between current theories of divorce, Jesus answered:

> Have you not read that the one who made them at the beginning made them "male and female," and said, "For this reason a man shall leave his father and mother and be joined to his wife, and the two shall become one flesh"? So they are no longer two, but one flesh. Therefore what God has joined together, let no one separate. (Mt 19:4-6)

The disciples who heard this and Jesus' subsequent, quite restrictive view of divorce made this very modern response, "If such is the case with a man with his wife, it is better not to marry" (Mt 19:10).

If marriage is such a serious, permanent and sexually exclusive commitment—perhaps the risk is too great and it is better not to get married at all. Those who have understood marriage truly, have understood the enormous step of trust and commitment that it is and have been daunted by it. This teaching is a warning designed to give us a powerful preemptive suspicion of tendencies to slide, drift or jump into marriage. The hope for marriage is that people who approach it will be both *more afraid* of its commitments and at the same time *more attracted* to its unique blessings.

The problematic vows. Christian wedding vows are themselves a call to suspicion of any easy, romantic stereotype of married life. The vows include a comprehensive anticipation of what could go wrong, before the fact. Notice that these warnings are not in fine print on the back of the marriage license. They are the substance of the vows themselves. Vows usually include some variant of these promises: "to have and to hold from this day forward, for better for worse, for richer for poorer, in sickness and in health, to love and to cherish, and forsaking all others, keep yourself only to him (her), until we are parted by death."

The vows are intended for marriage in *this* bent and twisted world, not another. Think of what a man and woman who say and mean them are promising. The vows force an anticipation of their responses to the worst-case disasters that could ever happen to them. The vows will make anyone suspicious of their own and their potential partner's naiveté, hypocrisy, impatience, sentimentality, fickleness, rashness, lack of judgment, lack of love and inability to stick to commitments.

Why do the vows need to be so grim? Why force a poor couple on their wedding day to anticipate the worst things that could happen to them? You might think they should play dirges at weddings and wear black armbands! Why not let the wedding vows be upbeat, to go along with the flowers and pretty clothes? It is because marriage itself is not an oasis away from the twistedness of the world. Marriage can bring out our deepest brokenness and failures, put them under the heaviest of pressures and amplify them beyond what they have been in other relationships.

But weddings are usually times of great joy and hope, and for good reason. Why? Because a man and woman have reckoned with all these grim possibilities and, wonder of wonders, are still willing to bind themselves to each other with extraordinary vows of love and faithfulness! It is only the extreme gravity of the vows that makes them something to celebrate so seriously. It may bring people from all over the world to be part of the celebration.

The problem is, of course, that we are not naturally very good at the love which will make a long marriage beautiful—even when we try. But hope in any marriage can never be that the partners will be so pure and loving that they will not hurt each other. This is why Jesus spoke so often and so uncompromisingly about forgiveness. If we are properly suspicious of ourselves, we realize that we will hurt those we love most—sometimes by accident, sometimes on purpose. But we can ask forgiveness, or we can grant forgiveness and start again with a love that as a result will not be brittle or fragile. We should expect to do both many times.

The better wine. Jesus' first miracle was at a wedding reception where the family ran out of wine. He turned a lot of water into wine and saved them from humiliation, but the caterer had not seen where the new wine came from. He explained that the way everyone did it was to give the best wine first and then when people were feeling no pain, give them any dregs and they would not know the difference. He scolded the groom because this last wine was better than the first (Jn 2:1-11).

Jesus probably meant this as a lived-out parable. The way everyone does it is to start with the best wine—great promises, high expectations and excitement. Most advertising promises instant success, gratification, happiness. How you pay the bill is discussed later. But when you look at the human life cycle through the stereotypes of our mass culture, you see dreams fading and people being satisfied with less and less. Of course this is not surprising when the initial dreams were those nurtured by advertising itself—dreams of youth, beauty, health, wealth, power, popularity and possibility.

Nowhere is this pattern more prominent than in today's mass culture stereotypes of marriage, in which marriage itself is an idol. Life's grand prize is a honeymoon in Hawaii, on the beach, backed by a sunset. Marriage starts in the stratosphere, but living happily ever after is not part of the bargain. Within a few years those feelings have faded. A couple can become skilled in ignoring or undermining each other. Then it is divorce or forty years of holy deadlock as they get gradually accustomed to less and less communication and intimacy. All this is seen as sad but more or less normal. Cynicism about marriage seems justified.

Jesus taught the opposite pattern for life in general. He never promised instant happiness. He discouraged people from following him, warning that it would mean trouble with their families and friends, sleeping out a lot and saying goodbye to their possessions. They would also have to face their own self-deceptions and sin. But they would not stay the same. They would grow. Jesus said of those who would follow him, "my yoke is easy, and my burden is light" (Mt 11:30), and "I came that they may have life, and have it abundantly" (Jn 10:10).

So also, in a Christian view of marriage the better wine is at the end. The true hope for a marriage is not the naive expectation that a couple will not fall out of the love they had for each other on their wedding day. The hope is that their love on that day will grow, that at the very beginning of a marriage, a long, brutally realistic look is taken at the demands of these extraordinary and improbable vows. Am I really willing to love and support him or her in chronic illness, accident, bankruptcy, betrayal, disappointment, suffering and loss—all the while knowing that we will both change in unpredictable ways? Am I willing to face my own sin, vanity, jealousy, selfishness in the confidence of God's forgiveness, but also in my own willingness to forgive and be forgiven by my spouse? The realism and humility that makes a relationship to God possible will also start a couple in the direction of honest love for each other. As they continue in this direction the wine will get better as they go.

A lot of cynicism about marriage surrounds the permanence and exclusiveness of the marriage vows. Some are cynical because they think that such vows are wonderful but unrealistic, and therefore bound to disillusionment. Others feel that the vows are not wonderful at all but are destructive and restrictive to growth and honesty.

To the first objection the realism of a biblical vision of marriage anticipates the disillusioning brokenness and, as much as is possible, prepares to meet it. It also can provide a foundation in a solid relationship for healing and change in that brokenness.

To the second, those who feel that the permanence of the vows is a curse, there is a lot of evidence going in the other direction. Nationwide studies have shown that it is this very commitment that is more likely to bring both men and women greater fulfillment than singleness or other more conditional arrangements—relationally, sexually, financially and in physical health and longevity.[1] That is, the permanence of the marriage vows should not be seen as a no-exit trap for the unwary. For those willing to embrace the vows with their eyes open by informed suspicion, they are a positive source of strength, confidence and growth.

Marriage and idolatry. Idolatry occurs when we inflate anything within creation to the place of God in our loyalties, priorities, expectations. This both dishonors God and destroys those who do it. There are two kinds of marriage problems related to idolatry. The first happens when marriage itself becomes an idol or God substitute. In this case our marriage partner must carry far more weight than he or she is able. The partner cannot be the main source of meaning in life without it crushing him or her. The second problem happens when there is another idol in our lives, because it will undermine loyalty to the marriage. Think of the marriages destroyed by idols of work, money, social status, sex or self-fulfillment. If anything is an idol to us, we will be willing to sacrifice our marriage on its altar.

If God is allowed to be God, marriage is part of his creation and is a way to serve and honor him. Its ultimate purpose is not to maximize emotional and sexual fulfillment or even self-esteem. Its ultimate purpose is beyond both partners and will mean honoring the One who made us.

What About the Alternatives?

I could write many more things in defense of marriage, but in a broken world there always can be a matching list of agonizing examples of abuse, which can fuel cynicism. What are the choices for something better?

We are living at a time when there are all sorts of alternatives to marriage, some tried and others less tried. There is no end to the variations of coupling and uncoupling, sexual cohabitation, serial monogamy, and polygamy, with all combinations of sexes and expectations. These are all in rhythm with the pace and transience of modern life, with its mobility and obsolescence, but even more with its commitment to individualism and freedom, especially sexual freedom. I fear for the long-term fulfillment that this freedom brings to those who choose it, but fear more for those who do not get to choose the family or other arrangement into which they were born. I am thinking of the children who have not yet appeared in our discussion.

Children, more than a special-interest group. In too many discussions of marriage and family, children are ignored. They are spoken of as if they were a special-interest group. One thing that does make them special is that they have no voice, they are powerless. But children are not a special-interest group. Children are the entire human race at the most fragile and vulnerable time of its existence.

There is simply no other social organization that can care for, provide for and nurture children as well as a stable mother and father can who are committed to their children and each other. Too often children have been considered resilient to the divorces and dislocations in their parents' lives. They do not object, or if they do, they usually forgive or excuse neglect or even abuse. This is not necessarily because they are really resilient and unaffected by it, but because this insecurity is the only story they know, so they have nothing to compare with it. They believe that their experience is normal, and parents can easily mistake silence for resilience.

The recent studies of Judith Wallerstein, Julia Lewis and Sandra Blakeslee make this point clearly. Their book, *The Unexpected Legacy of Divorce*, is a longitudinal study, meaning that they have followed children of divorce over a long period of time.[2] What they found was that divorce was not just traumatic for children in its immediate aftermath, after which they recovered. It affected them in countless ways for the full twenty-five years studied, often in difficulties forming romantic relationships themselves.

Sometimes divorce is necessary and is the best option for all concerned. There is no question either that some single parents do a marvelous job raising children who thrive. But divorce now has such cultural resonance that it is a regular theme on *Sesame Street* and is seen as just the normal way of doing things. Serial monogamy has become a perfectly acceptable way to express our relational freedom.[3] Divorce has statistically become quite normal. But what is helpful to children is not determined by what happens to be a current trend or a statistical norm in adult behavior. The Wallerstein study makes it hard to ignore or sidestep the divorce fallout for our children.

Family as a strategy for an unpredictable world. The backdrop of our discussion of cynicism has been the assumption that we live in a world, most of whose events we cannot predict. Many of the events that profoundly affect our lives are largely out of our control. There is no believable strategy for a pain-free, frustration-free existence. However, the biblical institution of marriage and family does a good deal to provide us with a safety net to cope with the storms that will come on us, not alone, but with those who are committed to stand with us in sickness and in health, in joy and sorrow. Those aspects of marriage and family that seem hard and jar against modern and postmodern freedom and mobility are exactly the things that make it strong enough to be a foundation for growth and a safety net when things go wrong.

Theologian and ethicist Gilbert Meilaender wrote an intriguing piece called, somewhat tongue-in-cheek, "I Want to Burden My Loved Ones." He had been troubled by the many discussions of medical ethics in which the refrain was how to avoid putting any burdensome decisions on family members when a person was no longer competent to make them. He felt something was missing. I will quote him at some length:

The first thought that occurred to me in my musing was not, I admit, the noblest: I have sweated in the hot sun teaching four children to catch and hit a ball, to swing a tennis racket and shoot a free throw. I have built blocks and played games I detest with and for my children. I have watched countless basketball games made up largely of bad passes, traveling violations, and shots that missed both rim and backboard. I have sat through years of piano recitals, band concerts, school programs—often on very busy nights or very hot, humid evenings in late spring. I have stood in a steamy bathroom in the middle of the night with the hot shower running, trying to help a child with croup breathe more easily. I have run beside a bicycle, ready to catch a child who might fall while learning to ride. (This is, by the way, very hard!) I have spent hours finding perfectly decent (cheap) clothing in stores, only to have these choices rejected as somehow not exactly what we had in mind. I have used evenings to type in final form long stories—longer by far than necessary—that my children have written in response to school assignments. I have had to fight for the right to eat at Burger King rather than McDonald's. Why should I not be a bit of a burden to these children when I am dying?

This was not, as I have already granted, the noblest thought, but it was the first. And, of course, it overlooks a great deal—above all, that I have taken great joy in these children and have not really resented much in the litany of burdens recited above. But still, there is here a serious point to be considered. Is this not in large measure what it means to belong to a family: to burden each other—and to find, almost miraculously, that others are willing, even happy, to carry such burdens? Families would not have the significance they do for us if they did not, in fact, give us a claim upon each other. At least in this sphere of life we do not come together as autonomous individuals freely contracting with each other. We simply find ourselves thrown together and asked to share the burdens of life while learning to care for each other. . . .

It is, therefore, understandable that we sometimes chafe under these burdens. If, however, we also go on to reject them, we cease to live in the kind of moral community that deserves to be called a family. Here more than in any other sphere of life we are presented with unwanted and unexpected interruptions to our plans and projects.

Meilaender concludes, wondering if one day his wife will have to make difficult choices about his medical care when he is unable to make them for himself.

> No doubt this will be a burden to her. No doubt she will bear the burden better than I would. No doubt it will be only the last in a long history of burdens she has borne for me. But then, mystery and continuous miracle that it is, she loves me. And because she does, I must of course be a burden to her.[4]

I find many people today caught in an agonizing crossfire. From one side comes their own cynicism about marriage. From the other side comes a deep loneliness that longs for what marriage can provide. My intention in this chapter has not been to persuade anyone to get married. There are many reasons not to marry, some of them given in the New Testament itself. My purpose has been rather to provide a different perspective for anyone tempted to cynically dismiss marriage and family as institutions so intrinsically corrupt and destructive that they can only be held up to ridicule. The commitments that rightly inspire fear are at the same time the very components of marriage that are its essence and strength. There is an honest and realistic hope that marriage and family can be life-giving and beautiful.

CYNICISM AND THE CHURCH

I hate, I despise your festivals,
and take no delight in your solemn assemblies. . . .
Take away the noise of your songs;
I will not listen to the melody of your harps.
But let justice roll down like waters,
and righteousness like an ever-flowing stream.

AMOS

We need to draw ever nearer to the reality of Christian faith and
witness in our time, however burdensome, however heavy with
failure, limitation, and disappointment. The reason is simple. Our
Lord Jesus Christ comes to us in the flesh. We can draw near to
him only in his body, the church. Loyalty to him requires us to
dwell within the ruins of the church.

R. R. RENO

At least five times . . . the Faith has to all appearances gone to
the dogs. In each of these five cases it was the dog that died.

G. K. CHESTERTON

Christ loved the church and gave himself up for her.

APOSTLE PAUL

AS WITH THE FAMILY, I will not try to outline a full description of the
Christian church. We will look at some of the cynic's grievances about

the church and also the warnings in the Bible's suspicions. They are God's preemptive strikes against potential abuses of his truth and of human lives.

What This Chapter Is *Not* About

A common source of cynicism about the church is from those who do not believe in the church's God. They see through the church by definition because in their view it builds its life, message and hope on something that is only a human fabrication and self-deception. This creates a necessary cynicism that is sometimes directly hostile to the church, seeing it as a social club designed to sustain a massive illusion. Their argument is by now familiar to us. The church helps to provide a crutch for the security and comfort of the weak and a smokescreen for those wanting to hide selfishness behind religious respectability.

Yet there is also a less obvious cynicism beginning from the same ideas but which seems much more friendly to the church. It says: No one can know ultimate truth as it really is, but the Christian church has a very powerful and wonderful story and tradition. Its symbols and metaphors give vibrant meaning to the lives of many people. It is valuable because it means so much to those people. This view seems much more amicable. It is nonetheless cynical about God because it presumes to see through and deconstruct God's basic claim to have revealed himself truly in words. It then reduces Christian faith to a generic human response to the mysterious unknown. Open cynicism comes out of the closet whenever the church is clear that it actually believes the story to be true.

I will not be dealing with this cynicism here because it is at root not cynicism about the church but a prior cynicism about the church's God. Nonbelief in the God of the Bible makes seeing through the church understandable if not inevitable, whether it is done with hostility or a more apparently friendly relativism. If this is where you are, your issues are with part three of the book, where cynicism about God has been addressed directly.

So for this part of the discussion, we will assume the church's God and consider cynicism that targets the church itself, although this is rarely a clean distinction. If you are cynical enough about the church, it might drive you out of the church and to cynicism about God himself. So the influence of cynicism can be a two-way street between the church, its God and back again.

The Bible itself teaches that the people of God will provide evidence to the non-Christian world *for* or *against* the truth of Christ, depending on the quality of their thinking and living.[1] The church cannot preach good news, be bad news and still expect to be taken seriously.

The Church and Its Failures

The church of Christ is an institution that stands solidly astride the paradox of the human condition—simultaneously glory and ruin. It is made up of people who have acknowledged their ruin but who have found forgiveness, purpose and hope of glory in the mercy of God. This means that by its very identity or definition, the church is people who come together in a common acknowledgment of failure but also a common hope for something better.

Church failure. God has appointed many different callings for the church. His people are to trust and worship him, to study his truth, to persuasively tell the gospel of Christ to those who do not know him, to faithfully administer the sacraments, to be a community of growth among themselves and also to reach out in service to the surrounding world. The very diversity and scope of these defining tasks for the church and the high standards for them make it a difficult institution to evaluate fairly. For that reason it is a deceptively easy target for cynicism.

The churches that we can see in the world, from whole denominational traditions down to individual congregations, vary from glorious faithfulness in significant areas of this vision to abject failure. The church is so diverse, lives in so many places, faces so many different problems and challenges, we cannot possibly evaluate its success or integrity in general.

We could make a list of the church's failures—of corruption, hypocrisy, disobedience, apathy, tribalism, self-righteousness, self-satisfaction, accommodation and perversion of its own ideas and ideals—together with all the suffering that has resulted. Then we could make a list of its great strengths and its impact for good in the world—the courage in persecution, the clarity of its message and life that has freed countless people from superstition, ignorance, poverty, fear, revenge and ultimately lostness from God, as well as motivating them positively to love, forgiveness, equality and justice.

My purpose here is not to try to establish that one of these lists is longer or more important than the other. A fair response to the cynic is certainly not to minimize the church's failures but to admit with all the honesty we can that the church is a mixed bag. It always was and still is.

How did Jesus see the church? As we look at the New Testament, it turns out that Jesus saw the church in much the same way. In his letters to the seven churches in Revelation, he said:

> I know your works, your toil and your patient endurance. I know that you cannot tolerate evildoers; you have tested those who claim to be apostles but are not, and have found them to be false. I also know that you are enduring patiently and bearing up for the sake of my name, and that you have not grown weary. But I have this against you, that you have abandoned the love you had at first. (Rev 2:2-4)

> I know your works; you have a name of being alive, but you are dead. Wake up, and strengthen what remains and is at the point of death, for I have not found your works perfect in the sight of my God. (Rev 3:1-2)

These letters show that the church is for people who are failures, even failures at doing church. But the church is a community of people under God that is a place of grace, where God is still working in that wreckage to change us. Dietrich Bonhoeffer struggled mightily with his disappointments over church failure, but with a helpful perspective.

> Just as surely as God desires to lead us to a knowledge of genuine Christian fellowship, so surely must we be overwhelmed by a great disillusionment with others, with Christians in general, and, if we are fortunate, with ourselves.

> By sheer grace, God will not permit us to live even for a brief period in a dream world. . . . God is not a God of the emotions but the God of truth. Only that fellowship which faces such disillusionment, with all its unhappy and ugly aspects, begins to be what it should be in God's sight, begins to grasp in faith the promise that is given to it. The sooner this shock of disillusionment comes to an individual and to a community the better for both.[2]

Bonhoeffer's point is that as we recognize serious failures in the church, it is not the time to walk out the back door in cynicism. A deeper honesty suggests that it is time to look for growth to begin—in ourselves and in the church community.

Grievances with the Church

As we think of our grievances with the church, we may need to realize that what we object to, the prophets and apostles probably objected to long before. Think of Amos's words at the start of this chapter, "I hate, I despise your festivals, / and take no delight in your solemn assemblies" (Amos 5:21). Usually it is not the people of God following Jesus faithfully that make people cynical about the church.

We cannot address every grievance about the church. But the more familiar we are with the New Testament, the more we will realize that it plants in us healthy suspicions, warning us to anticipate mistakes and abuses that wait for us in the church's life. We will look at some of the God-planted suspicions given to help us avoid the most common grievances.

Hypocrisy. Perhaps the most common invitation to cynicism about the church is hypocrisy. Cynicism's standard cliché about the church is that it is "filled with hypocrites." This is a curiously powerless criticism. Of course it is filled with hypocrites. What else is new? Hospitals are filled with sick people. Hypocrisy is a human problem, not a distinctively Christian problem. Is anyone suggesting that there is no hypocrisy outside the church?

Hypocrisy invites cynicism, which unmasks and exposes its posturing, hollowness and self-righteousness. We can, for example, find churches that have sanctioned slavery, racism, sexism, economic injustice and class prejudice all in the name of God and love. Revelations of sexual abuse of children by priests in the Roman Catholic Church have only encouraged cynicism. Cynicism is all the sharper because the church claims to speak with such an authoritative moral voice into the world. Then there are the hypocrisies within any church congregation as members and leaders do not walk their talk.

Just because hypocrisy is so widespread, almost normal, this does not lessen its seriousness. Jesus reserved some of the most stinging rebukes for hypocrites. He repeated, "Woe to you, scribes and Pharisees, hypocrites!" no less than seven times in one chapter (Mt 23) as he denounced one hypocrisy after another in the religious leadership. They crucified him at the end of that week.

We have already discussed his warnings of the hypocrisy of using prayer, fasting and almsgiving as means for self-marketing (Mt 6:1-18). He said, "Beware," "Watch out," "Be suspicious" of hypocrisy in ourselves first and also in others.

Because people of the church are hypocrites, a grotesque dissonance is set up between them and their Master and his teaching. The church has the words of Jesus and the whole Bible, which expose hypocrisy, rebuke it and call it to repentance. Christians have prophetically challenged themselves and other Christians to repent of hypocrisy, with profound consequences. Think of William Wilberforce in England working against slavery and Martin Luther King Jr. working against institutionalized racism in the United States. They were able to apply the moral leverage of biblical teaching on those who had respect for the Bible but had rationalized away its prophetic force—and they changed the world.

The church's stance in the world. Another grievance is the church's tendency to feel alienated from society and then to respond by turning in either of two opposite directions—blending in to society's ways to minimize conflict, or tribalizing into a subcultural community to maximize safety. The cynic sees the church blending in and behaving like a chameleon. It seems to have no backbone or identity as it assimilates, accommodates and compromises its distinctive beliefs and ethics to suit whatever is acceptable in society. The cynic asks, Isn't the church irrelevant if all it does is what is already being said and done by those outside the church? But cynics also expose the opposite response. A different part of the church separates itself from society and forms a ghetto, speaking in what sounds to them like a tribal dialect, circling the wagons or forming a quarantined fortress.

When Jesus spoke of how the church should function in society, he used two images. The church is *salt* and *light.*

You are the salt of the earth; but if salt has lost its taste, how can its saltiness be restored? It is no longer good for anything, but is thrown out and trampled under foot. You are the light of the world. A city built on a hill cannot be hidden. No one after lighting a lamp puts it under the bushel basket, but on the lampstand, and it gives light to all in the house. In the same way, let your light shine before others, so that they may see your good works and give glory to your Father in heaven. (Mt 5:13-16)

Jesus alerted them to anticipate the danger of failing to be salt and light. Salt acts as flavoring and also as a preservative. Light shows the ideal of Christlikeness and also illuminates and exposes what is in the darkness. Again he is planting suspicions in their minds to warn them. Saltless salt is diluted and therefore resonant with its surroundings, losing its taste. A light under a basket has the opposite problem, retreating into a subculture and not allowing the light of Christ to shine out.

Sociologists point out that these are the two options for any minority group in a majority culture. I live near Boston, Massachusetts, where Irish and Italian immigrants have assimilated and now nearly run the place politically. On the other hand, Chinese immigrants have built Chinatown. There are perfectly legitimate reasons for an ethnic minority to go in either of these directions. But Jesus warned the church against both assimilation and tribalism. His church must live as salt and light, and in doing that it must defy both of those enormous social forces. It was meant to be"in the world"but not"belong to the world" (Jn 17:11, 16).[3]

The betrayal of grace. Grace is at the core of the Christian faith, so when people are searching for grace and instead get rules and rejection from a church, they often become cynical. The apostle Paul's writings are filled with preemptive suspicion about betraying God's grace. The arguments of his letters to the Romans, Galatians, Ephesians, Philippians and Colossians reveal that he was in a constant battle to articulate, clarify, argue and defend salvation that was by the grace of God, plus nothing. Any denial or attempt to add to grace was unmasked and rebuked.

We can see the same theme in the older brother in Jesus'parable of the prodigal son (Lk 15:11-32). When the older brother heard the sound of the banquet given in honor of his brother, he became so angry that he refused to come in. Despite his father's invitations, he stayed outside and complained that he, who had worked so hard, had never been as honored as this useless"son of yours."In the older brother of this story, Jesus was giving the people who had just rebuked him a portrait of themselves. It has stood as a warning ever since. Here is one who refused to either give or receive grace. He is recognized as a mean-spirited loser, missing out on the joy of the great party to end all parties.

Mountains and molehills. Another closely related cynical grievance is the church getting "mountains" and "molehills" backward. The trivial is lifted high; the profound is trivialized. Tribal churches tend to specialize in the micro-morality of issues that the New Testament does not even raise—length of sermons, styles of music, church buildings, choir robes, hair length and tattoos. Both liberal and conservative churches can easily allow particular political agendas to eclipse biblical teaching on biblical ethics and even salvation itself. When molehills are turned to mountains, inevitably mountains are reduced to molehills—forgetting humility, truth, justice and love. People can easily conclude that the church is all about molehills, not about mountains.

Again, the irony is extreme, given whose church it is. Jesus warned against it so often that it allows little excuse for his followers who invert mountains and molehills. He spoke of those who are so meticulous that they tithe right down to the amount of the harvest of their herb gardens, but who "neglect the weightier matters of the law: justice and mercy and faith." He called them "blind guides" who "strain out a gnat but swallow a camel" (Mt 23:23-24).

The character of church leaders. Of course there are church leaders who are guilty of all of the vices just described and more, providing an invitation to cynicism about the church itself. Complaints seem to focus on arrogance, highhandedness and authoritarian leadership. I hear grievances about the minister as a CEO, who does not listen and who tolerates no criticism or alternate views. One might conclude that the church is a private club to uphold his ego and career. Painful personal experience can back this cynicism.

Jesus was highly attuned to the danger of arrogance in the leadership of the church, so much so that he even warned about certain titles for future leaders. He called for an alternative to the contemporary "leadership styles," cautioning them:

> But you are not to be called rabbi, for you have one teacher, and you
> are all students. And call no one your father on earth, for you have   ✶

one Father—the one in heaven. Nor are you to be called instructors, for you have one instructor, the Messiah. The greatest among you will be your servant. All who exalt themselves will be humbled, and all who humble themselves will be exalted. (Mt 23:8-12)

Jesus was so sensitive to the problem of pride in leadership that he warned them of the dangerous power of even the words they used to address their leaders. They were to avoid titles and names that might elevate those leaders above the rest of the church, undermining their true identity as its servants. He even implied that with such titles leaders would be more likely to usurp the authority of God.

Jesus also taught the disciples to suspect that people would falsely claim to be the Messiah. He anticipated future challenges, "Beware that no one leads you astray. For many will come in my name, saying 'I am the Messiah!' and they will lead you astray" (Mt 24:4-5). He warned especially about these bogus claims when they came with predictions of an imminent apocalypse.

The apostles Peter and Paul gave many guidelines of suspicion for Christians choosing future leaders. These were in the form of attributes and gifts for qualification, and vices and liabilities for disqualification. In just one example, the apostle Paul wrote, "Now a bishop must be above reproach, married only once, temperate, sensible, respectable, hospitable, an apt teacher, not a drunkard, not violent but gentle, not quarrelsome, and not a lover of money" (1 Tim 3:2-3).

He was saying, beware of a potential leader who lacks humility, loves money, drinks too much, quarrels and fights. Watch out if this person is inhospitable, promiscuous, unstable or cannot explain matters of faith clearly and with gentleness.

Can you imagine how different the history of the church might have been if these warnings had been carefully heeded? But it is not as if they have been completely or even substantially ignored, although we can certainly think of flagrant examples. Honesty requires us to recognize that there are also many times and places when the leadership of the church has stood out, not attracting attention to itself, but demonstrating Christlikeness to both the church and the world.[4] In the months after hurricane Katrina devastated New Orleans and the Mississippi coast, the news was filled with the failure of government agencies, mired in corruption and bureaucracy. Slowly and quietly, though, the story has emerged of the countless churches and church groups that offered prodigious amount of help in food, clean water and open homes.

Worldview and Failure in Perspective

Given the tendency for cynicism about the church to ricochet back to cynicism about God, we need to be very careful about the conclusions we draw from the church's failures. I have tried to point out that the church's worst failures have always been when it denies its Lord and ignores its book. This is no small point.

It becomes very important when we contrast the church's failures to, for example, the well-known failures of institutions inspired by Marxism and Nazism. On the one hand, catastrophic failures are catastrophic failures, whoever makes them. But on the other hand, we must realize that along with the enormous differences in the scale of human destruction, the barbarities of Marxism and Nazism are clear and congruent expressions of those worldviews.

Both Marxism and Nazism called for the elimination of anyone who would stand in the way of their evolutionary, social or economic ideals and dreams. In fact, within the ethical frameworks of their respective worldviews, what most of us would call their worst atrocities cannot be considered failures at all. We cannot honestly say that because all human societies have their ideals and all fall short of them, they are all somehow "in the same boat" of moral equivalence. Although there is a superficial truth to this, it obscures a far larger truth—that the institutions of Marxism and Nazism failed morally because of how *well* they fulfilled their ideals. From within the teachings of Marx and Engels or Hitler and Goebbels, there is no significant reform or correction to the momentous butcheries of Marxism and Nazism.

By contrast, the barbarities of the church of Christ, whether they were crusades, inquisitions, witch trials, apartheid or whatever else, stand in jarring opposition to the life and teaching of Jesus Christ and his apostles. Understanding the Bible with greater depth, context and integrity has been the baseline for the call to repentance and correction of the sins and aberrations of God's people from the church's beginning.

History provides one of the best reasons to question cynicism about the church. Churches have improved, reformed, been renewed and gained new life, strength and truth after sinking very low. G. K. Chesterton spoke of the Christian faith going to the dogs at least five times, but it was always the dog that died.[5] He was saying that the church can fall into appalling compromise and sin, but it has had within itself the ability to outlive both its enemies and its own self-destruction to rise again. This is because God has given the church the Bible and the Holy Spirit. In these resources it has always had the means for its own self-correction and new life.

If you are a Christian and cynical about the church, there are probably many reasons for that cynicism. But you may have lost a sense of solidarity in brokenness with the rest of us in the church. Jesus taught, "Blessed are those who mourn, for they shall be comforted" (Mt 5:4). Mourning is not about overconfident suspicion. It is about grieving. Nehemiah wept for the city of Jerusalem in ruins, but that is not all he did. He asked the king, "Send me to . . . the city of my ancestors' graves, so that I may rebuild it" (Neh 2:5).

The final and most important reason not to be cynical about the church of Jesus Christ can only be convincing to those of us who believe in the church's God. The church is God's church and "Christ loved the church and gave himself up for her" (Eph 5:25). It is a community of grace, which many of us have experienced as a reality. He is not finished with us.

CYNICISM AND GOVERNMENT

The preservation of a democratic civilization requires the wisdom of the serpent and the harmlessness of the dove. The children of light must be armed with the wisdom of the children of darkness but remain free from their malice. They must know that power of self-interest in human society without giving it moral justification. They must have this wisdom in order that they may beguile, deflect, harness and restrain self-interest, individual and collective, for the sake of the community.

REINHOLD NIEBUHR

It's easy to preserve your integrity in opposition, and tempting to hoard it by remaining in opposition under any circumstance. Scarier and indeed riskier is engaging your integrity by investing hope in flawed politicians operating in an imperfect world. The cheap pleasures of cynicism are always in plentiful supply. Abandoning them is like going on a diet or giving up smoking. Hope, in other words, is the thing that takes work.

MICHAEL KINSLEY

CYNICISM ABOUT GOVERNMENT SEES THROUGH the operation of the state to expose only self-interest, manipulation and abuse of power to the point that it can seem useless for a citizen to be involved at all. I saw some graffiti on a Cambridge, Massachusetts, wall, commanding us all, "Don't vote. You'll only encourage them!" Most versions of the daily news provide some support for this perspective with revelations of political dishonesty, greed and moralistic spin.

I will not be addressing the pamphleteers in this chapter. They are the attack dogs of politics and journalism who assault politicians on the opposing side of any divide with cheap shots, invective and satire. They are certainly cynical—about the people in government, but not about the institution of government itself. On the contrary, they obviously believe that good government is worth fighting for because change is still possible if they can only"get those idiots out of office."

The majority of cynical complaints, as we saw in chapter four, have to do with the electoral process having become a circus of media-bathed impression management with little room left for substance. Remember *Wag the Dog* (see pp. 36-37)? These are real grievances, but they need historical perspective. Despite the theatrics of the electoral system in the United States, people who live here or in other modern democratic nations have the sort of opportunity to influence political events never dreamed of by most people in known history.

In questioning cynicism about the state, we cannot possibly disagree with many damning complaints against particular governments. But the cynical charge is far more totalizing—it is that government itself is so corrupt as an institution that it is not worth trying to improve it. This view in the democratic West owes more to apathy than to honesty. Surely a place to address the prevalent cynical complaint would seem to be in the reform of the electoral system in its domination by media and money. But the challenge of cynicism about government itself needs to be met before we can expect motivation to reform any part of it.

Insofar as we have the possibility to be involved in our political world, how do we respond to the aura of cynicism about government itself? The question is raised starkly by the political scientist Glenn Tinder:

> How can one be as steadily critical as our historical circumstances require us to be without living in embittered solitude? How can one be fully cognizant of the human depravity and the terrifying dangers our historical situation so starkly display without falling into despair? Where can one stand between cynicism and sentimentality, apathy and fanaticism?[1]

The Christian hope is not in finding a golden mean somewhere between cynicism and sentimentality, a half-way balancing act between two false choices. Any approach must come from a deeper theological grasp of human nature and the human condition.

The Larger Picture

We must return yet again to the two sides of human nature. Humans have value because of who we are by creation, but because of our predisposition to evil and corruption we are dangerous to ourselves and one another. God has given people authority in the name of the state to use force to resist evil and accomplish good, even sanctioning the taking of human life to do it (Rom 13:1-7). The apostle Peter also taught Christians to honor and respect the governing authorities and to obey them, even though he knew perfectly well that his emperor was Nero (1 Pet 2:13-17).

Yet examples abound in Old and New Testaments of the abuse of political power. Think of the prophet Samuel's warning to the people of Israel, who demanded a king. He predicted that a king would make high-handed use of their sons and daughters, their real estate and their harvests, and before long they would be crying for deliverance from the one who was meant to be their deliverer (1 Sam 8:10-17). One of the most perceptive of Christian novelists, Fyodor Dostoevsky, reflected on the corrupting power of power itself:

> Whoever has experienced the power, the unrestrained ability to humiliate another human being, . . . automatically loses power over his own sensations. Tyranny is a habit, it has its own organic life, it develops finally into a disease. The habit can kill and coarsen the very best man to the level of a beast. Blood and power intoxicate. . . . The man and citizen die with the tyrant forever; the return to human dignity, to repentance, to regeneration, becomes almost impossible.[2]

Any biblical perspective of the state will include a vision for political power used well—to encourage righteousness and discourage evil (1 Pet 2:14)—but also suspicion anticipating this intoxicating corruption of power that sin produces. It presents us with a qualified but positive vision of the state and its role in society. Modern Western democracies, which are profoundly influenced by the Christian worldview, have tried, albeit very imperfectly, to enable governments to have the power to pursue the well being of their people. But at the same time they try to guard against unchecked power, most easily abused if it is held by too few people or interests.

Justice, equality and prejudice. Equality is one of the great ideals of Western democracy, and it is at the basis of its notion of justice. People should be treated equally before any law of the land, not with favoritism or prejudice. Actually, this is quite a strange and counterintuitive idea. Why should people be treated as equals when they are so obviously not equal by any measurable standard? Think of the ways we rank each other—according to wealth, race, sex, beauty, creativity, strength, popularity, intelligence, moral virtue and so on. We might as well say that all cars are equal. Where did this strange idea of equality come from? It did not come from Greek philosophy. For Aristotle, slaves and women were not at all equal to free men.

The idea of the equality of all people came to the modern world from the Bible, beginning in Genesis 1, with the story of creation of man and woman equally in God's image. They and their progeny were equal to each other because they were equal in dignity and value in the sight of God. Although Christian people have sometimes disregarded this teaching in catastrophic ways, such as in race-based slavery, apartheid and institutionalized sexism, it has been a benchmark to which they have been brought back as they respected biblical truth. If we have equal dignity and value before God, that gives a transcendent foundation for the idea of equal human rights and freedoms.

God calls us to have preemptive suspicions about whether justice is really being done. He measures justice not by abstract definitions but by how our society treats the poor, the widow, the orphan and the stranger. Why these people? Because the rich and powerful can make it hard for us if we treat them badly. The poor and disenfranchised cannot do this on their own. So if the orphan and the stranger are treated well, policies and practices are likely to be motivated by obedience to God and not just by self-interest. Typical of the commands of God are: "You shall not deprive a resident alien or an orphan of justice; you shall not take a widow's garment in pledge" (Deut 24:17); "Cursed be anyone who deprives the alien, the orphan, and the widow of justice" (Deut 27:19). This is a God-planted suspicion that sees the treatment of the powerless as the weathervane indicating respect for justice.

God and Caesar: Suspicion That Goes Both Ways

In an interchange with Pharisees and Herodians who were trying to trap him, Jesus was asked about whether to pay taxes to the emperor. Jesus pointed to the image of Caesar on a coin, and said, "Give therefore to the emperor the things that are the emperor's, and to God the things that are God's" (Mt 22:21). From this statement, Jesus' followers have understood two things among others: First, that it is not against God to pay taxes to a civil government, even—as was the case then—a government that was also a false religion. Second, they understood that loyalty to Caesar was not absolute but limited. They could not give to Caesar their ultimate loyalty because that belonged only to God.

Suspecting the state's misuse of faith. Jesus was teaching respect for the state, but at the same time suspicion that the state might demand from people what they should give only to God. This suspicion anticipated what turned out to be a recurrent crisis from the first days of the church through to today. Early Christians had to choose whether to obey the political authorities who told them to renounce their faith or face death. Modern Christians have often faced not only the demand to deny Christ directly but also the problem of a government demanding disobedience to God. Christian people have, for example, refused to fight if they believed a war (or all war) was wrong. They have refused to obey laws that they considered immoral, such as the Fugitive Slave Law in the United States or the state's demand to relinquish Jewish refugees in Nazi occupied Europe.

Suspecting religion's misuse of the state. Early Christians, with their complete lack of political power, might have thought it strange to worry about the danger of their faith having an undue influence on the political process. But Jesus' teaching anticipated the future. After the emperor Constantine himself became a Christian (at least in name), it became a very real issue. Jesus forewarns of a time when his people would have political power and might want to use it in his name, drawing wrongly on his moral authority for their highhanded political or military actions. In the parable of the wheat and the weeds he speaks of the kingdom of God being like a field in which good wheat was sown, but then an enemy sows weeds into the same field (Mt 13:24-30). The servants ask permission to pull up the weeds. They are told, "No; for in gathering the weeds you would uproot the wheat along with them" (v. 29). God would direct the harvest himself at the end of the season.

The political implications of this parable are far-reaching (see Jesus' interpretation in Mt 13:36-43). The servants represent the people of God offering to pull all those who are weeds out of the world—the weeds being God's presumed enemies. But Jesus' point is that God does not trust his servants to do that. They cannot tell the difference between wheat and weeds, and the final harvesting is not their job anyway.

I believe that this parable does not prohibit a just war, fought to defend a nation against armed aggression. But it does prohibit a holy war—followers of Jesus thinking they are serving him by killing those that they decide are God's enemies, to weed them out of the world. Although there was holy war at God's direction during a specific place and time of Old Testament history, the New Testament is clear that the sword of God has now become the Word of God (Eph 6:17), spreading the gospel by telling the good news, not by military action. If Christians try to fight a holy war, it is an arrogant preemption of the final judgment of God.

There is an instructive example in American history of a national leader struggling to follow God's moral order but not presuming to have a straight line of communication from God: the second inaugural address of Abraham Lincoln. The Civil War was drawing to an end with horrifying carnage on both sides. Lincoln, the head of state, considered the war morally just. But as a believer in God, Lincoln also had the humility to not equate his cause directly with God's, nor did he see himself as God's infallible representative on earth.

> Both read the same Bible and pray to the same God, and each invoked His aid against the other. It may seem strange that any men should dare to ask a just God's assistance in wringing their bread from the sweat of other men's faces, but let us judge not, that we be not judged. The prayers of both could not be answered. That of neither has been answered fully. The Almighty has his own purposes. . . .
>
> With malice toward none; with charity for all; with firmness in the right, as God gives it to us to see the right, let us strive on to finish the

work we are in; to bind up the nation's wounds; to care for him who shall have borne the battle, and for his widow, and his orphan—to do all which may achieve and cherish a just and lasting peace, among ourselves, and with all nations.[3]

As president, Lincoln would have represented "Caesar" in Jesus' teaching. But as a believer in God, Lincoln claimed only what was due to Caesar under God. He recognized that the "Almighty has his own purposes" and also that as president he would pursue the right "as God gives it to us to see the right," acknowledging his limited authority and moral insight. Lincoln also saw that the pursuit of justice had to be tempered and followed by charity. He did not expect this speech to be popular, and wrote about it in a letter to Thurow Weed two weeks later: "Men are not flattered by being shown that there has been a difference of purpose between the Almighty and them. . . . To deny it, however, in this case, is to deny that there is a God governing the world."[4]

Cynicism About Christian Political Involvement

Suspicions of unwanted entanglements between "Caesar" and God are current in the political discussions in the United States as I write. Many fear that Christians in high places of leadership, who might assume that God is on their side, would presume to force their faith on the nation, disregarding the separation between church and state. While some of these fears are hysterical, not all are, given the rhetoric of some Christian leaders. Theocracy, a form of government in which its leaders claim direct divine inspiration, violates the deepest principles of democracy, which have, for good reason, gained respect in much of the world. If Christians look at the biblical story and at political history, it should warn them against any theocratic temptations and inspire them to work hard to mitigate suspicions of their ambition for theocracy.

Sins and crimes. The fear is that Christians will use the law to push as much of their faith down the collective throat of the pluralistic public as they can. For example, people fear that Christians will force more and more of what they believe are sins to be criminalized and what they believe is righteous to be privileged. But we need to ask, What is the difference between a sin and a crime?

Christians must distinguish between moral principles rooted in creation and moral principles rooted in redemption. The ethics of creation include the value of human life created in God's image; care for the creation (the environment); the institutions of work (the economy) and marriage/family; and truth telling. Biblical morality in these areas applies to all people in the fallen world, whatever they might believe. Creation is something that all citizens have in common. It is appropriate that the coercive power of laws should be used to lead a society toward the Creator's view of the good in each of these areas, because this leads to the common good (although not all will agree). Sufficiently serious sins against these moral principles should be treated as crimes. Laws do not necessarily demand God's ideal, but a good law leads a given society from wherever they are toward God's ideal. Therefore, a good law for one society might not be the same as a good law for the other, although the ideal they are aiming for is the same.

The ethics of redemption, by contrast, do not apply to everyone, just those who are followers of Christ. They include belief in Christ, the sacraments, prayer, church membership and a confession of faith. No state should force these on anyone. Such coercion would violate an individual's freedom of conscience to make up his or her own mind about the deepest personal commitments. Real faith cannot be coerced.

Many of the disasters in Christian history and much cynicism about Christian political involvement have been caused by Christians who have ignored the distinction between creation and redemption ethics. It has led the church to usurp powers of the state, or the state to use religious moral authority for purposes of personal or political power.

Baptism at sword point, the crusades and the Inquisition are examples of such coercion. At one time admission to Oxford and Cambridge universities was denied to all but members of the Church of England. In the Massachusetts Bay Colony in the early seventeenth century a resident had to be a member of the local Congregational church to vote in town meetings. This not only created fierce resentment against the church but also diluted it with nonbelievers who made up bogus conversion stories to be able to vote. The history of institutional anti-Semitism is rooted in the same problem. Refusal to confess Jesus as Lord and Messiah resulted in the denial of many basic human rights to Jewish people throughout much of Western history.

The attempts to serve God by using the power of the state to coerce ethics of redemption have always backfired against the cause of Christ, bringing lasting confusion and bitterness. They have been both theologically wrong and cruel, as well as self-destructive for the church. Had the church followed more biblical principles, missionaries, not crusaders, would have gone to the Middle East. There is no holy land, holy city, holy mountain or holy building that Christians can justify fighting for with holy war in God's name. The cause of Christ has been served far better by state toleration of religious pluralism than by state establishment of any one Christian tradition.

However, while denying any aspirations of theocracy, Christians still have a responsibility to be engaged in political life. Of course they will want to "legislate morality." Everybody does. Everyone wants the laws and policies of their country to reflect what they believe is morally right. This does not constitute the "establishment" of religion in violation of the First Amendment of the U.S. Constitution. The transcendent source of creation's moral values does not disqualify those values from the public square. Is there any reason why the state should be influenced only by values derived *without* explicit reference to God? But the morality that Christians want to legislate must be the moral principles of creation ethics, not redemption ethics. So, it is surely legitimate, even mandated for Christians to be involved at some level in the legal issues of life and death, marriage and family, environment, economics and truth telling. (I have much less sympathy for trying to force prayer into public schools against the will of people who do not believe there is a God to pray to.)

Christians who are involved in the political process need to persuade the majority that their views are best for the common good—just like anyone else. Using hardball politics or throwing Bible verses at people who do not believe the Bible is not persuasion. To get traction in the minds and hearts of people in pluralistic cultures, Christians have to be persuasive in new ways, using nonreligious vocabulary and arguments for the common good.[5]

Hope

The best challenge to cynicism is history. That is, it is simply untrue that political history reveals unrelieved decline, increase in corruption, injustice and collective suffering. Efforts to reform political systems have not always been futile, though some political systems have been so corrupt that they have either collapsed or been destroyed from the outside before there could be improvement.

Here is a thought experiment. Imagine yourself back in the cold war era, around 1985. You are relatively well informed about the world political situation of that time. Imagine meeting someone who informs you that in less than ten years the iron curtain in Eastern Europe will fall without major bloodshed and South Africa will be ruled by a black man after a peaceful transition of power. What would you think? I know perfectly well what I would have thought. This person is naive, incompetent and perhaps delusional. And yet, there it is.

It is not a coincidence that many Christian people who had not given in to cynicism had important parts to play in the collapse of Communist Eastern Europe and the reshaping of South Africa. The hope that inspired years of hard work and sacrifice for positive change was not foolish, sentimental or utopian. Sometimes the hope was slender and the risks were great, but that slender hope for the future was necessary for the changes to have taken place.[6]

Dietrich Bonhoeffer argued against political cynicism even from his cell in a Nazi prison. He had given up hope of reforming the existing Nazi government from within, so he had decided to actively resist it, was imprisoned and ultimately executed. He opposed Christian defeatism or resignation that abandoned the future to the enemy. "In sheer resignation or pious escapism they surrender all responsibility for the preservation of life and for the generations yet unborn. Tomorrow may be the day of judgment. If it is, we shall gladly give up working for a better future, but not before."[7]

Bonhoeffer's perspective is valuable for all three institutions we have discussed: family, church, and state. Christians do not hope for utopia in this world order. There is plenty of mud still to throw at all three institutions. Christian hope enables people with well-informed suspicions to work hard for significant but less-than-total solutions to the problems of the world.

HOPE AND THE COSTS OF CYNICISM

*For me it is amazing to experience daily the radical difference be-
tween cynicism and joy. Cynics seek darkness wherever they go.
They point always to approaching dangers, impure motives, and
hidden schemes. They call trust naēve, care romantic, and forgiveness sentimental. . . . They consider themselves realists who
see reality for what it truly is and who are not deceived by "es-
capist emotions." But in belittling God's joy, their darkness only
calls forth more darkness.*

HENRI NOUWEN

*From the cross the Christian sees the world with all its values in-
verted, with vice conquering virtue, with chaos winning out—or
so it seems. From the door of the empty tomb, all is changed.
Death has been swallowed up in victory! The risen Lord reigns!
So, the world-and-life view of the Christian is neither victimized
nor pessimistic nor neutral nor even optimistic; the Christian
world-and-life view is* hopeful, *focused on hope because of the
redemption and resurrection of Jesus Christ.*

D. BRUCE LOCKERBIE

*With this faith we will be able to hew out of the mountain of de-
spair a stone of hope.*

MARTIN LUTHER KING JR.

WE HAVE TRACKED THE ELUSIVE CYNICAL WAY OF SEEING. One person
can be drawn to cynicism by temperament, another by painful personal

experience, another by the style of humor of a circle of friends and still another by his or her ideas about human nature. When we bring these variables to the three theaters of cynicism—God, individuals and institutions—it becomes more complicated still, because for most people, their cynicism behaves differently in each of these theaters.

It is interesting to notice, for example, the way cynicism is scattered through the ideas of some important thinkers. Karl Marx was deeply cynical about God and human nature, but wildly unsuspicious and optimistic about one institution in particular—the state. Nietzsche was cynical about God and most people (who were mere sheep), but held up "superman" status for a very few exceptional people. Rousseau was very positive about the possibilities of the unfettered individual, was ambivalent about God but cynical about society that held the individual in institutional chains.

Despite the diverse forms that cynicism takes, we started with the bottom line of cynicism as confidence in being able to see through surfaces to what is corrupt and self-serving beneath the surface. Cynicism can sometimes provide necessary suspicion to see things as they are in a broken world. But it resists putting limits on suspicion, leaving us with an overconfident mistrust that is an unreliable guide.

The Promises of Cynicism

Cynicism presents itself to our society with three very attractive promises: sophisticated enlightenment, guaranteed honesty, and self-protection. I will summarize my evaluation of cynicism by reversing the flow of suspicion and suggesting serious doubts about these three promises.

The promise of enlightenment. It may be called "enlightened," but cynicism seems as vulnerable as any other perspective to being unmasked and exposed. This is apparent especially when cynicism is pressed to come out from behind its moods, innuendoes, jokes and oblique references to actually explain the trustworthiness of its strategy of unmasking other people. Like its victims, cynicism is open to being the target of an ideology critique, even to the discovery that some of its driving motivations are things the cynic might be ashamed of. Cynicism seems to lose its privileged position and reputation for sophistication as it takes its own medicine.

It would be possible to see cynicism as a source of wisdom if cynicism were a judicious and limited suspicion. But cynicism does not limit suspicion and so sees through everything with confidence. Seeing *through* too much means *seeing* very little.

The promise of honesty. The association of cynicism with honesty is very deep in our society, but we have already seen that honesty can lead beyond cynicism. This is clear if we notice the overbite of cynicism, its claim to know more than it can really know. The overstatements "All work is motivated by envy," "All politicians are corrupt" and "Everybody has their price," although casually tossed into conversations, require virtual omniscience to be justified. Perhaps the association of cynicism with honesty owes less to the reliability of cynicism and more to the way we associate honesty with the willingness to make negative evaluations.

Remember the observations made by Søren Kierkegaard: We talk of the fear of being mistaken in our evaluations of people, but our fear is lopsided. We are much more afraid of being wrong about thinking too well of a person than we are of being wrong about thinking too badly of him or her. Though both mistakes are equally in error, we are much more afraid of the former. Our preference for a negative evaluation is not driven by honesty or commitment to truth, but by other motivations—most likely by self-protection, competitiveness or vanity.[1]

The promise of self-protection. Some people very consciously use self-protection as a rationale for their cynicism and withdrawal from other people, society and God. This response to pain, betrayal and disappointment is certainly understandable but has enormous hidden costs. Cynical self-protection is shallow, short-lived and ultimately self-crippling.

To evaluate its promise for self-protection fairly, we must look at the personal, practical consequences of long-term cynicism. Think, for example, of the impact of cynicism on the three theological virtues: faith, hope and love. A person who embodies these virtues must live in a place of risk and vulnerability. Cynicism in its self-protection sees through them all as bogus, dangerous, naive and without integrity. (I am not suggesting that every cynical person sees them in this way, but that the voice of cynicism is there to unmask each one.)

When we see through *faith* we exclude God from our lives. He is indifferent, malicious, unknowable or absent. Any faith in him is explained as a compensating projection or some kind or a smokescreen to hide selfishness.

There is a cynical attitude to faith in both popular culture and more so-phisticated society that encourages us to sleepwalk through momentous choices in our lives, unconscious of their content or consequence. Are we created or are we accidents? Are we alone in an impersonal universe that is deaf and blind to our hopes, fears, suffering and crimes, or is there a Person there? Are we accountable to anyone? Is there any meaning beyond the meanings that I invent for myself? Cynicism about faith shuts down our grappling with these questions. Cynicism about God also makes us vulnerable to cynicism or sentimentality about everything else.

When we see through *hope*, as cynicism does, it appears naive, an easy target to expose. It is "escapism,""blind hope,""pie in the sky." There are admittedly plenty of blind and foolish hopes, but to undercut all hope is to undermine any positive connections that we might have to the future. It means that we are not allowed to imagine any improvement in the world. This cuts off the light that hope might shine into our present experience and makes it an artificially dark place. It is only safer in that it provides a shriveled immunity from immediate disillusionment, while guaranteeing a deeper disillusionment over the long term.

One of our paradigms of cynicism, that "all toil and all skill in work come from one person's envy of another" (Eccles 4:4), shows what cynicism can do to hope. If we believe the totalizing word *all*, we should never allow ourselves to hope that our own work (or that of our friends) might ever have a motivation beyond the competitive struggle for status. Given the time and energy we expend in our work, this is an appalling conclusion to take seriously.

When we see through *love* with cynical vision, the consequences are momentous. If cynicism looks at love and always sees some vice or selfishness beneath it, what happens to relationships? When a kind word is said, the cynic thinks, *What is she after?* or *What does he want from me?* At the workplace there's confusion about job responsibilities, and the cynic thinks, *He's trying to cheat me and get out of work himself.* This attitude pushes others away and pushes the cynic backward into angry isolation. This becomes clear when we are on the receiving end of such cynicism. Every positive effort is deconstructed. We try to help and are met with accusation of ulterior motives. If we protest, that only seems to prove the cynic's point: now we have gotten "defensive," the sure proof of guilt. When our love is met with cynicism, it is a powerful disincentive to keep on loving. Not many people are able to swim against that current for very long.

The promise of self-protection is surely one of the cruelest illusions offered by cynicism. Cynicism about a person or an institution can actually be a self-fulfilling prophecy. If we distrust others and do not believe that there is any possibility of lasting human solidarity or community, our individualism will isolate us: *They won't care for me so why should I care for them?* Michael Lerner reflects on the results of this attitude at a political level:"When this fear becomes widely shared, we find it impossible to mobilize people to defend one another's interests, leaving each of us with considerably less power than we might have had."[2]

Cynicism about government or any other institution can keep people from an effort to make a difference, even at local levels. If individuals trust each other enough to work together, they can actually make changes. Cynicism says it is not worth the risk to stand together because nothing will change anyway. This makes us powerless to resist destructive forces, whether political, theological, economic, social or environmental. Our consequent powerlessness then confirms our cynicism.

So, we need to seriously question the ability of cynicism to deliver on the promises that make it so attractive. Cynicism makes a false promise of sophisticated enlightenment, a false claim to honesty, and offers a false hope of self-protection. Like Nietzsche's worm that has been stepped on, cynicism is a curling up of the soul away from all that is brightest in the world, leaving us too often in the grip of loneliness.

Christian Hope

In daring to hope the Christian finds some of the greatest tension with cynicism. Christian faith directs us to look to a better future in this world and the next. Hope is our connection to this future, which shines light back into the present, becoming part of the change that it promises.

Hope is not optimism. Christian hope is having a good reason to believe that a better future is coming. Hope is not optimism, which is often a matter of having a more buoyant temperament than most or a willingness to ignore what is tragic when it gets in the way of good feelings about yourself.

Christian hope is tied entirely to its anchor, God, whatever our temperament. This means that hope is in what God will do. It also means that God's truth radically shapes the character of hope itself. If hope has this theological mooring, it will live with humility's awareness of limitation and sin. Hope will see through the secular utopia just around the corner—inevitable moral progress or entitlement to happiness on earth.

Hope and suspicion as interdependent. Christian hope and suspicion are interdependent. Without an informed mistrust, hope is sure to be naive. Hope is solid when it has passed through the many preemptive suspicions of Christian awareness.

The marriage commitment is a good metaphor for the nature of hope in general. The marriage vows are bristling with suspicions and anticipations of trouble, yet there are very few events more predictably hopeful than weddings. It is not that hope survives despite the suspicions in the grim vows. Hope is solid because it has looked the grim possibilities in the face.

So it is with Christian hope itself. Hope is grounded in God and also in suspicions taken seriously. Trouble is anticipated. We are given plenty of warnings about our own sin and the brokenness and tragedy of the world. Yet we have the hope that when we trust in him, God will bear his fruit through us in this life and take us to be with him in the next. Christian hope, with humility, prepares us as much as we can be prepared for the unpredictability of our futures.

This hope is against the backdrop of a confidence that we know the ultimate trajectory of history and that it is in God's hands. As the historian Christopher Lasch wrote, "Hope does not demand a belief in progress. It demands a belief in justice: a conviction that the wicked will suffer, that wrongs will be made right, that the underlying order of things is not flouted with impunity."[3] Hope includes the confidence that the Creator in his goodness will ultimately deal with the many problems that we are unable to resolve or even understand ourselves.

Hope against cynicism. Think about some of the influential people whose lives we have noted. Try to imagine the temptation to cynicism experienced by Martin Luther King Jr. He was on the receiving end of a culture of entrenched racism and hatred. Even some of the African American community resisted his efforts. Yet for years he worked tirelessly and at great risk, suffering for justice, which he pursued without violence to the end. He was assassinated, but not before he had changed the world. Can you imagine him doing this if cynicism had left him without hope?

Imagine Nelson Mandela's possible reasons for cynicism. He spent twenty-seven years in South African prisons, also for pursuing racial justice. What would he have accomplished after his release if he had given up hope and given in to cynicism?

Finally, think of Alexandr Solzhenitsyn. He served eight years in Soviet prisons because of careless remarks about Stalin in a letter to a friend. In his attempts to tell the story of his experience and that of his nation, he was endlessly harassed and threatened by its authorities, who could not bear the truth. But he was one of the most significant individuals in bringing down the iron curtain. Consider how attractive cynicism would have been for him, yet he persisted in his writing because he knew God was calling him to tell the truth, and he dared to hope that the truth would get out.

It seems that these men had overwhelming reasons to be cynical, but in fact they were heroic for their sustained hope and the actions built on that hope. Cynicism about God, individuals or the institutions of society—any one of these three—would have neutralized the extraordinary impact of their lives.

Faith and Paradox

As we conclude our journey through the alleyways of cynicism, we must be clear about its relationship to the alternative we have proposed—faith in Jesus Christ. Faith in Christ is not the opposite of cynicism. In fact many of the cynical voices we have heard bear a striking resemblance to the sound of Jesus and the prophets as they exposed sham, spin, hypocrisy and instrumental religion.

Biblical faith is not a simple message of optimism and triumph in a simplistic, predictable world. Within its victory there is much tragedy, and this paradox runs through the entire biblical story. This is paradoxical, not as some have meant the word (meaning forever ambiguous, unclear and celebrating contradiction) but in the coexistence of victory and defeat, strength and weakness, already and not yet while God's truth and his providence regularly blind-side us with the unexpected.

The whole Christian story is deeply ironic—in the original sense of irony—from start to finish. Who would ever expect that the God who made the forty billion galaxies (at last count) would bother to create such tiny creatures as human beings, put us on this small blue planet and then take us seriously even after we had betrayed him? In this interaction, who would have guessed that he would have mercy on us? We would never have predicted that in order to receive us back after our betrayal, God would join the human race himself, live thirty years in obscurity, get in trouble with the authorities and be tortured to death! We know that dead people do not recover, but somehow, he was alive, walking around on Easter morning.

The paradoxes continue. He expects us to be both wise as serpents and innocent as doves. The poor in spirit are blessed with the kingdom of God. Mourners are comforted. The meek inherit the earth. The happiest people are those who have given up their entitlement to happiness. It should not surprise us that this God should require of us both suspicion and hope, to be wise as serpents and innocent as doves.

Henri Nouwen reflected on our choice.

People who have come to know the joy of God do not deny the darkness, but they choose not to live in it. They claim that the light that shines in the darkness can be trusted more than the darkness itself and that a little bit of light can dispel a lot of darkness. They point each other to flashes of light here and there, and remind each other that they reveal the hidden but real presence of God. They discover that there are people who heal each other's wounds, forgive each other's offenses, share their possessions, foster the spirit of community, celebrate the gifts they have received, and live in constant anticipation of the full manifestation of God's glory.[4]

Although it is often well hidden, that glory can shine out from God, in individuals and through the family, church and government. God teaches us preemptive suspicions about the world. With them we can recognize the brokenness that the cynic sees—but without losing the hope that the cynic rejects. With them we can recognize the glory in the world that the cynic cannot see—but without the sentimentality that the cynic fears.

We have tracked Job's search for wisdom throughout this book. I will give him the last word. It is from a reflective interlude between the more argumentative parts of the book of Job. He has discovered that wisdom is not easily learned by the living or the dead. It is not lying around to be found by those who trip over it, who are mildly curious or who think they can buy it. God sees everything in heaven and earth, not just more than but infinitely more than the human cynic sees. He sees and understands even those things that are specifically beyond human prediction and control—wind, waters, rain and lightning. Wisdom is found in him. It was this conviction that kept Job from sinking under the weight of a cynicism that otherwise might have drowned him.

> Where then does wisdom come from?
>   And where is the place of understanding?
> It is hidden from the eyes of all living,
>   and concealed from the birds of the air.
> Abbadon and Death say,
>   "We have heard a rumor of it with our ears."
>
> God understands the way to it,
>   and he knows its place.
> For he looks to the ends of the earth,
>   and sees everything under the heavens.
> When he gave to the wind its weight,
>   and apportioned out the waters by measure;
> when he made a decree for the rain,
>   and a way for the thunderbolt;
> then he saw it and declared it;
>   And he said to humankind,
> "Truly, the fear of the Lord, that is wisdom;
> and to depart from evil is understanding." (Job 28:20-28)

NOTES

Chapter 1: Introducing Cynicism

Epigraphs are from William Chaloupka, *Everybody Knows: Cynicism in America* (Minneapolis: University of Minnesota Press, 1999), p. 27, and Søren Kierkegaard, *Works of Love* (New York: Harper & Row, 1964), p. 240.

[1]"Cynic" and "cynical" in *The Random House Dictionary of the English Language*, unabridged ed. (New York: Random House, 1966).

[2]Peter Sloterdijk, *The Critique of Cynical Reason* (Minneapolis: University of Minnesota Press, 1987), p. 4.

[3]Gary Trudeau, "Doonesbury," *Boston Sunday Globe*, July 7, 1996.

[4]Edward Martin, *H. L. Mencken and the Debunkers* (Athens: University of Georgia Press, 1984), p. 7.

[5]William E. Woodward, *Bunk* (New York: Harper, 1923), p. 229, cited in ibid.

[6]*L'Abri* is the French word for "shelter." An American theologian and his wife, Francis and Edith Schaeffer, began the work in French-speaking Switzerland in 1955 by opening their home to anyone wanting to study and discuss questions of the truth and the implications of the Christian faith. It was a residential environment—a shelter—from the relentless secularism of society, from toxic religious expressions but also from a general atmosphere that can find no time to reflect openly on the most serious of questions. L'Abri has established branches in England, Holland, Sweden, the United States, Canada and South Korea.

Chapter 2: Cynicism

Epigraphs are from Jeffrey Goldfarb, *The Cynical Society* (Chicago: University of Chicago Press, 1991), p. 2, and Harry Truman, cited in Richard John Neuhaus, "Understanding Evangelicals," *First Things* 147 (November 2004): 65.

[1]R. Bracht Branham and Marie-Odie Goulet-Caze, *The Cynics* (Los Angeles: University of California Press, 1996), pp. 7-8.

[2]William Chaloupka, *Everybody Knows: Cynicism in America* (Minneapolis: University of Minnesota Press, 1999), p. 3.

[3]D. R. Dudley, *A History of Cynicism* (Chicago: Ares, 1980), p. 37.

[4]Diogenes, cited in ibid., p. 43.

[5]Crates, cited in Branham and Goulet-Caze, *Cynics*, p. 10.

[6]Branham and Goulet-Caze, *Cynics*, p. 10.

[7]Farrand Sayre, cited in Branham and Goulet-Caze, *Cynics*, p. 121.

[8]"Odes to Joy,"*Time*, January 17, 2005, pp. A42-43.

[9]Oscar Wilde and Antov Chekov, cited in Peter Sloterdijk , *Critique of Cynical Reason*, p. xxxii.

[10]Douglas Coupland, *Life After God* (New York: Pocket Books, 1995), p. 286.

[11]Daniel Boorstin, *The Image* (New York: Atheneum, 1977), pp. 3-4.

Chapter 3: Seeing Through People

Epigraphs are from Michael Lerner, *The Politics of Meaning: Restoring Hope and Possibility in an Age of Cynicism* (Reading, Mass.: Addison-Wesley, 1997), p. 3, and Robert Wright, *The Moral Animal* (New York: Vintage, 1994), p. 194.

[1]Christopher Hitchens, *The Missionary Position: Mother Teresa in Theory and Practice* (New York: Verso, 1995).

[2]Joe Kelly,"Fathers and Daughters,"*Fatherhood Today* 5, no. 3 (2000): 7.

[3]Dick Keyes, *True Heroism* (Colorado Springs: NavPress, 1995), chap. 3.

[4]E. O. Wilson, *On Human Nature* (New York: Bantam Books, 1982); E. O. Wilson, *Consilience* (New York: Vintage Books, 1998); Robert Wright, *The Moral Animal* (New York: Vintage Books, 1994); Richard Dawkins, *The Selfish Gene* (Oxford: Oxford University Press, 1989); Richard Dawkins, *The Blind Watchmaker* (New York: W. W. Norton, 1996).

[5]Wright, *Moral Animal*, p. 194.

[6]Ibid., pp. 325-26.

[7]Erving Goffman, *The Presentation of Self in Everyday Life* (Garden City, N.Y.: Doubleday, 1959), pp. 208ff.

[8]Ibid., pp. 4-5.

[9]Richard M. Huber, *The American Idea of Success* (Wainscott, N.Y.: Pushcart, 1987), p. 231.

[10]Dale Carnegie, cited in ibid., p. 238.

[11]Huber, *American Idea of Success*, p. 244.

[12]Richard Stivers, *The Culture of Cynicism: American Morality in Decline* (Oxford: Blackwell, 1994), p. 26.

[13]Kenneth Gergen, *The Saturated Self* (San Francisco: Basic Books, 1991), p. 139.

[14]Tom Wolfe, *Bonfire of the Vanities* (New York: Bantam Books, 1988).

[15]"The Commodification of Everything" is the theme of entire issue of *The Hedgehog Review* 5, no. 2 (2003).

Chapter 4: Seeing Through Institutions

Epigraphs are from William Chaloupka, *Everybody Knows: Cynicism in America* (Minneapolis: University of Minnesota Press, 1999), p. 212, and Michael Lerner, *The Politics of Meaning: Restoring Hope and Possibility in an Age of Cynicism* (Reading, Mass.: Addison-Wesley, 1997), p. 313.

[1]For reflection on some of the causes and consequences of the loss of cultural author-

ity, see Os Guinness, *The American Hour* (New York: Free Press, 1993); Peter Berger, *Facing Up to Modernity* (New York: Basic Books, 1977); David Wells, *No Place for Truth* (Grand Rapids: Eerdmans, 1993); Craig Gay, *The Way of the (Modern) World* (Grand Rapids: Eerdmans, 1998).

[2]William Chaloupka, *Everybody Knows: Cynicism in America* (Minneapolis: University of Minnesota Press, 1999), p. 202.

[3]Jedidiah Purdy, *For Common Things: Irony, Trust and Commitment in America Today* (New York: Alfred E. Knopf, 1999), p. 43.

[4]Roger Ailes, cited by James Q. Wilson, "Stagestruck," *The New Republic,* June 21, 1993, p. 33.

[5]Chaloupka, *Everybody Knows,* p. 8.

[6]Douglas Coupland, *Generation X* (New York: St. Martin's Press, 1991), p. 36.

[7]Thomas Morgan, cited in Amitai Etzioni, "How to Make Marriage Matter," *Time,* September 6, 1993, p. 76.

Chapter 5: Seeing Through God

Epigraphs are from C. S. Lewis, *A Grief Observed* (London: Faber & Faber, 1961), p. 17, and Thomas Carlyle, quoted in Paul Erland, *The Cynic's Almanac* (Nashville: Cynic's Ink, 1996), p. 99.

[1]Archibald MacLeish, *J.B.* (Cambridge: Riverside Press, 1958), p. 10.

[2]C. S. Lewis, *A Grief Observed* (London: Faber & Faber, 1961), pp. 9-10, 17, 26.

[3]Stephen Crane, "The Open Boat," in *The Norton Anthology of Short Fiction,* shorter ed. (New York: W. W. Norton, 1978), p. 243.

[4]Ibid., p. 244.

[5]Mark Twain, cited in Bruce Lockerbie, *Dismissing God* (Grand Rapids: Baker, 1998), p. 126.

[6]MacLeish, *J.B.,* p. 11.

Chapter 6: Seeing Through Human Knowledge of God

Epigraphs are from Friedrich Nietzsche, *Daybreak: Thoughts on the Prejudices of Morality,* trans. R. J. Hollingdale (Cambridge: Cambridge University Press, 1982), no. 95, p. 54, and Sigmund Freud, *The Future of an Illusion* (New York: Anchor Books, 1964), p. 30.

[1]Peter Sloterdijk, *The Critique of Cynical Reason* (Minneapolis: University of Minnesota Press, 1987), p.15.

[2]Ludwig Feuerbach, *The Essence of Christianity* (New York: Harper & Row, 1957).

[3]Peter Sloterdijk, *Critique of Cynical Reason,* p. 29.

[4]Friedrich Nietzsche, *Thus Spoke Zarathustra,* trans. R. J. Hollingdale (London: Penguin Books, 1988), p. 141.

[5]Ibid., p. 190.

[6]Friedrich Nietzsche, *Daybreak: Thoughts on the Prejudices of Morality,* trans. R. J. Hollingdale (Cambridge: Cambridge University Press, 1982), p. 54.

[7]Susan Neiman, *Evil in Modern Thought* (Princeton, N.J.: Princeton University Press, 2002), p. 228.

[8]Walter Lippmann, *A Preface to Morals* (London: George Allen & Unwin, 1929), p. 47.

[9]Peter Sloterdijk, *Critique of Cynical Reason*, p. 16.

[10]Ibid., pp. 16-17.

Chapter 7: Seeing Through Meaning to Power

Epigraphs are from Kevin J. Vanhoozer, *Is There a Meaning in This Text?* (Grand Rapids: Zondervan, 1998), p. 135, and Jeffrey Goldfarb, *The Cynical Society* (Chicago: University of Chicago Press, 1991), p. 17.

[1]Robert Bellah, *The Good Society* (New York: Alfred A. Knopf, 1991), p. 44.

[2]Jonathan Culler, cited in David Lehman, *Signs of the Times* (New York: Poseidon, 1991), p. 265.

[3]Jackson Lears, "The Birth of Irony," *The New Republic*, November 12, 2001, p. 47.

[4]Frank Gannon, "Endpaper—Seeking Certitude," *New York Times Magazine*, October 2, 1994, p. 100.

[5]Jonathan Rauch, "Let It Be," *Atlantic Monthly*, May, 2003, p. 34.

Chapter 8: Seeing Through Everything Else

Epigraphs are from John Barton, cited in Stanley Cohen and Laurie Taylor, *Escape Attempts: The Theory and Practice of Resistance to Everyday Life*, 2nd ed. (London: Routledge, 1998), p. 43, and Derek Bok, "The Purely Pragmatic University," *Harvard Magazine*, May-June 2003, p. 81.

[1]For a study of the particular modern characteristics of boredom, see Richard Winter, *Still Bored in a Culture of Entertainment* (Downers Grove, Ill.: InterVarsity Press, 2002).

[2]Richard Stivers, *The Culture of Cynicism: American Morality in Decline* (Oxford: Blackwell, 1994), p. 173.

[3]Ibid.

[4]Dave Wintsch, "The Church, Missions and Youth," unpublished paper (Amherst, Mass., newsletter).

[5]Stivers, *Culture of Cynicism*, pp. 174-75.

[6]Douglas Coupland, *Generation X* (New York: St. Martin's Press, 1991), p. 143.

[7]Stephen Crane, "The Open Boat," *The Norton Anthology of Short Fiction*, shorter ed. (New York: W. W. Norton, 1978), p. 230.

[8]Frank Ganon, "Endpaper—Seeking Certitude," *New York Times Magazine*, October 2, 1994, p. 100.

[9]Richard Rorty, *Contingency, Irony and Solidarity* (Cambridge: Cambridge University Press, 1995), pp. 73-74.

[10]Stanley Cohen and Laurie Taylor, *Escape Attempts: The Theory and Practice of Resistance to Everyday Life*, 2nd ed. (London: Routledge, 1998), pp. 53-54.

Chapter 9: Suspecting Our Suspicions
Epigraphs are from Reinhold Niebuhr, *Leaves from the Notebook of a Tamed Cynic* (San Francisco: Harper & Row, 1980), p. 105, and Merold Westphal, *Suspicion and Faith* (Grand Rapids: Eerdmans, 1993), p. 284.
[1]Merold Westphal, *Suspicion and Faith* (Grand Rapids: Eerdmans, 1993), p. 284.
[2]Edmond La B. Cherbonnier, *Hardness of Heart* (Garden City, N.Y.: Doubleday, 1955), p. 173.
[3]Ibid., p. 173-74.
[4]G. K. Chesterton, quoted in Alzina Stone Dale, *The Outline of Sanity* (Grand Rapids: Eerdmans, 1983), p. 66.

Chapter 10: The Vulnerability of Cynicism
Epigraphs are from William Chaloupka, *Everybody Knows: Cynicism in America* (Minneapolis: University of Minnesota Press, 1999), p. 30; Søren Kierkegaard, *Works of Love* (New York: Harper & Row, 1964), p. 219; and R. R. Reno, *In the Ruins of the Church* (Grand Rapids: Brazos, 2002), p. 42.
[1]Friedrich Nietzsche, *Twilight of the Idols/The Anti-Christ*, trans. R. J. Hollingdale (Harmondsworth, U.K.: Penguin, 1986), p. 26.
[2]Douglas Coupland, *Generation X* (New York: St. Martin's Press, 1991), p. 150.
[3]I am indebted to a friend and filmmaker Paul Reuter for his insights about the function of cynicism and perceived underachievement in a world where there are many stars.
[4]Søren Kierkegaard, *Works of Love* (New York: Harper & Row, 1964), p. 219.
[5]R. R. Reno, *In the Ruins of the Church* (Grand Rapids: Brazos, 2002), p. 32.
[6]Ibid., p. 38.
[7]Kierkegaard, *Works of Love*, p. 264.
[8]Stanley Cohen and Laurie Taylor, *Escape Attempts: The Theory and Practice of Resistance to Everyday Life*, 2nd ed. (London: Routledge, 1998), p. 54.
[9]Helmut Thielicke, *The Waiting Father*, trans. John Doberstein (San Francisco: Harper & Row, 1959), p. 135.
[10]Herman Melville,"Benito Cereno," *Billy Budd and Other Tales* (New York: New American Library, 1979), p. 221.
[11]Nick Hornby, *How to Be Good* (New York: Riverhead, 2001), p. 164.

Chapter 11: Suspecting Contemporary Suspicion About God
Epigraphs are from Jackson Lears,"The Birth of Irony,"*The New Republic*, November 12, 2001, p. 50, and Tom Stoppard, *Jumpers* (London: Faber & Faber, 1976), p. 69.
[1]Os Guinness, *Long Journey Home* (Colorado Springs: Waterbrook, 2001), p. 18.
[2]Stephen Crane,"The Open Boat," in *The Norton Anthology of Short Fiction*, shorter ed. (New York: W. W. Norton, 1978), p. 230.
[3]See R. C. Sproul, *The Psychology of Atheism* (Minneapolis: Bethany Fellowship, 1974), p. 94.

[4]Tom Stoppard, *Jumpers* (London: Faber & Faber, 1976), p. 69.

[5]W. H. Auden, cited by Edward Mendelson, *Later Auden* (New York: Farrar, Straus & Giroux, 1999), p. 207.

[6]Eugene Genovese, *Roll Jordan Roll* (New York: Vintage Books, 1976), pp. 232-55.

[7]David Aikman, *Great Souls: Six Who Changed the Century* (Nashville: Word, 1998), p. 68.

[8]Ibid., p. 177.

[9]G. G. Coulton, cited in Genovese, *Roll Jordan Roll*, p. 254.

[10]Douglas Johnston and Cynthia Sampson, eds., *Religion, the Missing Dimension of Statecraft* (New York: Oxford University Press, 1994).

Chapter 12: The Providence of God

Epigraphs are from E. La B. Cherbonnier, *Hardness of Heart* (Garden City, N.Y.: Double-day, 1955), p. 149, and C. S. Lewis, *The Problem of Pain* (Glasgow: Collins, 1977), p. 3.

[1]A common saying of Francis Schaeffer's.

[2]D. A. Carson, *How Long O Lord?* (Grand Rapids: Baker, 1990), p. 213ff.

[3]Keith Thomas, *Religion and the Decline of Magic* (New York: Oxford University Press, 1997), pp. 104-5.

Chapter 13: Living with the Providence of God

Epigraphs are from Lesslie Newbigin, *Proper Confidence: Faith, Doubt and Certainty in Christian Discipleship* (Grand Rapids: Eerdmans, 1995), p. 104; Fyodor Dostoyevsky, cited in *Notes from a Wayfarer: The Autobiography of Helmut Thielicke*, trans. David R. Law (New York: Paragon, 1995), book epigraph; and Dietrich Bonhoeffer, *Letters and Papers from Prison* (New York: Macmillan, 1962), p. 27.

Chapter 14: Providence Experienced

[1]Daisetz Teitaro Suzuki, *Mysticism: Christian and Buddhist* (New York: Harper, 1957), p. 133.

[2]Ibid., p. 136.

[3]Martin Luther, cited by William Placher, "Christ Takes Our Place," in *Interpretation*, January 1999, p. 6.

[4]C. S. Lewis, *A Grief Observed* (London: Faber & Faber, 1973), pp. 36-37.

[5]G. C. Berkouwer, *The Providence of God* (Grand Rapids: Eerdmans, 1961), p. 246.

[6]C. S. Lewis, "God in the Dock" in *Undeceptions*, ed. Walter Hooper (London: Geoffrey Bles, 1971), pp. 200-201.

Chapter 15: A Pointer to Transcendence

Epigraphs are from C. S. Lewis, *The Problem of Pain* (Glasgow: Collins, 1977), p. 12; Dietrich Bonhoeffer, *Letters and Papers from Prison* (New York: Macmillan, 1962), p. 17; and Glenn Tinder, *The Political Meaning of Christianity* (San Francisco: HarperCollins, 1991), p. 43.

[1]Armand Nicoli, *A Question of God* (NewYork: Free Press, 2002), pp. 36-37.

[2]Os Guinness, *Long Journey Home* (Colorado Springs: Waterbrook, 2001). Guinness examines a number of "signals of transcendence," such as thankfulness, evil and joy.

[3]Peter L. Berger, *Facing up to Modernity* (NewYork: Basic Books, 1977), p. 52.

[4]Robert Wright, *The Moral Animal* (NewYork: Vintage Books, 1994), p. 326.

[5]Mark Twain, *The Adventures of Huckleberry Finn* (New York: New American Library, 1959), pp. 92-95.

[6]C. S. Lewis, *The Problem of Pain* (Glasgow: Collins Fontana, 1977), p. 12.

[7]Stephen Crane, "The Open Boat," in *The Norton Anthology of Short Fiction*, shorter ed. (NewYork: W. W. Norton, 1978), p. 230.

Chapter 16: What If the Transcendent Has Come to Earth?

Epigraphs are from Lesslie Newbigin, *Proper Confidence: Faith, Doubt and Certainty in Christian Discipleship* (Grand Rapids: Eerdmans, 1995), p. 104, and Reinhold Niebuhr, *Leaves from the Notebook of a Tamed Cynic* (San Francisco: Harper & Row, 1980), p. 105.

[1]John Calvin, *Institutes of the Christian Religion* 1.1.1-2 (Grand Rapids: Eerdmans, 1964), pp. 37-38.

[2]One of the most prominent proponents of this idea is John Dominic Crossan. See, for example, his *The Historical Jesus: The Life of a Mediterranean Jewish Peasant* (San Francisco: HarperSanFrancisco, 1991).

[3]For a helpful evaluation of recent attempts to find the Jesus of history, see Ben Witherington III, *The Jesus Quest*, 2nd ed. (Downers Grove, Ill.: InterVarsity Press, 1997).

[4]Augustine, *Confessions*, trans. Henry Chadwick (NewYork: Oxford, 1992), p. 145.

[5]C. S. Lewis, *Surprised by Joy* (NewYork: Harcourt Brace Jovanovich 1955), pp. 227, 228.

Chapter 17: Questions About a Transcendent Message

Epigraphs are from Peter L. Berger, *A Rumor of Angels* (NewYork: Doubleday, 1970), p. 27, and Kevin J.Vanhoozer, *Is There a Meaning in This Text?* (Grand Rapids: Zondervan, 1998), p. 456.

[1]Kevin Vanhoozer, *Is There a Meaning in This Text?* (Grand Rapids: Zondervan, 1998), p. 462.

[2]Ibid., p. 458.

Chapter 18: What If God Is Not a Cynic?

Epigraphs are from Blaise Pascal, *Pensées* (NewYork: E. P. Dutton, 1958), no. 418, p. 111, and Will Campbell, cited in Philip Yancey, *What's So Amazing About Grace?* (Grand Rapids: Zondervan, 1998), p. 142.

[1]David Ader, "Survival Taught and Learned," *Massachusetts Wildlife* 53, no. 4 (2002): p. 13.

[2]Blaise Pascal, *Pensées* (NewYork: E. P. Dutton, 1958), p. 111.

[3]Merold Westphal, *Suspicion and Faith: The Religious Uses of Modern Atheism* (Grand Rapids: Eerdmans, 1993).

[4]Friedrich Nietzsche, *Daybreak: Thoughts on the Prejudices of Morality*, trans. R. J. Hollingdale (Cambridge: Cambridge University Press, 1982), p. 54.

Chapter 19: Seeing Through Cynicism

Epigraphs are from Merold Westphal, *Suspicion and Faith* (Grand Rapids: Eerdmans, 1993), p. 286, and Søren Kierkegaard, *Works of Love* (New York: Harper & Row, 1964), p. 214.

[1]C. S. Lewis, *The Abolition of Man* (New York: Macmillan, 1955), p. 91.

[2]Rollo May, *Psychology and the Human Dilemma* (New York: D. Van Nostrand, 1967), p. 4.

[3]Michael Lesy, *Rescuers: The Lives of Heroes* (New York: Farrar Straus Giroux, 1991).

[4]Samuel Oliner and Pearl Oliner, *The Altruistic Personality* (New York: Free Press, 1988).

[5]Chapter seven of Mary Stewart Van Leeuwen's *My Brother's Keeper* (Downers Grove, Ill.: InterVarsity Press, 2002) contains a helpful explanation and critique of evolutionary psychology.

Chapter 20: Beyond Cynicism I

Epigraphs are from Merold Westphal, *Suspicion and Faith* (Grand Rapids: Eerdmans, 1993), p. 288; Flannery O'Connor, *Mystery and Manners* (New York: Farrar, Straus & Giroux, 1992), p. 35; and Blaise Pascal, *Pensées* (New York: E. P. Dutton, 1958), no. 527, p. 143.

[1]Iris Murdoch, *The Sovereignty of the Good* (New York: Ark, 1970), p. 95.

[2]Peter Sloterdijk, *The Critique of Cynical Reason* (Minneapolis: University of Minnesota Press, 1983), p. 40.

[3]Martyn Lloyd-Jones, *Studies in the Sermon on the Mount* (Grand Rapids: Eerdmans, 1967), p. 180.

Chapter 21: Beyond Cynicism II

Epigraphs are from Dietrich Bonhoeffer, *Letters and Papers from Prison* (New York: Macmillan, 1962), pp. 27-28, and G. K. Chesterton, *The Defendant* (London: R. Brimley Johnson, 1901), p. 6.

Chapter 22: Cynicism and Marriage

Epigraphs are from Denis de Rougement, *Love in the Western World* (Princeton, N.J.: Princeton University Press, 1983), p. 300, and Mae West, quoted in Nancy F. Cott, *Public Vows* (Cambridge, Mass.: Harvard University Press, 2000), p. 1.

[1]Linda Waite and Maggie Gallagher, *The Case for Marriage* (New York: Broadway Books, 2000).

[2]Judith S. Wallerstein, Julia M. Lewis and Sandra Blakeslee, *The Unexpected Legacy of*

Divorce: A 25-Year Landmark Study (New York: Hyperion, 2001).
[3]Barbara Defoe Whitehead, *The Divorce Culture* (New York: Vintage Books, 1996).
[4]Gilbert Meilaender, "I Want to Burden My Loved Ones," *First Things* 16 (1991): 13-14.

Chapter 23: Cynicism and the Church

Epigraphs are from R. R. Reno, *In the Ruins of the Church* (Grand Rapids: Brazos, 2002), p. 13, and G. K. Chesterton, *Everlasting Man* (Garden City, N.Y.: Image Books, 1962), p. 254.
[1]Francis Schaeffer, *The Mark of the Christian*, in *The Complete Works of Francis A. Schaeffer* 4 (Westchester, Ill.: Crossway, 1982), pp. 183-205.
[2]Dietrich Bonhoeffer, *Life Together* (San Francisco: Harper & Row, 1954), pp. 26-27.
[3]For a more thorough discussion of salt and light and its implications for the church, see Dick Keyes, *Chameleon Christianity* (Eugene, Ore.: Wipf & Stock, 2003).
[4]Charles Colson has written a helpful book, *The Body* (Dallas: Word, 1992), surveying both high points and pitfalls of what is happening in the contemporary church.
[5]G. K. Chesterton, *Everlasting Man* (Garden City, N.Y.: Image Books, 1962), p. 254.

Chapter 24: Cynicism and Government

Epigraphs are from Reinhold Niebuhr, *The Children of Light and the Children of Darkness* (New York: Charles Scribner's Sons, 1960), pp. 40-41, and Michael Kinsley, "Visiting a Place Called Hope," *Time*, April 19, 1993, p. 74.
[1]Glenn Tinder, *The Political Meaning of Christianity* (San Francisco: HarperCollins, 1991), pp. 10-11.
[2]Fyodor Dostoyevsky, *House of the Dead*, quoted in Paul Johnson, *Modern Times* (New York: Harper Collins, 1985), p. 86.
[3]Abraham Lincoln, second inaugural address, March 4, 1865.
[4]Abraham Lincoln, "Abraham Lincoln's Letter to Thurow Weed," March 25, 1865, cited in *Abraham Lincoln: His Speeches and Writings*, ed. Roy P. Basler (Cleveland: World, 1946), pp. 792-93, 794.
[5]See Don Eberly, *Restoring the Good Society* (Grand Rapids: Baker, 1994).
[6]Douglas Johnston and Cynthia Sampson, *Religion: The Missing Dimension of Statecraft* (New York: Oxford University Press, 1994).
[7]Dietrich Bonhoeffer, *Letters and Papers from Prison* (New York: Macmillan, 1962), p. 33.

Chapter 25: Hope and the Costs of Cynicism

Epigraphs are from Henri Nouwen, *The Return of the Prodigal Son* (New York: Image, 1994), p. 117; D. Bruce Lockerbie, *Dismissing God* (Grand Rapids: Baker, 1998), pp. 21-22; and Martin Luther King Jr., "I Have a Dream," in Jocelyn Goss, *Rhetoric and Readings for Writing* (Dubuque, Iowa: Kendall Hunt, 1981), p. 253.
[1]Søren Kierkegaard, *Works of Love* (New York: Harper & Row, 1964), p. 219.

[2]Michael Lerner, *The Politics of Meaning* (Reading, Mass.: Addison-Wesley, 1997), p. 11.

[3]Christopher Lasch, *The True and Only Heaven* (New York: W. W. Norton, 1991), p. 80.

[4]Henri Nouwen, *The Return of the Prodigal Son* (New York: Image Books, 1994), p. 117.

"INFORMED CONSENT" TO A WORLDVIEW 24
SOCIOBIOLOGY 28
LOSS OF AUTHORITY 36
3 MEDIA TARGETS 37
THE CHURCH'S MESSAGE 41
IMAGES OF GOD 44
DOUBT 45
BROKEN PEOPLE / BROKEN WORLD 46
CAPACITY AND FRUSTRATION 47
VOICING THE THOUGHTS OF OTHERS 51
IDEOLOGY 52
INSTRUMENTAL FAITH 55
ENLIGHTENMENT 55, 51, 119, 137
generalist / specialists
lumpers / splitters 59
CYNICISM / UTOPIANISM 65
OCS OF GOD / MEANING / AUTHORITY 65, 66
HIGH RISK CONVICTIONS 82
ROMANCE OF CYNICISM 85F
RECONSTRUCTING THE MOTIVES OF CYNICS 88
NO NEUTRALITY 89
WORLDVIEW STARTING POINT 90
IS IT TRUE? 91

MAN SEEKING IDOLS 92
GOD 93
INCENTIVES / DISINCENTIVES 94
ATHEISM AND OPPRESSION 95
THE FALL 102
CHOICES + NATURE 103
FINITE MAN 109
CYNICS SUPPOSED POSITION 110
THE CROSS AND SIN 114
SUFFERING 116
PROGRESS / PESSIMISM 119
CYNICISM / SENTIMENTALITY 124
LIVING OUT "ISMS" 126
WHO BENEFITS? / WHO PAYS?
NATURE DOES NOT "CARE" 127, 129, 131
IS / OUGHT 128
A PLACE TO THROW ROCKS 128, 130
UNNATURAL MORALITY 129
GROUNDLESS CYNICISM 130
MORAL AXIOMS 132
IDENTITY OF JESUS SEARCH 137
IDENTITY POMO STYLE
GOD HAS SPOKEN 146, 147
WORDS / LANGUAGE 148
CYNICS OMNISCIENCE 153
THERAPEUTIC / UTOPIAN 154
CHRISTIAN HOPE ASSUMPTIONS 154
PASCAL'S GREATNESS, BRUTENESS 156

...TICE

...

GOD IS NOT CYNICAL 163, 169

CONTEXT OF DECISIONS
164

TWO STYLES OF CYNICISM
174

THE META-NARRATIVE
176

IDOLS 178, 195

"BEWARE OF" 183

1 COR. 13 184F

CYNICS AND THE CHURCH
201

CHURCH MINISTRIES 202

CHURCH + WORLD 205

TITLES FOR LEADERS 207

TRANSCENDENT FOUNDATION
214

SINS/CRIMES 217

CREATION/REDEMPTION
ETHICS 217FF